T0339172

They Said No to Nixon

The publisher and the University of California Press Foundation gratefully acknowledge the generous support of the Constance and William Withey Endowment Fund in History and Music.

They Said No to Nixon

Republicans Who Stood Up to the
President's Abuses of Power

Michael Koncewicz

UNIVERSITY OF CALIFORNIA PRESS

University of California Press, one of the most distinguished university presses in the United States, enriches
lives around the world by advancing scholarship in the
humanities, social sciences, and natural sciences. Its
activities are supported by the UC Press Foundation and
by philanthropic contributions from individuals and
institutions. For more information, visit www.ucpress.edu.

University of California Press
Oakland, California

Library of Congress Cataloging-in-Publication Data

Names: Koncewicz, Michael, 1984– author.
Title: They said no to Nixon : Republicans who stood up
    to the president's abuses of power / Michael
    Koncewicz.
Description: Oakland, California : University of
    California Press, [2018] | Includes bibliographical
    references and index. |
Identifiers: LCCN 2018009981 (print) | LCCN 2018012425
    (ebook) | ISBN 9780520970960 (E-book) |
    ISBN 9780520299054 (cloth : alk. paper)
Subjects: LCSH: United States—Politics and
    government—1969–1974.
Classification: LCC E855 (ebook) | LCC E855 .K66 2018
    (print) | DDC 320.0973/0904—dc23
LC record available at https://lccn.loc.gov/2018009981

Manufactured in the United States of America

25 24 23 22 21 20 19 18
10 9 8 7 6 5 4 3 2 1

Contents

Acknowledgments

As a young fan of *The Simpsons*, my introduction to the cartoon Nixon was a gateway of sorts to a lifelong interest in the history of the 1960s and 1970s. Voiced by Harry Shearer, Nixon's hunchbacked, sad-sack demeanor and defensive attitude was admittedly a superficial caricature, but it made him unique, and more intriguing, than any other president I had encountered in popular culture. It is why I purchased a Nixon Halloween mask and dressed up as the thirty-seventh president for my first middle-school dance. I want to start off by thanking all of my friends, family members, and fellow scholars who tolerated, and in many ways helped nurture, this lifelong interest in Nixon. This book would not have been possible without you.

This project began during my time as a special assistant at the Richard Nixon Presidential Library and Museum, originating from numerous conversations with my boss at the time, Timothy Naftali. Tim's encouragement convinced me that there was still much more to uncover about the Nixon administration. His passion for good political history helped guide me through the research and writing of this book. In his dual role as a public historian and the director of a presidential archive, Tim's contribution to Nixon scholarship is immeasurable.

A special thanks also goes out to the Nixon Library's former education director Mindy Farmer and her assistant, Summiya Ilyas. Both worked incredibly hard to transform the museum's school tours, creating a nonpartisan program for thousands of students in Southern California. Mindy first hired me as an intern in 2010, and later included me in her efforts to produce better public history within a presidential library. Working with them and their team of student interns was a formative experience that showed to me that the Nixon era was still alive.

My research for this book began when I was a doctoral student at the University of California, Irvine, where I was afforded the opportunity to work with a stellar team of historians. My adviser, Jon Wiener, was the other key figure who initially inspired me to tackle this topic. His prior work on Nixon, the Nixon Library, and the politics of public history always reminded me of the pertinence of my own research. As an always reliable source for feedback, he has played an important role in shaping this book. I also thank Alice Fahs, Emily Rosenberg, and Norm Rosenberg for their consistent support and for their thoughtful comments on the earliest versions of the manuscript.

During my time at New York University, I have greatly benefitted from a community of activists and scholars based around the Tamiment Library's Center for the United States and the Cold War. Over the last four years, my work has been shaped and improved by a wide range of conversations with archivists, librarians, historians, and other scholars, inside and outside of NYU. I thank Kyle Burke, Andrea Chiampan, Robert Cohen, Christopher Dietrich, Luca Falciola, Sean Fear, Irene Gendzier, Frank Gerits, Marjorie Heins, Tony Hiss, Timothy Johnson, Masha Kirasirova, Teishan Latner, Henry Maar, Andrew Needham, Mary Nolan, David Parsons, Kim Phillips-Fein, Ellen Schrecker, Lydia Walker, and Talya Zemach-Bersin. I especially thank Marilyn Young for her support before she passed away in February 2017. Marilyn's work will always serve as an inspiration to generations of historians.

Over the last few years, different parts of this project have been reviewed by several political historians who were generous enough to provide their feedback. Thank you to Kathryn Brownell, Mark Feldstein, Ken Hughes, Geoffrey Kabaservice, Robert Mason, Rob Rakove, Scott Spitzer, Tim Thurber, Tom Vance, Leah Wright Rigueur. Thank you also to the anonymous readers who helped me produce a better book.

As a researcher seeking to locate textual documents, I was helped immeasurably by the Nixon Library's archival staff. Their excellent service made those visits to their research room especially productive. I specifically thank Carla Braswell, Gregory Cumming, Pamla Eisenberg, Craig Ellefson, Melissa Heddon, Abigail Malangone, Dorissa Martinez, Meghan Lee-Parker, Ira Pemstein, and Jason Schultz for their assistance. Their service has made the campus at Yorba Linda a fantastic place to do research.

My research also received financial support from the Gerald R. Ford Presidential Foundation. Through winning a travel grant from the Ford Foundation, I was able to dig deeper into the post–Nixon administration history of Paul H. O'Neill, Elliot Richardson, and William Ruckelshaus. Thank you to the Ford Foundation, the director of the Ford Library Elaine Didier, and their archival team, specifically Mark Fischer and Jeremy Schmidt.

Outside of the presidential library system, I was aided by the staffs of MIT's Institute Archives and Special Collections, the Library of Congress's Manuscript Division, the Special Collections Department at the University of Massachusetts Amherst, and the National Archives at College Park. I would like to thank Katie Moore and Dorothy Walker at the University of South Carolina's Political Collections for helping me find relevant materials within Johnnie M. Walters's papers. I was also quite fortunate to have had the chance to interview John W. Dean, Jonathan Moore, William Morrill, and John Thomas Smith II. As veterans of the Nixon administration, they were each extremely generous with their time and gave me a better understanding of my own research.

Thank you to UC Press history editor Niels Hooper, editorial assistant Bradley Depew, jacket designer Claudia Smelser, production editor Dore Brown, and copy editor Paul Tyler for making this book a reality.

Finally, I would like to thank my family for all of their love and support. My parents and my sister have always provided important support throughout my academic career, and I could not have finished this book without them. From the very beginning of my research, my best friend, Stephanie, has played an invaluable role in helping me complete this project. The summer of our wedding, she had to deal with me spending far too much time listening to the Nixon tapes. When we moved from California to New York, she made sure I had enough time to write while we stayed in motels in the middle of the country. With her love and support, I was able to complete this book while we raised our first daughter. This book is for Stephanie and Penelope.

Introduction

"Too Many Nice Guys"—What Brought About Resistance in the Nixon Administration

"I think the trouble is that we've got too many nice guys around who just want to do the right thing," said an exasperated Richard Nixon on August 3, 1972. Sitting in the Oval Office with his two closest advisers, Chief of Staff H. R. Haldeman and Assistant for Domestic Affairs John Ehrlichman, the president vented about his cabinet's lack of toughness. He was especially enraged over the unwillingness of certain administration officials to bend the rules to go after his political enemies. Earlier in the conversation, Nixon exclaimed, "We have all of this power and we're not using it!" He asked, "Who is doing this full time? Who is running the IRS? Who is running over to the Justice Department? . . . With all of the agencies of government, what in the name of god are we doing about the McGovern contributors?" Haldeman responded, "The short answer to your question is nothing." Nixon retorted, "Part of the problem is the bureaucracy, part of the problem is our own goddamned fault. There must be something we can do." Although he griped about several different individuals in his administration during the discussion, the president specifically blamed his recently appointed secretary of the treasury George P. Shultz. During that summer, Shultz and the then commissioner of the Internal Revenue Service (IRS) Johnnie Walters had resisted the White House's efforts to use the agency to harass and punish their opponents. "He's not being political enough," said Nixon. "I don't care how nice of a guy he is. I don't care how good of an economist he is. We can't have this bullshit!"[1]

The conversation was not an isolated one—Nixon regularly brought up his frustrations with Shultz and Walters throughout the rest of that summer and into the fall of 1972. These were not tantrums, but rather the culmination of his prolonged struggle to politicize the federal bureaucracy. The president's taped tirades were not just expressions of his inner demons; they were representative of Nixon's increasingly sinister views of governance, particularly the powers of the presidency. Nixon's White House recordings are extremely valuable artifacts as they capture the beleaguered president behind closed doors and expose his uncensored views on a wide range of topics. Taken together, they are much more than just a collection of entertaining sound bites. While they do not capture the totality of the Nixon presidency, the tapes provide indisputable evidence that Nixon created and took great pains to develop a strident culture of loyalty that ultimately led to the crimes of Watergate.

In an attempt to counteract cartoonish depictions of Nixon in popular culture, some scholars and media figures have recently attempted to dismiss the importance of the White House tapes in assessing his presidency. "He needed to vent and blurt—cut that damn agency in half!—before settling down and shrewdly estimating what was possible and what was not," argues Evan Thomas in Being Nixon: A Man Divided.[2] This broader view of the White House tapes obscures the fact that Nixon's "blurts" were sometimes the starting points for many of the White House's plots to control and politicize the administration's bureaucracy. When it came to trying to use the federal government for political purposes, Nixon was firmly at the center of many of the White House's operations. Those who study Nixon must confront the fact that his private conversations were often the driving force behind many of his staff's more sordid schemes. There were times when Nixon's rants led to real action.

The president's anger was also emblematic of a deep division within his own administration over the White House's attempts to fully institutionalize its abuses of power during Nixon's first term. The president's vision of a government where he could more readily punish his enemies never came to fruition, but that was only because of the Republicans who said no to Nixon. While many are familiar with the Republicans who turned against the president during the final stages of Watergate (Barry Goldwater, Hugh Scott), there were also Republicans within the Nixon administration who opposed the White House without the limelight that others received.[3] The substantial resistance that the president faced from the IRS was not the only case, as several other Republican appointees also opposed Nixon's attempts to politicize their work and dramatically transform their offices. Well before the American public became aware of the White House's dirty tricks, there were Republicans who quietly blocked Nixon's orders and provided an important, yet fragile, check on the imperial presidency. Although many others within the White House followed through on Nixon's dirty tricks to varying degrees, some had enough courage to resist the White House's plots to further expand the power of the presidency. Officials within the newly created Office of Management and Budget (OMB) said no to the president's orders to cut federal funds to universities. Elliot Richardson and his staff also resisted the White House while they were at the Department of Health, Education, and Welfare (HEW) in small battles that mostly stayed out of the public eye. They later famously stood up to Nixon during the Saturday Night Massacre, a crucial turning point in the Watergate saga, but a moment that was also rooted in Richardson's previous conflicts with the White House.

Taken together, these acts of resistance show that before there was a public bipartisan consensus on Nixon's impeachment in 1974, opposition to the president was not purely political. Instead, it was sometimes driven behind the scenes by the very people who worked for him. The administration officials who opposed the president were not spurred on by political gain; they were concerned primarily with Nixon's very real threat to the federal government. For these men, Nixon's plots to attack his political opponents were also an attack on their ethics and the nonpartisan culture that had shaped their work within the government.

The individuals who refused to carry out Nixon's orders were, like the president, Republicans, but they were also civic-minded officials who were shaped by the broader technocratic culture of the postwar era. Most of them were ideologically moderate within the context of the Nixon era, but some were philosophically conservatives. Still, they shared an even-keeled and nonpartisan approach to civil service, one that placed them at odds with Nixon and the emerging conservative movement's culture of loyalty. While they were not all moderates in terms of their policy beliefs, and came from significantly different backgrounds, they were moderates when it came to their views on how to run the federal government.

Based on his comparatively liberal domestic record, many recent scholars have labeled Nixon as either a moderate or even a liberal when evaluating his entire presidency. Nixon's legislative record is certainly a complex one that does not follow the conservative mold, but it should not completely define his approach to the presidency nor his legacy.

When comparing the men who resisted Nixon's illegal orders with the president, one can see that the true moderates within the administration did not reside within the Oval Office. Although the men who said no to Nixon were in tune with certain elements of the president's domestic agenda, they were often at odds with his temperament and his willingness to abuse his power.

Above everything else, the individuals who opposed Nixon valued public service over the president's cutthroat view of politics. Whereas Nixon was shaped by the politics of the early Cold War, these men were shaped by a nonpartisan culture that had permeated much of the federal bureaucracy. Within certain sectors of the federal government, it was this nonpartisan culture that contributed to the resistance to Nixon. It was a technocratic culture that was largely rooted in postwar consensus values, one that led some conservatives and many moderates to adopt a noncombative approach to the liberal bureaucracy that had been solidified during the New Deal era. Coming up in the age of Eisenhower, a moderate Republican who had little to no interest in rolling back the New Deal, the men who stood up to Nixon did not share his animosity toward the postwar bureaucratic state. Although Nixon was at times in line with the more moderate segments of the Republican Party, especially as Eisenhower's vice president, his recurring bellicosity collided with the nonpartisan technocrats within his own administration. Instead, Nixon's rigid emphasis on loyalty created the conditions where some of his own appointees would end up resisting his orders. As products of a nonpartisan culture that was not invested in targeting the "other"— namely, the liberal establishment and the New Left social movements of the era—the men who resisted Nixon stood in direct contrast to the culture of loyalty that led to Watergate. Unlike the president's men, they did not believe there was a conspiracy to bring down the administration. As a group, they were more than just "nice guys." The individuals who said no to Nixon helped prevent the White House from doing further damage to the federal government and the American people.

Nixon scholars and other historians of the postwar era have often struggled to define Nixon's worldview. Given his mercurial nature and ideological pliability, Nixon remains difficult to fully characterize, even in 2018. In his pre-presidential career, he was both a vocal anticommunist and the man who sought to distance the Eisenhower administration from McCarthyism. He often adopted a form of right-wing populism in his campaigns, but also famously condemned right-wing extremists in California during his failed bid to become governor in 1962. As president he made peace with both China and the Soviet Union, but continued the nation's war against North Vietnam, bombed sovereign nations such as Cambodia and Laos, and supported the coup against the democratically elected Salvador Allende in Chile. On the domestic side, Nixon's record was also marked by notable achievements that could best be described as either "liberal" or "moderate," while also playing to conservative elements in the GOP. For example, the Environment Protection Agency was created under Nixon's watch, but he later vetoed the Clean Water Act and sought to rein in the new agency behind the scenes. His administration did much to desegregate schools across the South, but Nixon also maintained a "Southern Strategy" in an effort to appeal to disaffected white Democrats through Supreme Court appointments and the White House's public opposition to school busing. Nixon's attempt to reform welfare, the Family Assistance Plan, would have introduced a guaranteed income for poor families, but he later jettisoned the plan and deemed it too costly. These are just a few examples to demonstrate Nixon's complicated domestic and foreign policy records that have contributed to an unsettled legacy.

The stories of Republicans who said no to Nixon do not completely define the totality of Nixon's presidency, but they do collectively offer up a better sense of the thirty-seventh president's worldview. Focusing on these acts of resistance sheds new light on not only who Nixon considered to be his enemies, but also on who he believed would be a part of his "new establishment." In numerous White House meetings, Nixon criticized the post–New Deal liberal establishment that over time had shaped much of academia, the mainstream press, and the federal bureaucracy. Although Nixon's "new establishment" was never fleshed out in terms of its ideology, it was meant to stand in opposition to the liberal establishment, the American left, and the dramatic cultural changes of the late 1960s and early 1970s. Nixon's brand of conservatism was primarily defined by what he opposed. This was true throughout his political career, from his anticommunist crusades in the 1940s to his persistent attempts to enhance the powers of the Oval Office. In the absence of a well-defined ideology, Nixon often adhered to a Manichean form of cultural conservatism when dealing with his opponents in his public campaigns, but also in private. Since he firmly believed that his presidency was under attack by his enemies, administration officials who refused to carry out his orders were quickly labeled as a part of the old "establishment." They had violated a core part of his new establishment—loyalty to his presidency. This culture of loyalty was at the center of what eventually led to Watergate.

In addition to viewing any type of resistance as a blatant example of disloyalty, Nixon was quick to question the masculinity ("toughness") of officials who showed any signs of hesitation in carrying out one of his orders. Listening to the White House tapes, one can often hear the president directly tie an individual's loyalty to the White House to his crude understanding of masculinity. Whether it was labeling the federal bureaucracy as having "no guts," concluding that the nation's intellectual and political establishment had "gone soft," or demanding that the new head of the Bureau of Labor Statistics be someone "who has balls," Nixon regularly used gendered terms that denoted his need for more masculine individuals in his administration.[4] While these types of conversations have sometimes been dismissed as Nixon's desperate attempts to sound tough, it should not be ignored that Nixon's simplistic views on masculinity and loyalty had an impact on how he governed, especially when dealing with internal resistance.

Nixon's emphasis on masculinity can be situated within a broader history of gender and American history, particularly within the confines of the Cold War. As K.A. Cuordileone's *Manhood and American Political Culture in the Cold War* demonstrates, Nixon's political career was deeply connected to the nation's anxiety over the state of manhood in the postwar era. Cuordileone specifically points to Nixon's use of the phrase "pink" in his attacks on Helen Gahagan Douglas, his opponent in the 1950 Senate election, as he infamously claimed that the congresswoman was "pink right down to her underwear." However, Cuordileone also includes a compelling analysis of the 1960 presidential election that some saw, in the absence of significant policy differences, as a battle of personalities, namely Kennedy and Nixon's masculinity. The media saw the former's sense of masculinity as "genuine," while the latter was viewed as inauthentic.[5]

For Nixon, taking action to harass and even punish his enemies was a true sign of masculinity. It would prove whether a member of his administration was either a "tough guy" or a "nice guy," whether that individual was with "us" or "them." Despite their many past instances of showing loyalty to the president, officials such as Elliot Richardson and George Shultz were consistently dismissed as weak whenever their independent streaks got in the way of the White House's plans. Richardson and Shultz did in fact receive cabinet posts, but they were mostly appointed to these positions because of the prestige that they brought to the administration. This sense of prestige was often connected to their reputations as Ivy League–bred experts who had ties with Washington's political establishment and/or social scene. Once they were appointed, they were expected to follow through on Nixon's demands and exhibit a certain level of toughness. There was an almost automatic tension between these types of presidential appointments and the White House's more nefarious plots. When Nixon unleashed an illegal order, it was a test of that particular individual's loyalty. The moderates who opposed such orders failed that test, and proved to not be tough enough to trust with sensitive projects.

For Nixon, it was further evidence that he could not trust individuals who were tied to the Ivy League liberal establishment. In Nixon's mind, these types of officials were more loyal to their elite social networks than to the presidency. Unlike more recent conservative presidents, what was known as the liberal establishment held significantly more influence in the Nixon era, even within the GOP. With the Democrats controlling both the House and the Senate throughout his presidency, and an influential moderate wing within the Republican Party, several of Nixon's appointments were partially driven by an attempt to placate the D.C. establishment during a time when their ranks truly mattered. Nixon resented the establishment, and wanted to build a new one, but he begrudgingly accepted their influence, especially during his first term.

Nixon's heightened sense of loyalty, combined with his skewed understanding of masculinity, eventually led to the development of a bunker mentality that persisted throughout much of his presidency. Although he began his presidency with a healthy amount of ideological diversity, with a significant number of liberal and moderate Republicans in high-level positions, that mentality eventually led to the diminishment of dissenting voices. By the end of his first term, Nixon's growing suspicions about some of the less politically inclined moderates who did not aggressively pursue the White House's enemies turned them into his enemies as well. The president came to the conclusion that they were not fit to lead in the White House's war on the "establishment," including its enemies in the media, the antiwar movement, and even those who were embedded within the federal bureaucracy.

The battles between Nixon and the civil servants who opposed him are not only stories about the Nixon and the authoritarian culture he built inside the White House—they are a part of a larger history of the Republican Party. By looking at the officials who said no, along with the ones who were loyal to the president, one can better understand the significant cultural and ideological shifts that occurred within the GOP during the 1970s. While Nixon is hard to pinpoint when it came to his ideological views, his approach to dealing with his political opponents aligned him with some of the more aggressively partisan elements of the New Right of the 1970s. "I didn't like Nixon until Watergate," admitted M. Stanton Evans to historian Rick Perlstein in 2005.[6]

It is important to note that unlike Evans, who cofounded the seminal organization Young Americans for Freedom, Nixon was never a movement conservative. In fact, much of his foreign and domestic policies angered the right and kept him from ever being fully embraced by large segments of the conservative movement of the 1970s. Heather Hendershot's recent book on William F. Buckley includes a chapter that focuses on the conservative commentator and Richard Nixon, showing that the former generally saw the latter's presidency as a "long detour." Hendershot also shows Buckley taking great pains to downplay Nixon's allegiance to the conservative movement, writing at one point that "the traditional liberal sin is lust for power, so that Nixon's sins tend to be Democratic sins." For Buckley and many others in the conservative movement, Nixon's presidency was one defined by compromise of the movement; Reagan was always their future.[7]

Nevertheless, Nixon's attempts to use the government to punish his foes on the left placed him alongside the far right of the Republican Party. During his presidency, Nixon firmly believed that the country was in the middle of a period of cultural chaos and political instability, one that had not been seen since the Civil War. He felt that his willingness to bend the rules was justified during a period of civil unrest that was caused by the Left. Whatever ideological disputes he may have had with the more conservative elements of the GOP, they were frequently overridden by his desire to squash the American Left and destroy the influence of the nation's liberal establishment. It was not a coincidence that when it came to issuing controversial orders, the president often relied on some of the more conservative members of his team. Whenever Nixon's controversial orders were rejected by a more moderate member of his administration, there was often a conservative who was willing to display his loyalty to the president. "I'd rather take a dumb loyalist than a bright neuter. I really would," said Nixon during a meeting about his second-term reorganization. "I'm frankly bored to death with dumb loyalists. I love them. They drive me up the wall. On the other hand, believe me they're damn comfortable to have around here in a crunch."[8]

When the president felt that he was under siege, he veered aggressively to the right, particularly when he was mapping out his second term. He was explicit in his desire to move the country further to the right in his private discussions in the final few weeks preceding the 1972 election. "What McGovern stands for, the eastern liberal media stands for, the eastern intellectuals stand for . . . must be crushed," said Nixon in a meeting with Haldeman and his former treasury secretary John Connally on October 17, 1972. "It cannot come back and have an opportunity to have much influence in American life for a while." He later argued that a landslide victory would weaken the major mainstream print and television media outlets and that it would also be "a terrible blow to the eastern establishment, the university types, all of them of that kind." Nixon's views on the nation's establishment were also tied to regional politics. It was a way for the president to divide the nation in rather simplistic terms when plotting out the future of the Republican Party. "And it will be a great encouragement to the decent people in this country. There's decent people in every state, but to speak regionally, they're in the South, they're throughout the Midwest, out in California, a lot of strong people out there."

Nixon's views regarding the decency of the American public and its elite institutions were tied to his repeated desire to create a new, more conservative establishment. His goals went beyond winning a second term, as he wanted to develop a new cultural and political establishment that would move the country in a more conservative direction. "And what we've got to do after this election is to build a new establishment." Nixon's plan for a new establishment were somewhat amorphous, but they were decidedly driven by his deep-seated anti-Semitism, as he believed that there were too many Jewish employees in his administration who were connected to the liberal establishment. "We have our share of them. They're very good. . . But there are too many Jews in the government." Instead of recruiting from the Ivy League, Nixon wanted to "go out in the heartland" and avoid the nation's elite universities.[9]

In many ways, Nixon wanted to build a government during his second term that resembled J. Edgar Hoover's FBI. He believed that the longtime FBI director had succeeded in creating a more disciplined island within the federal government, one that was shielded from what he felt was "an attitude of permissiveness" that had seeped through the post–New Deal federal bureaucracy. In recent years scholars have shown that Nixon had a complicated relationship with Hoover, as the two greatly differed when it came to responding to the cultural and social revolts of the late 1960s.[10] In his book on the FBI, Timothy Weiner points to Hoover's refusal to adopt the Nixon White House's plan to dramatically increase the government's surveillance of left-wing radicals (the "Huston Plan") in 1970 as a key turning point in the

Watergate saga. It is the moment where Hoover began to scale back the FBI's covert operations, spurring the president to bring the planning of those types of activities in-house—i.e., into the halls of the White House. Following Hoover's death in the spring of 1972, Nixon became even more focused on filling the void left behind by the controversial cold warrior. Beverly Gage's work on Hoover and Nixon further demonstrates the importance of the split between Hoover and Nixon in understanding Nixon's eventual downfall. Like Weiner, she presents Hoover's refusal to carry out the "Huston Plan" as a turning point for the Nixon presidency, one that was shaped not only by Hoover's anxiety over changes in American culture, but also by Hoover's desire to protect the FBI. In a 2012 article, she stresses that Hoover must be understood as a bureaucrat who saw himself as nonpartisan, and that Watergate should primarily be seen as "a bureaucratic conflict within the executive branch itself." Through this lens, Gage argues, one can better understand just why Watergate had a "limited impact on broader political trends," namely the rise of conservatism.[11]

Gage is correct to point out that Hoover's resistance to the Nixon White House should be situated within a larger story of the presidency versus the bureaucracy. That story, despite its ideological complexities, is still connected to politics as Nixon's antibureaucratic views fit alongside the rise of the conservative movement of the late twentieth century. The Nixon-Hoover split makes Nixon's private views of Hoover's FBI all the more fascinating as the president consistently held Hoover's past leadership in high regard. Just as Hoover's view of himself as a nonpartisan figure matters when studying the FBI, Nixon's own simplified view of Hoover's past leadership is also important when examining his plans for a new establishment in his second term. In his October 17 conversation with Connally and Haldeman, he specifically targeted HEW, the State Department, and the CIA as agencies that had been corrupted by the establishment. The president looked to Hoover's FBI as the ultimate model for his second term. "You take the FBI . . . Everybody says Hoover . . . made them cut their hair and so forth. Great integrity, great ability. He never picked boys from Harvard." He added, "Most of them . . . he got them from the Midwest, he got them from the southern schools and they are the best you ever saw. That's the thing that we're going to do."

In reality, Hoover's FBI was not completely in line with Nixon's appraisal. Still, the agency's history of cracking down on dissent meant that the president saw Hoover as a source of inspiration. After more than twenty-five years in politics, Nixon was convinced that the nation needed a federal government that would replicate Hoover's fascistic tendencies in attempting to squash all forms of left-wing protest. For the president, it was personal, as he brought up his own humble upbringing in order to offer up a stark contrast with the liberal elites. "We underestimate the ability of the good people of this country. . . I've never been one of these bunch, and I'm never going to be."[12]

Nixon's attempt to bring in a slew of Hoover-style operations under his supervision made his abuses of power exceptional when compared to his predecessors. Previous presidents, including Democrats, participated in operations that used the CIA and FBI to monitor and punish their political opponents. Watergate was partially the culmination of decades of wrongdoings, both in and outside the White House. No president since FDR was left untarnished by the dramatic growth of the federal government during the mid-twentieth century. It would be naïve to completely disconnect Nixon's crimes from the abuses of power that were carried out in previous administrations. For example, historians have shown that the Roosevelt administration had little use for civil liberties and supported the FBI's crackdown on left- and right-wing radicals in the 1930s and 1940s.[13] The Kennedy and Johnson administrations actively participated in the CIA and FBI's wiretapping of individuals, including journalists.[14]

Historians can and should quibble with the moral nature of these and numerous other unethical actions, but most of these activities differed from Nixon's misdeeds for one very important reason. Other presidents had kept a certain level of distance from the state's covert operations, especially when it came to the domestic realm, whereas Nixon was determined to bring them into the Oval Office. Part of this was the product of historical circumstance, with Nixon seeking to fill the void left by Hoover because the FBI director resisted the White House's Huston Plan. The other factor, which can be heard on the White House tapes, was Nixon's strong impulse toward authoritarianism. Viewing his presidency as one that was defined by a moment of civil strife, he sought to consolidate power in ways that tested the nation's democracy. While prior presidents largely used the power of the state to preserve the status quo, Nixon was obsessed with creating a new establishment that expanded his power. Pointing out the exceptionalism of Nixon's presidency and offering up a longer history of the imperial presidency are not mutually exclusive. The two narratives are intertwined, but the actions of other presidents should not be used to excuse Nixon's during his presidency.

The men who said no to Nixon varied in terms of their personal links to the nation's elite institutions and a broader establishment, but they did not share Nixon's sheer hatred of the establishment, its institutions, or its general tolerance of the New Left. When confronted with a refusal to carry out illegal orders, Nixon pointed to an individual's education or other ties to the establishment. Figures like Richardson, Shultz, and many others represented the old guard of the GOP, one that was partially driven by moderation, was open to ideological diversity, and came from a culture that did not completely combine politics with the power of the state. Their decisions to stand up to Nixon were illustrative of a tradition within the Republican Party that was under attack by a growing conservative movement in the 1960s and 1970s. Nixon was a complex figure, but his various plans to expand the power of the presidency to punish his enemies placed him at odds with many of the moderates whom he had hired. As principled civil servants, they were able to limit governmental abuses of power that would have helped conservatives gain more power inside of the Nixon administration. Their shared resistance to the president helped prevent a dramatic expansion of the federal government's ability to silence dissent from the left in the 1970s. Their battles with the White House show the true depths of Watergate and Nixon's ambitious expectations for a second term. More importantly, the civil servants who said no to the president offer up an important counternarrative to revisionist takes on Nixon that depict his time in the Oval Office as being disconnected from the modern conservative movement. These stories show that the moderates were an important roadblock to a conservative movement that shared Nixon's views on mixing politics with civil service. They were resisting not only specific orders, but also a culture that promoted a more cynical approach to government, one that was openly hostile toward opposing viewpoints.

Over the last two decades, numerous scholars have written about the rise of the Right in American politics in the latter half of the twentieth century. Work such as Lisa McGirr's study of grassroots Orange County activists, *Suburban Warriors: The Origins of the New American Right*, and Kim Phillips-Fein's focus on the influence on conservative financial elites in *Invisible Hands: The Making of the Conservative Movement, From the New Deal to Reagan*, have shown that both top-down and bottom-up approaches are important to fully explaining the evolution of the modern conservative movement.[15]

More recently, Kevin Kruse's work on the religious right, Jason Stahl's book on conservative think tanks, and Nicole Hemmer's detailed history of conservative media have examined the rise of conservatism, but all three hold up Nixon as a key character within their narratives.[16] Nixon is shown to play a crucial role in advancing conservatism, particularly when it comes to the cultural front. For Kruse, Nixon's campaign to aggressively woo evangelical voters during his presidency was an important part of his quest to create a new Republican majority. In Stahl's study of conservative think tanks, Nixon and Haldeman are shown to have been obsessed with attacking liberal think tanks such as the Brookings Institution. The president also regularly reached out to leaders of early conservative organizations such as William J. Baroody in an effort to maintain a healthy relationship with the conservative movement. "Until your pioneering efforts, the institutions of public opinion molding were largely monopolized by spokesmen for centralized big government who felt that every public policy program could be solved by massive federal spending programs," wrote Nixon to Baroody.[17] Nixon was distrusted by many conservative media figures who grew frustrated with the thirty-seventh president's ideological flexibility, but Hemmer points to the fact that Nixon was the first presidential candidate to openly court conservative media in 1968. Figures such as William F. Buckley would turn against Nixon following his trip to China in February 1972, but Hemmer shows that Watergate made Nixon more popular among many movement conservatives. "The right believed he was being brought down for his conservatism, that liberals were using Watergate as a pretense to reverse the results of the 1972 election." In the end, "Watergate granted Nixon a reprieve from his conservative critics."[18]

Less attention has been paid to the Republicans who were at odds with the New Right of the 1960s and 1970s, the liberals and moderates of the Eisenhower tradition who were in no way a part of the conservative movement. Recent works by Geoffrey Kabaservice and Leah Wright Rigueur offer compelling accounts of the moderate Republicans who opposed the growing influence of the Right. Kabaservice focuses on some of the more prominent moderate leaders and organizations of the 1960s and 1970s, while Rigueur spends much time examining the liberal/moderate African American voices within the GOP. Both historians show that there was significant resistance to the conservative takeover of the party, and encourage readers to further explore the role of the moderate in the Republican Party.[19]

The main subjects of this study also represented a different part of the GOP. They were the figures who in many ways felt isolated from the New Right's culture and ideology. Overall, they were able to work with

Democrats, and could best be described as bureaucrats who believed that they could find sensible nonpartisan solutions to society's problems. Ideologically Nixon may have been a moderate Republican, especially by today's standards, but his rhetoric, temperament, and ultimately his obsession with his political battles prevented him from being a truly moderate president. Nixon may not have been in tune with the conservative movement, and was occasionally at odds with some of its leaders and organizations, but his view of loyalty and politics fit within its worldview. Rick Perlstein's series of books on the rise of the Right and American culture forgoes studying the policy battles within the Nixon administration, and instead captures Nixon's role as a cultural figure within the nation's broader ideological struggle of the 1960s and 1970s.[20] Nixon was not a product of the Right, but he played a crucial role in seizing on events to divide the nation in a manner that strengthened the conservative movement. When it came to politics, Nixon was a conservative.

This book looks at the culture of criminality surrounding Watergate and why it did not succeed. The instances where Republicans said no to Nixon took place at a moment in time where an older brand of Republicanism still had significant influence within the federal government and American political culture. However, it was also a moment where the core of the Republican Party began to gradually turn away from moderate-tempered Republicans who fashioned themselves as analytics-based experts. Although Watergate was heralded by many in the press as a moment of bipartisan unity, many Nixon loyalists and conservatives saw it as a partisan witch hunt of a Republican president and proof of the media's liberal bias. The president, who had a far from perfect relationship with the conservative movement, became a martyr for the cause, whereas the men who stood up to Nixon were seen by some conservative Republicans as traitors to the cause. It was by no means the only reason many moderates and other civic-minded figures lost influence within the GOP in the latter half of the 1970s, but it was symbolic of a sea change within the party not only on ideological issues but with respect to partisan politics.

In addition to interacting with the broader arguments set forth by histories of the conservative movement, this book expands on the historiography of Richard Nixon, his presidency, and Watergate. Nixon scholarship has largely been shaped by memoirs of former Nixon staffers, journalists who covered the White House, government investigators, and other Watergate veterans.[21] Aside from the numerous memoirs, a disproportionate amount of the literature has been infused by present-day politics, taking the Nixon presidency outside of its historical context.

The Nixon revisionists of the late 1980s and 1990s presented an alternative to the early judgments of the Nixon administration, which were initially inspired by the nation's shock over the Watergate scandal. Much of the original wave of Nixon scholarship was driven by emotionally charged journalism, and seized on the public's anger about Watergate. Whether from the immediate reactions of the mainstream press or the best-selling memoirs from figures such as John Dean and Bob Woodward and Carl Bernstein, the earliest drafts of the history of the Nixon presidency revolved around his abuses of power. Historians, however, are trained to have an almost natural inclination to challenge dominant narratives, especially when they are shaped by journalists. Given the onslaught of negative appraisals of Nixon, it was not surprising that historians began to seek alternative approaches to studying his presidency. Writing in the wake of the Reagan administration's comparatively more consistent attack on New Deal liberalism, scholars began to trumpet Nixon as a figure who may have been the country's last liberal or even progressive president. Most of the first wave of major Nixon biographies that were published in the late 1980s and early 1990s were arguably shaped in various ways by Nixon revisionism. Works such as Stephen E. Ambrose's three-volume biography (1990–91) and Tom Wicker's *One of Us: Richard Nixon and the American Dream* (1991) sought to showcase some of the more positive accomplishments of the Nixon administration as opposed to further investigating Watergate. Wicker's book in particular marked a very noticeable shift for the former *New York Times* columnist/reporter who had gone from being placed on the White House's enemies list for his critiques of the president to encouraging a more forgiving depiction of the Nixon presidency.[22]

Following Nixon's death in 1994 and President Clinton's failed attempts at progressive reforms, journalists, political commentators, and historians increasingly argued that the real Nixon bore little resemblance to villainous "Tricky Dick." Rather, liberals should have held the president in high regard for his domestic policy accomplishments, from the creation of the Environmental Protection Agency to the passing of Title IX. In *Nixon's Shadow: The History of an Image*, David Greenberg devotes a chapter to the rise of the liberal Nixon trope within academia. Writing in 2003, Greenberg surveyed the trend and correctly pointed out: "Just as the unsparing Watergate-era judgments of Nixon reflected the spirit of those embattled years, so the verdicts of the

Reagan-era Nixon revisionists reflected, if unconsciously, the temper of their own times."[23]

Perhaps the clearest attack on the earlier Watergate-based depictions of Nixon can be found in Joan Hoff's revisionist examination of the Nixon presidency, *Nixon Reconsidered*. Published in 1994, the book was originally titled *Nixon without Watergate*, as it argued that historians should look beyond Watergate and instead focus on Nixon's domestic accomplishments when evaluating his legacy of his presidency. Looking back at Watergate, Hoff argued that the scandal was little more than an extension of the postwar presidency run amok and his crimes were not all that exceptional when compared to other presidents. She argued that Nixon's domestic achievements far outweighed any of his wrongdoings. "Nixon was so much more than Watergate and Watergate so much more than Nixon that his diehard critics can only simplistically conflate them by resorting to political correctness," and concluded, "Thus, they continue to lament rather than learn from Watergate and the Age of Nixon." Hoff, a self-described former New Left critic of Nixon, also targeted those who she believed were simply clinging to the anger from the political battles of the Nixon era. "If anything, those who were (and are) most enraged by Nixon are probably those whose ideal views of themselves in an age of authenticity made them most uncomfortable and possibly vengeful, toward an exposed version of their real inner selves."[24]

The revisionist trend continued into the new millennium with scholars such as Dean J. Kotlowski and Melvin Small, each of whom argued for a more nuanced take on the thirty-seventh president, while stressing the importance of his administration's progressive civil rights record and pragmatic foreign policy.[25] Both of their books, along with several others, have made valuable contributions to the ongoing discussion on Nixon's legacy, but are limited by the fact that they were written before the bulk of the White House tapes were released to the public. With researchers being able to listen to Nixon's tirades about liberals and the Left, it has now become significantly harder to soften Nixon's combative side or argue that his legacy should be defined by anything other than his abuses of power.

Despite a steady stream of new revelations about Nixon's dark side and lagging poll numbers, the revisionist trend has persisted.[26] During the George W. Bush years, many media figures and scholars looked at Nixon in a more favorable light, often arguing that Bush's decision to invade Iraq far exceeded the crimes of Watergate.[27] The trend has continued on both sides of the ideological aisle, as Nixon's wrongdoings have often been diminished by pundits when attempting to elevate a present-day scandal. One only had to google Hillary Clinton–Nixon or Donald Trump–Nixon during the 2016 election to see that the specifics of Nixon's downfall are often glossed over in order to make a political argument. One popular meme circulated by conservative media featured an image of Nixon with the heading "I deleted 18 minutes of recordings and had to resign as President." Below the thirty-seventh president is an image of Hillary Clinton with the caption, "I deleted 30,000 emails and I'm running for President."[28] More often than not, comparisons to Nixon do little to inform or remind the public of the real reasons for the president's resignation.

Nixon revisionism can also be seen in certain segments of popular culture such as the *Colbert Report* and even in more recent biographies of the thirty-seventh president.[29] Published in 2015, Evan Thomas's *Being Nixon: A Man Divided* recently updated several of the revisionist tropes in an attempt to soften Nixon's image. Thomas sets himself up as the last person who would have anything nice to say about Nixon, given his background as a part of the liberal media establishment through his many years as a reporter and editor at *Newsweek*. Much like Hoff, Thomas argues against the "cartoon version" of Nixon and, wherever possible, attempts to offer up a more balanced portrayal of the inner workings of the man. "Nixon's inclination toward the dark side has long been a cliché," concludes Thomas.[30] Although Thomas does not agree that Nixon was a liberal—his domestic achievements are largely described as opportunism—he still attempts to move beyond Nixon's abuses of power and craft a more generous depiction of the president. Aside from a heavy reliance on pro-Nixon sources (family members, ex-staffers), the book also frequently gives Nixon the benefit of the doubt, and fails to fully confront Nixon's abuses of power. Instead of focusing on Nixon's actions, Thomas depicts the president as a tragic figure who simply succumbed to his own personal foibles. "Still, it's true that Watergate got out of hand in part because Nixon was too shy, too trusting to confront his own staff on exactly what happened and who was to blame . . . He was too averse to conflict and too distracted to tame heedless subordinates."[31] It is certainly a worthwhile goal to counteract some of the more simplistic and polemical depictions of Nixon, but Thomas too often resorts to forgiving the president, crafting a narrative that offers up a rehabilitation of sorts.

On the whole, Nixon revisionists do not entirely ignore Watergate, but they still have contributed to a gradual shift away from acknowledging the exceptional nature of the scandal and the danger that Nixon posed to the federal government. Although some of the Nixon revisionists have provided compelling studies that have added to our understanding of the era, they have also led readers away from fully comprehending just why Nixon had so many critics from both sides of the aisle. Certain strains in Nixon scholarship have been too cautious in their analysis and too reliant on comparisons with other presidents. Nixon's image has especially too often been molded by the disappointments of liberal scholars over the policies of the Reagan, Clinton, Bush, and even Obama administrations. This trend has led historians away from judging Nixon and Watergate by the standards of the thirty-seventh president's era. Stanley J. Kutler recognized the dangers of this trend as early as 1987, during a high-profile conference for Nixon scholars at Hofstra University. After presentations by figures such as Stephen Ambrose and Joan Hoff, Kutler argued against those who felt that domestic initiatives such as the Family Assistance Plan deserved more attention than Watergate: "We are, to some extent, in danger of forgetting—not forgetting Richard Nixon, but forgetting what he did and what he symbolized to his contemporaries. History, after all, is not just what the present wishes to make of the past for its own purposes. Historians must judge the past by the standards of that past, not their own."[32]

Kutler also directly addressed arguments made by scholars that Watergate was simply the culmination of the postwar imperial presidency, a continuation of a longer history of abuses of power conducted by prior presidents. He conceded that Watergate showed that the "Nation would tolerate an imperial president, but not an imperious one," but that claiming that every postwar president broke the law in a similar fashion ignored the exceptional nature of Nixon's presidency. "Watergate still happened," argued Kutler, who concluded his remarks with a statement on Nixon's legacy. "What did he do? Watergate is both the shortest and the longest answer."[33]

Kutler's remarks from more than thirty years ago still ring true because they offer up a seemingly obvious but necessary rebuttal to those who seek to look beyond Watergate. The argument is even more pertinent given the rise of comparisons of Nixon to recent presidents. These comparisons make for compelling debates and may even help academics track certain historical trends from the 1970s to today, but the not-as-bad-as Reagan/Clinton/Bush/Obama/Trump approach often leads to poor historical judgments. One can certainly make the argument that a certain policy or scandal did more damage to the nation than Watergate, or that Nixon is not the worst president in American history, but that does not erase the fact that the Nixon White House posed a clear and well-documented threat to the U.S. Constitution. Taken together with the substantial amount of literature devoted to Watergate-related conspiracies that tend to present Nixon's resignation as the end result of a secret deep-state coup, the revisionist scholars have contributed to leading the public away from a moment in American history that transcended traditional ideological battles.[34]

While many scholars grew weary of Watergate in the 1990s, Kutler's *Abuse of Power: The New Nixon Tapes* (1998) demonstrated that there was still much to learn from the scandal. Kutler presented numerous transcripts of the infamous tapes that displayed Nixon's guilt on several fronts, extending beyond the Watergate cover-up. The book was a product of Kutler's lengthy legal battle with the federal government. As a result of Kutler's settlement with the National Archives, the tapes began to be released to the public, dramatically altering the sources that are accessible to Nixon historians. After years of resistance from Richard Nixon and his estate, the National Archives was now forced to let the public hear the recordings that forced his resignation. Whereas the revisionist historians of the 1990s were working primarily from textual documents, the tapes have now offered researchers thousands of hours of conversations from the White House and Camp David.

Through continued pressure from Nixon scholars such as Stanley Kutler and the efforts of the Nixon Library's first federal director, Timothy Naftali, to accelerate the release of the tapes, nearly 3,000 out of 3,700 hours of conversations were made available to the public between 1996 and 2013. Despite the release of the tapes, very few have taken full advantage of this treasure trove of recordings. Instead, most have primarily relied on textual records to evaluate the Nixon presidency. There is certainly much to learn from the textual files, but the tapes offer up a raw, uncensored take on the Nixon White House, one that clearly shows the divisions between some of the more civic-minded officials in the administration and the president. While Nixon's defenders often focus on the size of the collection and insist that the "tapes can be excerpted or taken out of context to 'prove' just about anything," one cannot ignore the totality of Nixon's misdeeds and his broader views on governance that can be heard on the recordings.[35] Collectively, the White House tapes challenge some of the more forgiving takes that have shaped some of the more common narratives about Nixon.

Installed in February 1971, Nixon's voice-activated taping system recorded private conversations in several different offices inside the White

House, and was later expanded to capture the president's conversations at Camp David. The recording devices were a secret to everyone inside of the White House with the exception of the president, Haldeman, Nixon's aide Alexander Butterfield, and the Secret Service staff who helped maintain the system. The overwhelming majority of the people captured on the tapes, including key administration figures such as John Ehrlichman and National Security Advisor Henry Kissinger, had no idea they were being recorded. The system was quickly taken down in July 1973 shortly after the public first learned about the president's secret taping system during Butterfield's Senate Watergate hearing testimony.

Over the last two decades, the White House tapes have given researchers unprecedented access to the Oval Office, allowing everyone the chance to listen to Nixon's private discussions regarding everything from Vietnam to his thoughts on popular culture such as the 1970s sitcom *All in the Family*. Between the Richard Nixon Presidential Library and the work of outside scholars, the entire collection can be found online. Anyone can easily find some of the more lurid conversations through a simple YouTube search that will pull up tapes that feature the president sounding drunk, ranting about student protestors, or making blatantly racist and anti-Semitic statements. This level of access has left historians wrestling with how to properly use the tapes to situate his presidency within the era of the postwar imperial president. From FDR to LBJ, presidents recorded their private conversations inside of the White House, but unlike Nixon, their systems were not voice-activated. The sizes of their secret White House recordings varied, but they were much more selective with regard to which conversations they recorded for history. Because of Watergate, Nixon never had a chance to fully review and edit his collection for future generations. As a result, no other president has left us with such an unvarnished look into their day-to-day operations. While this does place Nixon at a clear disadvantage when compared to other presidents, historians must also acknowledge that this does not excuse Nixon from his actions. Instead of explaining away Watergate by focusing on other presidents, the Nixon tapes should force historians to fully confront Watergate. By doing so, scholars will be better equipped to not only explain the Nixon presidency, but also better address past, present, and future abuses of power.

Those who defend Nixon have frequently dismissed the White House tapes as a collection of moments where the president was simply letting off steam. White House aides were in fact often adept at handling and eventually ignoring many of the president's more unorthodox requests.

In a 1987 oral history, Ehrlichman compared Nixon's rants to the Queen of Hearts in *Alice's Adventures in Wonderland,* demands that he and his colleagues usually ignored.[36] There were in fact many instances where some of Nixon's closest aides chose not to follow through on some of his more sinister orders. "And there were times he'd get up in the night and couldn't sleep, and so I recognized the phone call was just handholding . . . There were times when I knew I couldn't and shouldn't," remembered Charles "Chuck" Colson, who served as special counsel to the president from 1969 to 1973. "If I sensed that it was one of those middle of the night deals where he was just ranting, I'd let him rant and listen." He added, "There were many times when I did not do what he said and got the person involved who should stop him."[37]

What Colson and other close advisers to the president often underplayed in their later recollections of their time in the White House was the fact that there were also instances where they carried out some of Nixon's more questionable orders. Figures like Colson may have attempted to delay and distract the president when it came to some of his unethical requests, but they also aided and abetted his dark side throughout his presidency. If Nixon brought up one of his more questionable orders on a repeated basis, and not just during a single rant, there were those, like Colson, who were more than willing to carry out the president's wishes.

The officials who said no also attempted to avoid confrontations with the president, as they hoped to maintain a diplomatic relationship with Nixon. The main difference between these officials and the president's men was their collective moral compass. Despite their initial sense of loyalty to the president, they all reached a point where they felt that they had no choice but to resist his orders.

This book uses the tapes as a key primary source in order to better document the Nixon presidency and reveal the overwhelming pressure that administration officials faced when dealing with the White House's illegal orders. It is not my goal to only focus on a few conversations where the president was at his absolute worst. Rather, this study of the Nixon presidency uses the tapes to highlight persistent attempts to expand the powers of the presidency, often in hopes of punishing political opponents. While this book will include plenty of colorful, lewd, and offensive segments from the tapes, there is an overriding emphasis on the numerous conversations that show the White House's protracted efforts to "screw" their enemies.

Most Nixon scholars have made little use of the tapes to further investigate the totality of Nixon's abuses of power and the culture that led to Watergate. Even among books that have incorporated the tapes into their narratives of the Nixon White House, too many have focused on the minutiae of the Watergate scandal or details surrounding the administration's foreign policy. Whether it is John Dean's recent book *The Nixon Defense*, voluminous collections of transcripts on the Watergate break-in/cover-up, or even books driven by conspiracy theories about Nixon's downfall, too many scholars have been too caught up in either explaining or debunking every single detail of the traditional Watergate narrative.[38] Focusing only on the time period between the break-in and the president's resignation obscures and diminishes the decisions that the president made prior to the arrest of the Watergate burglars in the early morning hours of June 17, 1972. It is partially this overemphasis on such a narrow time period that has led many to conclude that Watergate is a well-worn subject.

In addition to Kutler's work, Weiner's 2015 book on the Nixon presidency, *One Man against the World: The Tragedy of Richard Nixon*, and Ken Hughes's invaluable work on Nixon and Vietnam have both recently used the tapes to further explore the Nixon presidency. With a heavy emphasis on Nixon's foreign policy, they are among the very few authors who have taken advantage of recently released materials to uncover new information.[39] John A. Farrell's *Richard Nixon: The Life*, the most recent stab at a definitive Nixon biography, also makes excellent use of Nixon's presidential archives. While the book adopts an occasionally forgiving tone toward the thirty-seventh president, it does not brush aside the president's dark side.[40] For example, the book received a wave of publicity for uncovering a note from H. R. Haldeman that stated that Nixon had instructed him to find a secret way to "monkey wrench" peace negotiations in Vietnam during the final days of the 1968 campaign.[41] Historians had for many years speculated about the Nixon campaign's efforts to block President Johnson's attempts to negotiate a peace settlement, but Farrell's discovery brought scholars significantly closer to fully confronting one of Nixon's darkest moments.[42]

This book builds off of the work of these and others who have recognized the importance of the White House tapes and other recently released documents in exploring the depths of the Nixon presidency. The tapes provide scholars with much more than just anti-Semitic or racist sound bites—they are a valuable resource that further informs us on Nixon's worldview, and how he viewed both his political enemies and the moderates who refused to do his bidding.

In addition to the Nixon tapes, this book relies on textual documents from the Richard Nixon Presidential Library, the Watergate Special Prosecution Force files, the private papers of the individuals who resisted the president's orders, memoirs, oral histories, and recent interviews with Nixon administration officials. There are inherent limits to oral histories and other accounts of the era, but they have provided extremely valuable insider accounts of the Nixon administration. Most importantly, their memories of the individuals who opposed the president serve as a counterpoint to Nixon's rants about them on the tapes. Those memories, when balanced out with archival sources, further document the dissent that existed within the administration prior to Watergate.

Johnnie Walters's aforementioned refusal to audit political enemies in the summer and fall of 1972 provides the central story of the first chapter. Despite enormous pressure from John Ehrlichman, Walters protected the IRS from becoming a political arm of the White House. Soon after Nixon's special counsel John Dean met with the commissioner to hand over the White House's enemies list, with special instructions to initiate audits, Walters took the list to George Shultz and stated that he would not carry out the order. Shultz supported the decision to say no to the White House and encouraged Walters to do nothing with the list, thereby blocking the White House's attempt to control the nation's tax system. Aside from their rejection of the enemies list, both Shultz and Walters were independent figures within the administration and had previously stood up to the White House in smaller ways.

The first chapter also looks at the history of the relationship between Nixon and the IRS, dating back to the first year of his presidency. Through tracking the White House's many attempts to politicize the IRS, along with the president's increasing desires to control the agency, one can better appreciate Shultz and Walters's courageous actions. The IRS was a central component of Nixon's plans for his second term, and their shared opposition to the president prevented the IRS from engaging in systematic abuses of power. Aside from Walters's memoir and a few historians of the IRS who have mentioned Walters's stand in passing, this is the first full account of the commissioner's decision to not audit the White House's enemies.[43] Due to the cloud surrounding Watergate, many have understandably assumed that wide-scale audits on political opponents took place during the Nixon years. The story of Johnnie Walters and George Shultz is a corrective to that broader assumption, while also showing just how close the White House came to controlling the IRS.

The second chapter looks at how officials within the Office of Management and Budget stopped Nixon's attempt to cut federal funds to universities due to the presence of antiwar protests. While the enemies list project was arguably the most dangerous plot, Nixon's attempt to strip federal subsidies to elite schools was the plan that was the most representative of the cultural chasm between the president and the moderates within his administration. This section will look at the creation of the OMB under Nixon, its impact on the federal government, its internal culture, and most importantly the moment where three assistant directors within the OMB refused to carry out the president's plan to punish the Massachusetts Institute of Technology. Soon after the order was passed down, Kenneth Dam, William Morrill, and Paul O'Neill bypassed the current leadership within the OMB and went to their former boss George Shultz, who was then secretary of the treasury. After they told the secretary they would rather resign than carry out the order, Shultz agreed with their stance and told them there was no need to resign. The order was never carried out and Shultz once again helped block Nixon's order. With the exception of an oral history from Paul O'Neill and a memoir from William Morrill, very little has been published about Nixon's MIT order. This chapter uncovers entirely new materials that further add to the public's understanding of Nixon's contempt for the antiwar movement of the Vietnam era.

The second chapter also analyzes Nixon's obsession with the Ivy League establishment and its influence, both within academia and his administration. He was determined to create what he often referred to as a "new establishment," and lessen the influence of the academic elites across the federal government. As the largest recipient of federal aid, and a site of substantial antiwar protests, MIT was the president's number-one target. As historians such as Margaret O'Mara have shown, MIT was just one of many schools who became intertwined with the nation's postwar military industrial complex.[44] This chapter will explore the history of MIT's relationship with the federal government, the protests that occurred during the Vietnam era, and how the institution's approach to dissent angered the president. As an alumnus of MIT, Shultz was a product of the academic culture that Nixon detested. Shultz's efforts to protect federal aid to universities pitted him against his successor at OMB, the more loyal and more conservative Caspar Weinberger. As the new director of the OMB, and later as the head of the Department of Health, Education, and Welfare (HEW), Weinberger took preliminary steps to initiate the president's plan in late 1972 and early 1973. The plan was never fully carried out, but looking at the details of Weinberger's actions presents an important comparison with the resistance of Shultz and others within the OMB.

Elliot Richardson's iconic refusal to fire the Watergate special prosecutor, Archibald Cox, is arguably the most famous instance of an administration official saying no to President Nixon. Richardson's resignation, which was quickly followed by Deputy William Ruckelshaus's decision to resign, was soon dubbed the Saturday Night Massacre and marked a turning point in the public's overall perception of Nixon and Watergate. However, it was also an extension of the culture that shaped similar decisions made by those within the IRS and the OMB. The last two chapters examine Richardson's time in the Nixon administration, his quiet battles with the White House, and how those experiences helped shape his decision to resign in protest during the Saturday Night Massacre. This last section also emphasizes the importance of his staff—in the State Department, HEW, the Pentagon, and the Justice Department—in supporting and pushing Richardson to stand up to the White House. After four years of being a fairly loyal soldier within the Nixon administration, the establishment Republican from Massachusetts reached his breaking point with the Saturday Night Massacre. It was what transformed him from being a yes man to someone who said no to the president.

In many ways, Richardson embodied the culture of the Ivy League establishment that Nixon was determined to destroy. His place within the administration was often tenuous, but he consistently proved to be a valuable asset for the White House, giving Nixon more credibility with both moderates and liberals. Furthermore, Richardson was mostly loyal to Nixon on the larger issues, and kept his private disagreements with the White House to himself. This combination of credibility and loyalty led to Nixon's decision to appoint Richardson as attorney general in the midst of the growing Watergate scandal. The decision vastly underestimated Richardson's integrity and eventually resulted in a direct confrontation between the Justice Department and the president. Richardson's dramatic resignation during the Saturday Night Massacre marked the moment that the moderates could no longer remain silent in their dissent. The events surrounding the Saturday Night Massacre have been covered in several memoirs and histories of the Watergate, with Ken Gormley's biography of Archibald Cox, *Archibald Cox: Conscience of a Nation,* offering up the crisis's most thorough recounting.[45]

Even though Richardson's time as attorney general was closely watched by reporters in the summer and fall of 1973, and became a part of Watergate lore, there is still much to learn about the man and his relationship with the thirty-seventh president. The last section of this book offers up the first detailed account of Richardson's relationship with Nixon, and his flexible role within the administration. Relying on Richardson's personal papers and interviews with some of his closest advisers, this last section takes on a traditional narrative and fleshes it out with Richardson's closely guarded perspective on the events that led to Nixon's resignation.

During the initial stages of this project, I gained firsthand experience dealing with the politics surrounding Nixon's legacy, and the persistence of the campaign to rehabilitate his presidency. This project is deeply informed by my time working for the National Archives at the Richard Nixon Presidential Library and Museum in Yorba Linda, California. Originally opened in 1990 as a privately run facility paid for by Nixon allies, the Nixon Library became a part of the federal presidential library system in 2007. This agreement between the private Nixon Foundation and the National Archives led to the library obtaining Nixon's White House records, materials that had been seized by the federal government in the wake of Watergate due to fears that Nixon and his aides would tamper with the materials. I first joined the Nixon Library as a graduate student intern, giving tours to a wide range of school groups, from kindergarten classes to senior citizens. Working with the library's Education Department, I learned how to lead nonpartisan tours through a museum that was at the time made up of exhibits that were created by Nixon loyalists in 1990. Explaining the life and times of Richard Nixon in front of exhibits that aggressively defended his legacy made me intensely aware of the politics surrounding the Nixon era and public history. Discussing Nixon's abuses of power with students, when pro-Nixon docents, Nixon Foundation employees, and Nixon White House alum were sometimes in the vicinity, was a constant reminder that the thirty-seventh president's legacy is still contested and far from settled.[46]

I was hired in January 2011 as the special assistant to the director of the library. Timothy Naftali, a Cold War historian, who became the library's first federal director in 2007, was then in the final stages of putting together the museum's new nonpartisan Watergate Gallery. Written by Nixon loyalists, the library's previous Watergate exhibit was taken down in 2007 due to its polemical tone. For seventeen years, museum visitors were presented with an outright defense of Nixon that was meant to convince readers that Watergate was a coup carried out by the president's enemies to reverse his landslide victory over Senator George S. McGovern in 1972. Facing stiff resistance from the Nixon Foundation, and at times his supervisors within the National Archives, Naftali navigated the library through treacherous waters that at several points could have compromised the historical veracity of the exhibit. The exhibit opened in March 2011 and offered museum visitors a full-fledged look at the Watergate scandal, starting at the release of the Pentagon Papers and ending with the Frost-Nixon interviews. Whereas the previous exhibit had glossed over the details of Nixon's crimes, the new exhibit allowed the public to explore the multitude of evidence that brought down the president. With the opening of the new exhibit, students can now listen to uncensored segments of the White House tapes and listen to the president obstruct justice during the Watergate cover-up.[47] My research was born out of this experience: while I contributed to the Watergate exhibit, I learned more about the stories of the Republicans who said no to Nixon. The exhibit, which includes an oral history snippet with George Shultz discussing his refusal to have the IRS audit political enemies, convinced me that there was still much to uncover about Nixon's abuses of power.

Naftali left the Nixon Library in November 2011, but I stayed in Yorba Linda until 2014, assisting the library's interim directors and continuing to work with our office's Education Department. After a year where the library opened the new Watergate exhibit, formally declassified the Pentagon Papers, released Nixon's Grand Jury testimony, and hosted its first nonpartisan academic conference, I expected the National Archives to continue to promote nonpartisan public history with the appointment of an independent-minded historian to lead the library.

Instead, the search for a director dragged on for more than three years. A major cause for the delay was the Nixon Foundation's unwillingness to accept a candidate who had been openly critical of Nixon in the past. For nearly a year, the Nixon Foundation refused to meet with the National Archives's leading candidate, Vietnam War historian Mark Atwood Lawrence, due to his prior scholarly work that critiqued Nixon. Combined with the Archivist of the United States David Ferriero's refusal to make an appointment without the Nixon Foundation's approval, the foundation won out and Lawrence dropped out as the lead candidate in the summer of 2013. In the end, a mainstream Vietnam War historian was too much for the Nixon Foundation to handle and for the National Archives to support.[48] That same year, I was told that the Nixon

Foundation was complaining to my supervisor that my research was "anti-Nixon." I sometimes felt that I was living my dissertation research, as the complaints of the Nixon Foundation about a low-ranking government employee echoed Nixon's obsession with punishing bureaucrats within his administration. With the library rapidly losing the influence it had built up in terms of its control over the museum and public programming, I decided to leave the Nixon Library and accept a job offer from the Tamiment Library and Robert F. Wagner Labor Archives at New York University, where Naftali had become the director.

The Nixon Library eventually hired Naftali's successor in January 2015: Michael Ellzey, an assistant city manager from nearby Irvine who had accumulated plenty of experience at managing public-private partnerships. While most of the presidential libraries are led by either historians or archivists, Ellzey's selection signaled that the National Archives and the Nixon Foundation could not come to a consensus on a trained Nixon expert. "I think what they're trying to do is get managers," said Ronald Walker, a former Nixon aide and chairman of the Nixon Foundation. He added, "You have enough researchers at the National Archives."[49] The selection was made as the library and the foundation were preparing to update their museum galleries, with the latter raising $15 million for the project while also taking the lead in crafting the content. Leading the fundraising effort was Fred V. Malek, a longtime Republican operative and former Nixon White House aide. Malek's career was later tarnished by the discovery that he participated in providing a list of Jewish employees in the Bureau of Labor Statistics in the summer of 1971. Unlike the main characters of this project, Malek followed through on one of Nixon's unethical orders, as the initiative was the product of one of the president's frequent anti-Semitic outbursts.[50] At the opening ceremony for the new museum galleries, Malek was one of several featured speakers. "We are so proud . . . in creating this magnificent new library, the new exhibits, which tell the story and totality of the man who was a great president." He added that it was time to "start to repay a debt of honor to this great man." In honor of his fundraising efforts, the newly renovated Nixon Library now has a theater named after Malek and his wife.[51]

The Nixon Foundation also hired another Nixon White House aide, Dwight Chapin, and one of the president's ghostwriters for his memoir, Frank Gannon, as consultants who contributed to the museum's renovation process.[52] Chapin was notably one of several White House staff members who was sent to prison after being convicted of perjury when he lied to a grand jury during the Watergate cover-up. During a May 2017 appearance at the Nixon Library to promote his latest book on Nixon, former Nixon speechwriter and conservative commentator Patrick J. Buchanan thanked the two consultants for their work on the new museum: "[I have] just been on a tour of the library now that Frank Gannon and others, and Dwight Chapin and others and [CEO and president of the Nixon Foundation] Bill [Baribault] have really fixed it up."[53]

Unsurprisingly, the new museum galleries maintained a strong defense of Nixon's presidency. Thanks to the role that the National Archives played in editing the galleries, the overall tone of the museum had considerably softened when compared to the exhibits that were crafted in 1990. Gone are the exhibits that leveled petty attacks on the Kennedys, Woodward and Bernstein, and other liberal icons of the era. Still, the new galleries collectively seek to rescue Nixon's reputation from Watergate, Vietnam, and all of the negative stories that have shaped mainstream public's perception of his presidency.

The reopening of the museum in October 2016 ushered in the rebranded "New Nixon Library" and was praised by both local and national media outlets, which mostly focused on the technological innovations that would bring the Nixon era to life for millennials. "Our goal is honesty," stated Christopher Cox, the president's grandson. "Now the museum isn't just better. It's state of the art."[54] The few articles that mentioned the contentious institutional history of the library zeroed in on the seeming willingness to adopt a more even-handed approach. Based on the inclusion of exhibits that allowed visitors to view a selection of the president's archival records and come to their own conclusions regarding some of his more controversial decisions, the new galleries were presented as balanced. "People can take it all in and then make up their minds about his legacy," said John Barr, treasurer of the Nixon Foundation.[55] Reports often overlooked the pro-Nixon framing of the new galleries, choosing to focus more on a narrative of reconciliation than one of contestation. The *OC Register* declared that the library had "made peace with its past," and praised the museum for "morphing into the kind of jewel that suits both Orange County and a presidential museum."[56]

The new museum opens with an introductory film that begins with Nixon's resignation, but does not include any real explanation of why he chose to do so. There are no details when it comes to Watergate, only news clips that feature the Watergate burglars, a very brief mention of the cover-up, a few segments from Nixon's prime-time resignation speech, and a heavy emphasis on Nixon's distaste for giving up. "He would not quit," says Patrick Buchanan, one of the film's main talking heads along-side figures such as Henry Kissinger and scholars like Evan Thomas and Mark Updegrove. The museum galleries open with an exhibit on "The Sixties" with the subtitle "A Nation in Turmoil." The exhibit offers useful short descriptions of some of the major events and movements of the era, but the visuals place a heavy emphasis on the chaos of the era. Much like his 1968 presidential campaign, Nixon is shown to be a law and order candidate, but one who stressed unity over politics. In the exhibit, Nixon is not a part of the culture wars of the era. Instead, he is above the fray. One panel features a selection from Nixon's first inaugural address. "We cannot learn from one another until we stop shouting at one another." The 2011 Watergate exhibit survived the museum's renovation untouched, but whereas it used to sit at the end of the museum, visitors now walk by the president and the First Lady sitting inside their helicopter with a recording of the First Lady recalling, "It's so sad. It's so sad." The museum quickly transitions from Watergate to Nixon's hard-luck childhood. The very next room features an exhibit "Back to the Beginning" that seeks to evoke compassion, as we learn about the president's humble beginnings in Southern California alongside a photo of a young Nixon with his father at the family's general store. While the tone of the new galleries is not nearly as strident as what was produced in the 1990s, Nixon's final campaign lives on in the halls of the museum.

The recent history of the Nixon Library shows that the legacy of Richard Nixon is still contested ground and deeply tied to present-day politics. Even though debates surrounding Nixon are without a doubt more heated in Orange County, they are still firmly a part of our political culture. Although much has been written about Watergate, focusing on the moderates who said no to Nixon provides a new and deeper level of understanding about the president's downfall. Taken together, they provide a valuable reminder that acts of opposition to the president's abuses of power were not based purely on partisan politics. Those who refused to carry out Nixon's orders came from an older brand of Republicanism that placed a higher value on nonpartisan analytical thinking and a more ethical approach to governance. Watergate was not simply an extension of the deep-seated political divisions of the era; it was a very real test of the nation's democracy. These arguments about Watergate are not entirely new, but one gains a deeper insight into the constitutional crisis of the era by learning about the Republicans who said no to Nixon.

1

"An Independent Son of a Bitch"

Nixon, Johnnie Walters, and the IRS

"Mr. Secretary, I'm sick and tired," said Johnnie Walters, commissioner of the IRS, to Treasury Secretary George Shultz on August 29, 1972. "You can have this fucking job anytime you want it." That threat to resign followed a tense telephone conversation with John Ehrlichman, who had said he was "very impatient" with Walters over the IRS investigation of Larry O'Brien, chairman of the Democratic National Committee (DNC). Led by the president's repeated demands and leaks to the White House from the commissioner's assistant Roger Barth, Ehrlichman increasingly pressured Shultz and Walters for more information about O'Brien throughout that summer. Stationed at three different posts in Shultz's office, Barth, Shultz, and Walters each played very different roles in their August 29 conversation with Ehrlichman. Barth mostly remained silent, Walters clashed with Nixon's domestic affairs adviser, and Shultz attempted to act as the peacemaker. After Shultz spent some time carefully going over the details of the investigation, Ehrlichman set his sights on the commissioner. "I think there's been foot dragging, I think you've been way too lenient with this guy." Just in case there was any confusion he said, "That's directly to Johnnie and not anybody else!"

Walters was irritated and countered Ehrlichman's attack: "I'm busting my gut . . . to do everything to protect the president. . . . especially when we're playing with fire!" Unsurprisingly, Ehrlichman disagreed. "We've been protecting the president for years and years at the IRS and that's an excuse not to do something!" Barth did not say a word throughout the entire exchange. Sensing that the meeting was spiraling out of control, the secretary took over the final few minutes of the discussion and insisted that they would find an appropriate way to look at the returns.[1] It was the last conversation between Ehrlichman and Walters. Shultz never raised the O'Brien issue again with Walters, and the commissioner backed down from his threat to resign.[2]

Walters's threat to resign from his post was the culmination of more than a year of heated battles with the White House over their attempts to politicize the IRS. Even though the O'Brien issue was never brought up again, Nixon did not give up on his efforts to control the IRS. The O'Brien investigation was only one part of a full frontal assault on the IRS in the summer and fall of 1972. Shultz and Walters's tense conversation with Ehrlichman prefigured the White House's bid to have the IRS adopt their enemies list and carry out political audits in the weeks leading up to the election. When the president's counsel John Dean presented a list of hundreds of McGovern campaign contributors that the White House wanted the IRS to audit, both Shultz and Walters refused. The list was one of several that had been drafted within the White House, but it was the only one that had been delivered to the commissioner with specific instructions to audit individuals for their political contributions. The president had hoped Walters would be a "ruthless son of a bitch," who would "do what he's told."[3] But with the support of his superior George Shultz, Walters locked the list in a safe and never followed through on the White House's order. Although the Nixon White House did succeed in infiltrating certain parts of the IRS, Walters and Shultz's refusal to audit political enemies protected the greater integrity of the agency. The two men stood in the way of Nixon's most ambitious power grab, one that would have institutionalized his abuses of power.

The president's plans for the IRS ultimately failed, as the rise of the Watergate scandal brushed aside any of the White House's attempts for more control over the agency. The president's schemes could have easily been carried out had it not been for the leadership of Republicans within the IRS and the Treasury Department like Shultz and Walters. If they had decided to yield to the president's orders, the IRS would have turned into a direct extension of the Nixon White House by initiating hundreds of politically based audits on Nixon's enemies. These actions would have further damaged the integrity of the agency, as well as the nation's entire democratic process. With the enemies list in their hands, Shultz and Walters both acutely recognized the danger of the requests and fought to protect the IRS from the president.

The White House's actions in the months leading up to the 1972 presidential election were one part of a nearly four-year effort to transform the IRS. Since his first year in office, the president and his aides had tried to wrest control of the IRS from a bureaucracy that they felt was largely at odds with the White House. Whether it was going after the tax-exempt status of left-wing organizations or trying to promote Nixon loyalists, the White House regularly attempted to use the IRS as a tool to expand their authority. In numerous taped conversations, Nixon described the IRS as a vital part of his plans to dramatically reshape the federal government. As Nixon outlined his goals for a second term, appointing Walters's successor at the IRS was often a central part of his vision of the next four years. In a meeting with H.R. Haldeman and the then White House's personnel chief Fred Malek just weeks before his second inauguration, the president stated, "There's no appointment that I consider more important than the IRS appointment."[4]

Control over the sixty thousand civil servants within the IRS was at the forefront of the White House's attempts to establish a more dominant executive branch that could readily use the agency to stifle a wide range of political activities. In order to expand the power of the state through the use of the IRS, Nixon often relied on his most loyal, and often most conservative, supporters within the federal government. For the president, loyalty trumped any sort of conservative ideology, but the two were often in sync when it came to the White House's attempts to control the IRS. On the whole, several key conservative loyalists within the administration saw the IRS as an agency that could and should be used against liberal and left-wing organizations.

The White House initially viewed the Republicans who stood in their way as irritating roadblocks, but as time went on, they were grouped together with the president's enemies. Shultz and Walters were both Republicans, identified as conservatives, but they were efficient civil servants above everything else. Nixon's attempt to politicize the IRS is arguably the most representative of Nixon's tendency to conflate conservatism with presidential power. With very few exceptions, Nixon wanted to use the IRS to punish the left. Unlike Nixon's cultural approach to conservatism, which placed a high priority on loyalty, Shultz and Walters both demonstrated political independence and a strong desire to keep their work within the federal government separate from politics. Although they came from different backgrounds, their mutual decision to stand up to the White House with regard to the enemies list was connected to their shared belief in the value of civil service.

In order to fully understand the importance of Shultz and Walters's refusal to take action on the White House's enemies list, one must start with Nixon's relationship with the IRS during the early years of his presidency. The White House's earliest efforts to reshape the IRS included monitoring appointments, attempting to promote Nixon loyalists, and targeting left-wing organizations and their tax-exempt status. The president and his aides avoided a direct confrontation with the IRS, and chose instead to work around the edges in order to avoid a potential scandal. Embedded within these practices were signs of what became a more fully developed vision for the IRS and the role that it would play within the Nixon administration. Throughout his first term, Nixon frequently became embittered over his failed attempts to change the IRS, and subsequently adopted a much more aggressive approach to politicize the agency. Although the president's own advisers occasionally dragged their feet due to their fears of getting caught, it was the leadership of the IRS that directly resisted Nixon's orders. It is through the Nixon White House's earliest interactions with the IRS that it becomes clear just how important the agency would eventually loom in the president's ambitious plans for the agency following his reelection.

NIXON, RANDOLPH THROWER, AND THE WHITE HOUSE'S EARLY ATTEMPTS TO CONTROL THE IRS

In a three-hour meeting with Haldeman, Ehrlichman, and Kissinger on July 21, 1969, Nixon mapped out his thoughts on the overall direction of his administration. Sitting with the men whom he identified as his "hard-core inner circle," the president was inspired by the recent Apollo 11 mission, which had taken place the day before. Throughout the meeting, he was insistent that the White House should use the word "GO" as their theme for the next several months. Haldeman wrote in his daily diary that Nixon argued that the theme meant "All systems ready, never be indecisive, get along, take risks, be exciting," and argued that they should not "fall into dry rot of just managing the chaos better. Must use the great power of the office to *do something.*" While the rest of the nation celebrated the feats of the Apollo 11 astronauts, Nixon linked the event to the need not only to take a more proactive approach to the presidency in the broader sense, but also to use the power of his office to harass and intimidate his opponents. During the meeting, Nixon stated that the "Main thing is we haven't used the power of the White House, to reward and punish." Later in the meeting Nixon also mentioned that he wanted to "set up and activate dirty tricks."[5] While Nixon saw the first six months of his presidency as a period where his team had settled into the White House, he was now prepared to take action on solidifying his support within his administration and take certain steps to expand his reach within the government.

The previous spring, Nixon appointed Randolph W. Thrower, a Republican lawyer from Georgia, to be the new commissioner of the IRS. In the midst of his appointment, Congress began to pressure the IRS to take a harder line on tax-exempt groups, targeting newly formed left-wing activist groups. There was arguably a legitimate concern about the wave of antiwar and civil rights organizations that had sprung up in the late 1960s, as their political activities may have violated their tax-exempt status. In response, the Senate and the House's Committee on Ways and Means led separate investigations into the process of granting tax exemptions to activist groups.[6] Nixon naturally shared Congress's concern and began to encourage the IRS to begin cracking down on groups that actively opposed his presidency. Soon after his appointment, Thrower met with Arthur F. Burns, a counselor to the president, and discussed the president's interest regarding the tax-exempt status of activist groups. Based on Thrower's notes of the meeting, Burns said that Nixon was worried "over the fact that tax-exempt funds may be supporting activist groups engaged in stimulating riots both on the campus and within our inner cities."[7] The meeting coincided with a memorandum written by White House aide Tom Charles Huston on June 18, 1969, that directly notified the president that the IRS would now take "a close look at activities of left-wing organizations which are operating with tax exempt fund." Huston recommended the White House use the IRS to monitor left-wing organizations, and Nixon wrote back that he agreed.[8]

Arising out of the public pressure from Congress and the private conversations and memorandums within the White House, the IRS created the Activist Organization Committee, later renamed the Special Services Staff (SSS) in the summer of 1969. Under the leadership of Thrower, the SSS conducted many credible investigations, but the secret committee also became susceptible to attempts by other parts of the administration to target certain organizations. While other special committees within the IRS relied on internal investigations, the SSS was the only group within the agency that relied on reports from other agencies. Whether it was the FBI, the Justice Department, or even the White House, the SSS regularly responded to reports that focused more on the politics of a particular group rather than the details of their finances.

The FBI was the largest source, sending nearly twelve thousand individual reports to the SSS, some of which had come from its infamous COINTELPRO surveillance program that targeted the left. Overall, information from the FBI added up to 43 percent of the data collected by the SSS, leading to politicized investigations of the Black Panthers, the Vietnam War Moratorium Day Committee, and other left-wing organizations. Through the work of the SSS, the IRS audited many of the same groups that were targeted by Congress and the White House for full-fledged investigations.[9] The actions of the SSS were certainly not unprecedented within the history of the federal government, but they provided a crucial outlet for the White House to begin to expand its influence within the IRS.

Despite the agency's efforts to clamp down on tax-exempt groups, the president and his aides within the White House continued to feel powerless when it came to the IRS. Even with the high level of harassment of activist organizations, the White House often complained that the SSS was not aggressive enough in collecting damaging information about their enemies. A year and a half after the establishment of the SSS, Huston reported to Haldeman that the IRS had demonstrated a "lack of guts and effort." He concluded: "The Republican appointees appear afraid and unwilling to do anything with IRS that could be politically helpful."[10] The memorandum eventually reached Commissioner Thrower, who saw Huston as part of a group of "young men at the White House who were unaware of the proper function of the IRS," a trend that he identified as "a growing concern over the latter period of 1970."[11]

The White House's earliest attempt to have one of its own staff members gain access to private tax records occurred soon after they hired Clark Mollenhoff in the fall of 1969. Mollenhoff, a journalist whose reports on corruption within the Teamsters union earned him a Pulitzer Prize in 1958, was officially hired as a special counsel to the president. Mollenhoff only worked for Nixon for nine months, but during that time he oversaw special investigations that led to him obtaining access to the tax returns of several individuals. Thrower agreed to let Mollenhoff study certain tax returns under "limited circumstances," and only with written authorization from the president.[12]

The commissioner provided office space in the IRS for Mollenhoff, who went through the records of nine individuals over the period of seven to eight months. Based on the information he had collected, Mollenhoff submitted a request to Thrower for audits on thirteen individuals on March 31, 1970.[13] Mollenhoff's list had originally come from Haldeman, who had told him to have the IRS audit the thirteen individuals. When the request reached the IRS, Thrower refused to initiate any of the audits since there was not enough data to provide justification. The request for audits in the spring of 1970 did not lead to abuses of power, but the decision to allow a Nixon aide access to private records marked a new stage in the precarious relationship between the IRS and the White House. Although Mollenhoff later defended his actions and claimed that he primarily conducted background checks, his investigations set a dangerous precedent for the Nixon White House and opened the door to future attempts to politicize the IRS.[14]

Within the IRS, the White House relied on Roger V. Barth, a former advance man for the Nixon daughters during the 1968 campaign, to provide insider information about the agency and its investigations. Based on recommendations from the White House, Barth was hired as Thrower's assistant in the spring of 1969 and quickly established himself as Nixon's man. Barth's deep-seated loyalty to Nixon was not a secret to most of his coworkers, as he hung framed, autographed pictures of the president and his family on the walls of his office.[15] Despite objections from many within the agency who saw Barth as a White House spy, the commissioner relied on his assistant for meetings notes and for background research on potential appointees. Throughout his time at the IRS, Barth regularly discussed internal IRS investigations with White House staff members while also complaining about the commissioner's leadership. In a meeting with the president, Ehrlichman once described Barth as "not only our man, but he likes to snitch on people. . . . gets vicious hatred of anyone on the other side."[16]

While Barth proved to be a useful resource within the IRS, the White House also relied on information about the agency from one of their own political operatives, Jack Caulfield. A colorful character who had previously worked as a detective for the New York Police Department, Caulfield was initially hired by Nixon in 1968 as a campaign security official. He was brought into the White House the following year as a staff assistant to the president, but soon became responsible for special political investigations. Known as a "super sleuth" by Ehrlichman and others within the White House, Caulfield carried out dirty tricks for nearly three years, and only became a public figure through his connections to the Watergate cover-up in 1973.[17] His first major project for the White House involved working with another former NYPD detective, Anthony Ulasewicz, to monitor the activities of Senator Edward M. Kennedy following the Chappaquiddick incident. Caulfield hired

Ulasewicz as a private detective, using political funds to pay him to conduct the Kennedy investigation, among several other covert projects that targeted the White House's enemies. Caulfield also kept tabs on the IRS, paying special attention to any signs of Commissioner Thrower's perceived disloyalty. Beginning in late 1969, Caulfield began to meet with Barth in the White House to discuss their mutual frustrations with the IRS. The two former Nixon campaign aides typically met in Caulfield's White House office to vent about Thrower's unwillingness to stand up to the agency's liberal staff, among other issues. In the summer of 1970, Barth informed Caulfield that Thrower had selected William Connett as the assistant to the commissioner for tax-exempt organizations. The decision infuriated Barth, who told Caulfield that Connett was "not a person that the WH could do anything with."[18] Months later, Barth sent a memorandum to Ehrlichman arguing that Connett was "an ultra-liberal career Democrat who is an integral part of the Club that runs IRS."[19]

Caulfield was especially useful to the recently appointed White House counsel John Dean, who was assigned by Haldeman to come up with a plan to reorganize the IRS in the fall of 1970. Before coming up with his own report, Dean tasked Caulfield with drafting a proposal for agency-wide cooperation with the White House. Caulfield gave his plan to Dean, who then submitted a more comprehensive report to Haldeman three months later.[20] In the introductory memo, Dean warned that a major reorganization of the IRS was "neither necessary nor wise," due to the possibility of being accused of politicizing the IRS.[21] Instead of a large-scale effort to revamp the IRS, Dean and Malek both argued for minor organizational changes that could eventually expand their influence within the IRS. As the president was planning to force Thrower out of the IRS, Dean and Malek warned that such a move would have its limits. In a separate memo to Haldeman, Malek argued that while the IRS had caused "substantial political embarrassment to the White House," firing Thrower and finding a new commissioner would not solve all their problems. "Any Commissioner of IRS is highly susceptible to being 'captured' by the career-oriented bureaucracy," concluded Malek.[22] Dean and Malek had identified the agency's institutional nonpartisan culture as one that opposed the White House's interests.

With Nixon and his aides convinced that new leadership was needed at the IRS, the White House continued to push forward in trying to find a new IRS commissioner. Facing increasing pressure for his removal, Thrower turned in his resignation in January 1971. Caulfield offered up a strong recommendation for his friend Myles J. Ambrose, a New York lawyer who was a former assistant U.S. prosecutor in New York before working for Nixon's 1968 campaign. In a note to Ehrlichman, he stressed the need for a person like Ambrose whose loyalty to the president ran deep. Caulfield wrote that "this Administration cannot effectively control this most powerful bureaucracy until it places the proper candidate at the helm. There is no doubt in my mind that Myles is that candidate."[23] In a memorandum sent to Ehrlichman and Attorney General John Mitchell, Malek conceded that Ambrose had "no real particular competence in the tax area and no real knowledge of the IRS," but because of his "strong political sensitivity and managerial competence," he was to be "regarded as a leading candidate." In Malek's view, Ambrose fit the bill because he believed that the "primary criteria" for the next commissioner was "complete loyalty to the President, coupled with political sensitivity."[24]

Just weeks after the installation of the president's secret White House taping system, Nixon went over the candidates who were being considered to be the next commissioner of the IRS. In a taped conversation with the president, Ehrlichman brought up Johnnie Walters, the then assistant attorney general of the Justice Department's Tax Division. He described Walters to Nixon as one of John Mitchell's assistants and as a "tax man," with a "good track record." He added, "This fellow has the credentials and the standing."[25] Months later, Walters was named the next commissioner of the IRS. Based on his affiliation with Mitchell, a man the president trusted, Nixon and Ehrlichman felt they had chosen a rock-solid loyalist to head up the IRS. However, Walters soon proved to be much more independent than the president had hoped for that winter.

A NEW COMMISSIONER CLASHES WITH THE WHITE HOUSE

Born on December 20, 1919, Johnnie M. Walters, the son of a poor tenant farmer, grew up in Hartsville, South Carolina, a small rural community more than an hour outside of the state's capital of Columbia. Upon graduating from high school, Walters was awarded a local scholarship to Furman University in Greeneville, where he jumped at the chance of building up a career away from his family's farm. Once he graduated from Furman, he joined the Air Force, serving as a navigator on B-24 bombers during World War II and receiving both a Purple Heart and the Flying Cross. After the war, Walters resumed his studies at the University of Michigan, where he received his law degree. Soon after passing the bar, the IRS recruited the young lawyer to work for the

Legislation and Regulations Division of the chief counsel's office in Washington. During his first stint at the IRS, Walters distinguished himself within the agency and was eventually promoted to assistant head of the division. His stay at the IRS ended after four years when he left the agency for the private sector. Over the next sixteen years Walters remained out of the government, first at Texaco and then as a private attorney at a law firm that specialized in tax law in South Carolina.[26]

Just weeks before Nixon's inauguration, the soon-to-be attorney general John Mitchell asked Walters to join the administration as an assistant attorney general who would be responsible for the department's Tax Division. Walters accepted the offer, but told Mitchell and others in the administration that he would not politick for the job. Walters was a tax lawyer, and from the very beginning of his time in the Nixon administration, he made it clear that he was not a politician. Within a few days Walters moved to Washington for his second run as a civil servant. He returned to the federal government as a veteran lawyer in his late 40s, and as someone known for his confidence, efficiency, and willingness to stand up to authority. He was a loyal Republican and came from a conservative political culture, but was also fiercely independent and consistently nonpartisan in his approach to civil service.

As the head of the Justice Department's Tax Division, he oversaw more than two hundred tax lawyers who maintained an impartial approach to their investigations. During his more than two years as an assistant attorney general, Walters enjoyed the job and faced little pressure to politicize his division's work. At one point, John Dean asked Walters about the possibility of having the IRS investigate the Urban Coalition Action Council, the liberal advocacy group that eventually became Common Cause. Dean, who had just left the Justice Department to work in the White House, had become an acquaintance of the assistant attorney general while the two worked at the Justice Department. Dean later discussed his relationship with Walters in a 2013 interview: it was "more of a social than a working relationship. I used to talk to him as somewhat of a friend."[27] After Dean approached his former colleague about investigating the Urban Coalition Action Council, Walters stated his opposition to initiating an investigation and recommended that they should "discuss carefully the possible consequences of the projects." After Walters pushed back on the idea, Dean conceded that there was no concrete evidence to bring the request to the IRS.[28] Although their discussion did not result in any real action, the incident highlighted Walters's distaste for dirty tricks and foreshadowed his later clashes with Dean and the White House. "Not once did we do anything on a political basis," remembered Walters of his time in the Justice Department in a 2008 interview with the Nixon Library.[29]

In the weeks after Thrower turned in his letter of resignation, Walters began to hear rumblings that the White House was having trouble finding a new head of the IRS. Over the previous two years, Walters had become a friend of the outgoing commissioner and was aware of the underlying reasons behind Thrower's forced resignation. As others vying for the job were deemed either too controversial for their connections to the Nixon White House or potentially too disloyal, Ehrlichman and Mitchell believed that they had found the right candidate in Walters. With his past experience as both a private tax attorney and an employee of the IRS, Walters had the perfect resume for the job. More importantly for Ehrlichman, Walters was a Republican from the South whom Mitchell trusted. Mitchell raised the issue with Walters in his office in the spring of 1971, asking his assistant if he would be interested in leading the IRS. Walters agreed, and after a few conversations with Treasury Secretary John Connally, he emerged as the front-runner for the position.

While Ehrlichman and Mitchell were convinced that Walters was someone they could rely on to reshape the IRS and carry out the president's orders, Nixon expressed some doubts leading up to the official appointment in June. The president's uneasiness was partially due to the fact that he knew that the White House had only played a cursory role in the selection process. As with other IRS-related issues, Ehrlichman sought to avoid a direct confrontation with the agency, and chose to trust Walters since he was Mitchell's assistant. On April 13, Ehrlichman first informed the president that Walters would be moving over from the Justice Department to replace Thrower. When Nixon asked if Walters was "alright," Ehrlichman reassured the president that Connally had "a lot of confidence" in him.[30]

Nixon once again asked about Walters in another meeting with Ehrlichman on May 13. "Are we sure he is a good guy? Is he loyal to us?" asked the president. "Well, he's Mitchell's guy and Mitchell vouches for him. I can't vouch for him personally," replied Ehrlichman. Later on in the discussion, Nixon reiterated that he wanted someone who would "do what he's told. . . . Every income tax return I want to see, I see!" The president also insisted that Walters should "go after our enemies, and not go after our friends! Now it's as simple as that!" The discussion then turned to Nixon's suspicions that he was unfairly targeted by the IRS during the Kennedy years, exclaiming, "They went after me!"

Ehrlichman reminded the president that he was on the same page, stating, "We want a lawyer that tells us how to do things, and not that we can't do things." Nixon once again went back to his lack of knowledge about Walters and repeated his expectations for the new commissioner. "I don't know Walters at all, but we want a guy like Kleindienst (the then deputy attorney general) in there who will deliver."[31] Two weeks later, Ehrlichman attempted to calm the president's nerves about the new commissioner. "Apparently people are getting more satisfied that this guy is going to be alright," said Ehrlichman. "He damn well better," said the president.[32]

Walters was announced as the new commissioner of the IRS on June 21, 1971, and was officially sworn in later that summer by Supreme Court Justice Harry Blackmun at the Treasury Department. As he prepared to take on his new post, Walters almost immediately showed his independent streak. In June, Walters specifically argued with Ehrlichman and others within the administration over the role that Barth would play in the IRS. Prior to his meetings with Barth's supporters, Thrower warned Walters that his former assistant's "usefulness" had become "limited," due to his reputation for being a White House spy.[33] With his predecessor's advice in mind, Walters openly questioned whether he should keep the young assistant in his office. When the White House got wind that their inside source's position was in limbo, they sent Malek to make sure that Barth's job was safe.[34] Barth himself even began corresponding with Walters, informing his future boss that he would like to be promoted to be his deputy at IRS.

Walters met with Barth, but told him that he needed someone with more experience in the tax system.[35] In the aftermath of their conversation, Ehrlichman called to talk about Barth's status within the agency. According to Walter's own handwritten notes of the conversation, Ehrlichman asked about the rumors and chose to "level" with the next commissioner of the IRS, describing Barth as "very helpful to WH," and as someone who kept "track [of] the President very well." Walters told Ehrlichman that he would not accept Barth as his deputy due to his youth and inexperience, and insisted that he needed someone who was much more familiar with the inner workings of the agency.[36]

A week later, Walters met with Malek and Connally to sort out the Barth issue, with the three eventually agreeing to keep him as the assistant to the commissioner for a three-month trial period. "If [Barth] does not work out, Malek will support move," wrote Walters during the meeting."[37] Even though Walters agreed to keep Barth as an assistant,

FIGURE 1. Johnnie M. Walters with his wife, Dorothy, and Supreme Court Justice Harry Blackmun at his IRS commissioner swearing-in ceremony, August 6, 1971. (Johnnie M. Walters Papers, South Carolina Political Collections, University of South Carolina)

the White House was still anxious over the amount of influence that would be afforded to their ally within the IRS. In a memorandum sent to Ehrlichman, Tod Hullin, the associate director in the Domestic Council, reported that Walters had recently met with Barth to inform him that he would remain in the IRS, but was "very vague about a specific position." Hullin also wrote that Barth felt that he would be "shoved into a corner and not given any responsibility," and that he would push for a more powerful position in the agency and try to gain support from Secretary Connally.[38]

Barth's worst fears came true when Walters selected William Loeb, a Democrat, to be his deputy in August 1971. Prior to his promotion, Loeb was the assistant regional commissioner for collections in the Atlanta office, and had worked closely with Walters in the chief counsel's office in the early 1950s. Walters was aware that picking Loeb "did not please everyone," even though he was not privy to the various memos that passed through the White House.[39] Rather than earning praise for his nonpartisan approach to naming his deputy, the choice led to the deterioration of Walters's relationship with the White House. In one note that was sent to the White House, Barth described Loeb as "a career Democrat" who according to his sources did not have "any administrative ability." He also complained that Walters had decided to transfer "direct responsibility for all exempt organization matters to a liberal career Democrat (William Connett) with the title of Assistant to the Commissioner for Exempt Organizations." A frustrated Barth concluded that the IRS "was better off under Thrower. Lord help us in 1972."[40] Walters soon became aware that Barth was going outside of the agency in his attempt to stop the promotion of Loeb and other Democrats in the department. In a meeting with Barth, the commissioner made it clear that only he "would handle White House contacts," and that the agency was "trying to operate non-politically around here."[41]

In order to protect the agency, Walters consistently resisted opportunities to build a closer relationship with the White House and even the Treasury Department. At one point, Walters was offered an office in the Treasury building, but he said no. "I wanted to stay with my people," remembered Walters.[42]

THE BEGINNING OF THE ENEMIES LIST

On June 13, 1971, the *New York Times* featured a front-page photograph of Nixon walking with his eldest daughter, Tricia, at her White House wedding. To the right, readers were confronted with a very different story that led with the headline, "Vietnam Archive: Pentagon Study Traces 3 Decades of Growing U.S. Involvement."[43] The piece was the first of several installments of what became known as the Pentagon Papers, a secret history of the Vietnam War that was organized by the Defense Department. Daniel Ellsberg, a former Pentagon employee who had become an antiwar activist, leaked the documents to the *New York Times,* and later the *Washington Post,* in hopes of publicizing the lies the federal government had told the American people with regard to the war. Although the Pentagon Papers targeted previous administrations, Nixon requested a court order to block the publication of the Pentagon Papers in the *New York Times.* On June 30, the Supreme Court ruled in favor of the *Times,* which soon resumed the publication of the Pentagon Papers. "We're up against an enemy, a conspiracy," said an irate Nixon to Haldeman and Kissinger on July 1. The Ellsberg episode convinced Nixon that the White House now had to take even more drastic actions against their opponents on the left. "They're using any means. We are going to use any means. Is that clear?"[44] Soon after that conversation, Nixon authorized the creation of the "Plumbers Unit," a special investigations unit that was managed by White House aide Egil "Bud" Krogh and made up of men such as G. Gordon Liddy and E. Howard Hunt who had experience conducting covert operations. Later that summer, the Plumbers broke into Daniel Ellsberg's psychiatrist office in Beverly Hills in a failed effort to discredit him. The operation, which Ehrlichman approved, was the first of numerous illegal activities that sought to harass the president's opponents and sabotage the Democrats during the 1972 primaries. Less than a year after the Ellsberg mission, the Plumbers were caught breaking into the DNC headquarters inside of the Watergate complex.

As the White House began to adopt an increasingly extreme bunker mentality following the release of the Pentagon Papers, Nixon placed an even greater emphasis on controlling the IRS. In a meeting with Haldeman that took place ten days after the *New York Times* published its first installment of the Pentagon Papers, Nixon told his chief of staff to find ways to audit political enemies. The president specifically mentioned Clark Clifford, the former secretary of defense and longtime Democratic lawyer who opposed the Vietnam War. Haldeman's handwritten notes of the meeting read "Now have our man in IRS. . . . Pull Clark Clifford + top supporters of doves – full list." He also jotted down, "Full field audit – Let us see what we can make of it. Colson make list of the ones we want."[45] Nixon's order set off a larger wave of activity, as several White House officials took more serious steps to try to use the IRS to harass key Democratic donors and supporters of the antiwar movement.

As a young counsel to the president who was looking for ways to impress his superiors, John Dean became immersed in the White House's plan to politicize the IRS. During that summer, Dean spent significant time investigating the Brookings Institution, a liberal think tank that had earned the ire of the president. In a taped meeting, Nixon told Haldeman on June 30 that he wanted the White House to find a way to break into the Brookings Institution so that they could steal files related to President Johnson's bombing halt in Vietnam during the 1968 campaign. At one point, Chuck Colson even organized a plan to firebomb the building and take the documents while firefighters put out the flames. The plan was eventually rejected by Dean and others within the White House as too dangerous.[46] "There was a lot of papering over, a lot of dodging and ducking," remembered Dean.[47] While Nixon's order never came to fruition, Dean continued to look for ways to attack Brookings. A month after the president's rant about Brookings, Dean wrote to Krogh to notify him that he had sent over copies of their tax returns. He added,

"Please note the attached memorandum on what should be done about large number of government contracts now held by the Brookings Institution." In the note to Krogh, Dean offered to find a way to "turn the spigot off" with regards to Brookings' federal contracts.[48]

Dean captured the White House's mood that summer in his memo "Dealing with Our Political Enemies." In the widely circulated note, Dean argued for "a good project coordinator" who could go after the White House's enemies. "Key members of the staff should be requested to inform us as to who they feel we should be giving a hard time." The project coordinator would then "determine what sorts of dealings these individuals have with the federal government and how we can best screw them (e.g., grant availability, federal contracts, litigation, prosecution, etc.)." The memo also argued that the project coordinator would have "access to and full support of the top official of the agency or department in proceeding to deal with the individual." Dean then suggested coming up with a "small list of names" that would act as their "targets for concentration." Although some work had already been done with creating a list of the White House's enemies, Dean's plan fully articulated Nixon's increasing demands to request a move on initiating audits. The memo eventually reached Haldeman's desk, as Gordon Strachan, one of the chief of staff's assistants, attached it to his own note on August 17, 1971. After reading the note, Haldeman initialed the memo and approved Dean's recommendations.[49]

Dean's plan solidified the White House's interest in documenting their enemies in the antiwar movement, the mainstream media, and a wide range of liberal activist groups. In early 1971, Chuck Colson and his staff began compiling a list of Nixon's enemies that was initially meant to be used to identify people who were to be excluded from White House functions. By June 1971, the list had grown to two hundred names and the project began to become tied with Nixon's repeated requests to audit political enemies. Colson sent the list of two hundred to Dean in June, two months before he began to work on his own list of targets. In the weeks after Dean's "screw the enemy" project was approved, Strachan and another Haldeman aide, Larry Higby, pressed Dean to follow through on the list. Dean eventually delivered a list of twenty names to Higby on September 14, 1971, that included media figures such as journalists Mary McGrory and Daniel Schorr, actor Paul Newman, and former NSC staff member Morton Halperin. After he received the list, Higby delivered it to Haldeman, who once again approved the request to follow through on the audits.[50]

Nixon made sure to stay close to the issue, as he repeatedly brought up the IRS during his conversations with his closest advisers. "We have the power, but are we using it to investigate contributors to Hubert Humphrey, contributors to [Edmund] Muskie, the Jews," said Nixon to Ehrlichman on September 8, 1971. "You see, we have a new man [Walters] over there. I know the other guy [Thrower] didn't do anything." He later asked, "Are we looking into Muskie's return? . . . Hubert? Hubert's been in a lot of funny deals . . . Teddy? Who knows about the Kennedys? Shouldn't they be investigated?"[51] In a separate meeting with Haldeman on September 13, Nixon complained that the IRS was investigating his friend the Reverend Billy Graham and once again brought up the issue of investigating his enemies. "Now here's the point. Bob, please get me the names of the Jews, you know, the big Jewish contributors of the Democrats . . . Could we please investigate some of the cocksuckers?"[52] The very next day, Haldeman told the president that the White House had developed a list of enemies, the one that Dean had delivered earlier that day. Once he was informed of the list, Nixon replied, "Good," and asked, "What about the rich Jews?" The president explained, "You see, IRS is full of Jews, Bob . . . That's what I think. I think that's the reason they're after Graham, is the rich Jews."[53]

Three days later, Ehrlichman wrote down, "Walters – IRS – get enemies," after a meeting with the president and Mitchell.[54] Nixon's faith in Walters greatly diminished soon after the new commissioner had shown that he would not fit into the role the president had carved out for him. Walters's early battles with the White House were not minor squabbles over personnel, but instead sent a strong signal that he was not willing to play politics with the IRS. A note sent from Gordon Strachan to Haldeman on December 1, 1971, showed that the White House had given up on the idea that Walters would act as the president's attack dog. Strachan complained that "Johnnie Walters has not yet exercised leadership. Unevaluated reports assert he has been either reluctant or unwilling to do so." The report specifically cited Walters's decision to appoint Loeb, a "career Democrat" who had "asserted his democratic credentials in staff meetings according to reliable sources (presumably Barth)." Aside from the Loeb appointment, Strachan also mentioned that the new commissioner had resisted the White House's efforts to politicize the agency. "Walters appears oversensitive in his concern that IRS might be labeled 'political' if he moves in sensitive areas (e.g. audits, tax exceptions)."

In addition to his critique of the commissioner, Strachan also laid out a plan to address the Walters problem, recommending that Malek play a greater role in addressing personnel issues at the IRS. When it came to following through on requests for audits, Strachan stated: "Walters must be made to know that discreet political actions and investigations on behalf of the Administration are a firm requirement and responsibility on his part." Strachan suggested giving Dean greater access to Walters "for action in the sensitive areas," and that "Dean should have access and assurance that Walters will get the job done properly."[55]

The White House initially saw the new commissioner as a fresh start at the IRS. Walters was a loyal Republican, a southerner, and a former assistant to John Mitchell. In many ways, he matched the presumed credentials to become a commissioner who would follow through on Nixon's nefarious vision for the IRS. However, Nixon, Ehrlichman, and many others within the administration discounted the fact that Walters could check off many of their necessary boxes and still resist the president's orders on purely ethical grounds. Nixon and others within the White House had repeatedly discussed the importance of finding the right person to succeed Randolph Thrower, but they never actually checked to see if Walters would treat the IRS as a political agency. His long-held nonpartisan approach to civil service never came up in the White House's search for a new commissioner. Based on his background, Walters led the IRS the only way he knew how—in a nonpartisan manner. As a result, Walters was no longer the president's man.

Walters's appointment and his subsequent early battles with White House officials marked a turning point in how the president and his aides plotted against the IRS. Whereas White House staff members had previously attempted to work on the periphery when dealing with the IRS, the president would now repeatedly insist that they dramatically increase their efforts in the coming year. Nixon's interest in transforming the IRS dated back to the beginning of his presidency, but the White House's struggles to change the agency only enhanced its importance. The IRS was now at the center of the Nixon White House's attempts to stifle their political opponents and expand the powers of the president. Walters's early resistance was the beginning of a collision course between himself, a headstrong tax lawyer from South Carolina, and the president of the United States.

THE O'BRIEN INVESTIGATION AND GEORGE SHULTZ

As the Nixon administration began its fourth year in office, the president took on an even more active role in finding ways to control the IRS.

After the White House gave up on Walters as an agent of change, Nixon pushed his staff even harder to directly confront the IRS. As White House officials began to follow through on the president's demands, many of them began to adopt an even more antagonistic view of the IRS. Many, including Chuck Colson, held the IRS in sheer contempt by 1972. "If the Internal Revenue Service even considers McGovern's complaint against the VFW, I will personally detonate the dynamite that will blow the IRS building off the map," wrote Colson to Dean after a representative of the Veterans of Foreign Wars contacted his office.[56] In many ways, Colson and other aides now grouped Walters and his staff at the IRS with their other enemies across the federal government. The president adopted this view, firmly convinced that the agency's bureaucracy could only be changed through more forceful tactics.

While the White House sought audits on hundreds of individuals, President Nixon and his advisers developed a special interest in targeting Larry O'Brien. The White House first became interested in collecting information about O'Brien shortly after the longtime Democratic strategist began his second stint as DNC chairman in 1970. One of the president's speechwriters, William Safire, first suggested investigating Larry O'Brien's finances after he read a story in *Newsweek* that mentioned the chairman's ties to an international consulting firm. "Can't we raise a big fuss about this?" Safire wrote to Haldeman on August 18, 1970.[57] Months later, the president brought up O'Brien's financial connections to the infamous business magnate Howard Hughes in a note he wrote on board Air Force One. "It would seem that the time is approaching when Larry O'Brien is held accountable for his retainer with Hughes." He then wrote that his close friend and businessman Charles "Bebe" Rebozo had information that linked Hughes to O'Brien. "Bebe has some information on this although it is, of course, not solid, but there is no question that one of Hughes' people did have O'Brien on a very heavy retainer for 'service rendered' in the past." The president told his chief of staff that Colson should "make a check on this."[58]

As covered in Mark Feldstein's 2010 book on renowned investigative journalist Jack Anderson and Nixon, the president believed that O'Brien had previously leaked a story to Anderson about the then Republican presidential candidate's financial ties to Hughes during the 1960 campaign. Nixon's bitterness had built up for more than a decade, and he was determined to use the new evidence that linked Hughes with O'Brien to destroy his rival's career. "I want to put O'Brien in jail. And I want to do it before the election," said Nixon to Ehrlichman. In 1972,

Anderson eventually uncovered and reported on a new $100,000 gift from Hughes to Nixon, leading the president to push even harder to go after O'Brien. "That goddamned Hughes thing. Larry O'Brien, he was on the payroll too."[59]

Nixon's renewed interest in O'Brien coincided with the IRS's growing investigation of Howard Hughes's finances. Beginning in early 1971, the IRS conducted extensive civil audits of a wide range of Hughes's entities. After the investigation was designated a criminal case that fall, special agents within the agency's Intel Division began looking into allegations that individuals within Hughes's companies had received kickbacks from various individuals. By the spring of 1972, the IRS officially established a task force that was based in Las Vegas to further investigate the case. Throughout the investigation, the task force sent regular reports to Walters and Assistant Commissioner for Compliance John Hanlon. Barth was also aware of the details of the investigation as he was responsible for delivering the agency's monthly sensitive case reports to the secretary of the treasury.[60] As expected, the staff assistant regularly passed on information related to the Hughes case straight to the White House.

Meanwhile, in early 1972 Walters began to look for ways to keep the IRS independent. Since it was an election year, the commissioner was genuinely concerned about attempts to politicize the agency. At the time, the IRS had a program where the agency would select returns for audits based on income, the number of deductions that were claimed, and other trigger points. "It was not on a personal basis," remembered Walters.[61] Walters and other members of the management staff of the IRS discussed the issue and decided that the agency would adopt a firm policy of carrying out its affairs in an apolitical manner.[62] This policy proved to be difficult, especially after special agents linked Hughes to Bebe Rebozo and the president's younger brother, Don Nixon. According to handwritten notes of a March 1972 meeting between Walters and the soon-to-be secretary of the treasury George Shultz, the commissioner reported that Rebozo and Don Nixon were now a part of their O'Brien case, complicating the White House's interest in further exposing Hughes's political contributions. Two months later, IRS agents uncovered more details of O'Brien's relationship with Hughes, as they found that the DNC chairman had received payments of $160,000 for his legal services. The payments were not illegal, but were enough to raise some suspicions about O'Brien.[63]

During the early stages of the O'Brien investigation, Walters decided to postpone a full-fledged investigation until after the election. He also delayed the Nixon and Rebozo investigations so that he would remain impartial while overseeing a case that included both prominent Democrats and Republicans. That decision soon came under fire as Ehrlichman wasted no time in demanding that the newly inaugurated secretary of the treasury George Shultz move quickly to investigate O'Brien. Since his appointment as secretary of labor in 1969, Shultz had been a loyal and trusted adviser to the president, but one whose influence had very real limitations. Although his new role as secretary of the treasury was a significant promotion for the well-respected economist, the position also heightened the simmering tensions that had built up between him and the Nixon White House over the previous three years. Nixon's new secretary always sought to find a way to avoid a fight with the White House, but his intellectual pedigree and pragmatic approach to civil service sometimes pitted him against the president. "One thing about Shultz is that he's not longed for this life in the campaign," concluded Nixon in the summer of 1972.[64]

Born on December 13, 1920, in a midtown Manhattan hospital, George P. Shultz was raised in Englewood, New Jersey. An excellent student who also had a strong passion for sports, Shultz's lifelong interest in economics came from his father, who had a PhD in history from Columbia University. He further expanded his interest in economics as a student at Princeton University, where he wrote a senior thesis on the Roosevelt administration's Tennessee Valley Authority project. As with many others of his generation, Shultz's studies were interrupted by World War II, just as he was accepted to the PhD program in industrial economics at the Massachusetts Institute of Technology. He enlisted in the marines, served in Samoa, and participated in combat in the Pacific Islands.

When he returned to the United States, he enrolled at MIT, received his PhD in 1949, and was hired at MIT, teaching in the Economics Department and the Sloan School of Management until 1957. He left MIT for a year in 1955 to serve as the senior staff economist for President Eisenhower's Council of Economic Advisors, working in an office that was located in the Executive Office Building. It was during his first stint in government that Shultz first met then Vice President Nixon, as the two participated in many meetings regarding economic issues. In 1957, Shultz accepted an offer from the University of Chicago's School of Business, where he was a professor until he became a dean in 1962. In his academic career, Shultz promoted a free market–based approach to economics, aligning himself with other well-known conservative economists at the University of Chicago such as Milton Friedman.

Throughout his professional life he maintained his conservative principles, but was also known for his pragmatism, especially when it came to his various management posts.[65]

Shultz's reputation as both an economist and a manager earned him a spot in the Nixon administration when the president-elect appointed him to serve as secretary of labor in 1969. According to Shultz, Nixon was initially wary of him due to his academic background. "I think he was a little afraid when I started that I was an academic who a little leery [of him], which wasn't true," remembered Shultz. The new secretary was in fact a supporter of Nixon, but he also made sure to inform his new boss that he would not play politics with his new position, and would even try to cooperate with organized labor. Before officially accepting the position, Shultz remembered telling Nixon, "They're not the enemy for me, and it doesn't mean I agree with all their positions by a long shot. I don't. But we're going to talk to them and be friendly with them. That's me and if you don't want it that way, you don't want me."[66] Regardless of what he may have thought of Shultz, the conversation did not change Nixon's mind, as the president officially hired him in January 1969. Shultz's planned approach to dealing with labor did not clash with Nixon's views because the president sought to work with unions on several fronts. During his time as labor secretary, Shultz successfully convinced the president to avoid any form of government intervention in a major Longshoreman's union strike that had spread across the nation's East and Gulf Coasts. Shultz's expert advice, which greatly differed from previous administrations, eventually worked, the strike being settled without any form of intervention from the White House. Shultz also played a key role in successfully enforcing the administration's progressive Philadelphia Plan, where government contractors were now required to adopt an affirmative action policy when hiring new employees.

As a part of the president's broader reshuffling of his administration in the summer of 1970, Nixon appointed Shultz as director of the newly created Office of Management and Budget. The position gave Shultz a visible leadership role over a team of budget advisers, an office suite in the White House, and even more direct access to the president. Nevertheless, there was always a significant level of distance between Nixon and Shultz due to their differing interests and approach to government. "He didn't really like budgeting much," said Shultz of the president. "I mean, he knew how important it was, and he focused on certain things . . . and it's kind of dull in some ways unless you like it. Well, I liked it." Aside from their policy interests, Shultz also butted heads with the president over the issue of price and wage controls. Shultz publicly supported Nixon, but privately clashed with the president and Treasury Secretary John Connally over how to properly address inflation. The issue led to Shultz's resignation in 1974, just months before Nixon's own departure from the White House.[67] While Shultz was a useful economic adviser to the president, Nixon and many others in the White House believed he was too soft to fully trust when it came to politics. Shultz's OMB post had been a promotion, but it was one that would test his sense of ethics, negotiating skills, and loyalty.

Shortly after his move to the Treasury Department, Shultz met with Ehrlichman to discuss the O'Brien case. Ehrlichman, who had received detailed reports about the case from Barth, told the secretary that O'Brien had received a separate payment of approximately $200,000–$250,000 from Hughes and had failed to report it to the IRS. Ehrlichman asked Shultz to look into the issue and made it clear that his request came straight from Nixon.[68] The secretary caved to the White House's demands and asked Walters to move forward with the O'Brien investigation. Walters reluctantly agreed and sent a request to Hanlon to examine O'Brien's tax records, but made sure to not mention the White House's interest in the case in hopes of protecting the integrity of the investigation. When Walters later spoke to the Watergate Special Prosecution Force in 1974, the former commissioner conceded that without pressure from the White House, the IRS would have waited to pursue the O'Brien case. "To that extent, IRS did fold to the pressure by accelerating the interview," said Walters. He also offered up somewhat of a defense of his actions by arguing that if O'Brien was an "ordinary citizen," the IRS probably would have moved even faster with their investigation based on the amount of money involved.[69]

Even though they originally resisted Ehrlichman's orders, the IRS eventually succumbed to the White House's pressure and began an initial review of O'Brien's finances, while also delaying the Nixon and Rebozo cases. Walters soon informed Shultz that their investigation had found that O'Brien had in fact reported all of his income to the IRS, including a substantial payment from Hughes. Instead of finding damaging information, the report showed that there was a small deficiency in one of the returns which resulted in a small refund for O'Brien. When Ehrlichman was informed of the results, he was incredulous and insisted that the agency reopen the investigation so that they could find the alleged unreported payment. Shultz met with Walters again to pass on the order. After the IRS delivered a second report with the same exact results to Shultz, Ehrlichman told the secretary to have the IRS interview O'Brien as soon as possible. Despite Walters's repeated insistence on waiting until after the election, Shultz agreed and told the IRS to bring the DNC chairman into their office.[70]

While Shultz and to a lesser extent Walters caved when it came to the White House's demands on O'Brien, the president still believed that both men and the IRS's bureaucracy were blocking his plans. The investigation was moving along, but Nixon's appointees had caused much anxiety in the White House through their mild resistance. On August 3, Nixon met with Ehrlichman alone in the Executive Office Building to further discuss the O'Brien case. "And if they bring up that goddamn Hughes loan again, we ought to break this over O'Brien's head!" said Nixon. Ehrlichman then told the president that he would move quickly on the issue and meet with Shultz. "I'm going to get Shultz tomorrow and sit down and I'm going to ask him to have the IRS go behind that entry in that report we got. . . . And call for those returns—a perfectly legitimate thing for him to do." Nixon replied, "That's what we're going to do, and just tell George he should do it." He added, "George has got a fantasy. What is George's—what he's trying to do, say that you can't play politics with IRS?"

In the same meeting Ehrlichman also informed the president that he was actively trying to promote Barth to deputy general counsel, a position that would increase the young assistant's influence within the agency.[71] He also brought up the fact that Shultz recently complained about Barth: "George called up and said, 'Geez, I am really having trouble with this. My bureaucracy is really wild about this; this guy is known to be a loyalist and a hard ass and so on, so I've had a lot of flak.'" Hearing about Barth's negative reception among much of the agency's bureaucracy set Nixon off on a tirade as the president considered a massive overhaul of personnel at the IRS. "I want to know many of those people are . . . appointees. Aren't there several?" asked Nixon. "Oh, sure, at the top, six or eight guys," said Ehrlichman. "Out with them! Every one of those bastards out now! I think the whole bunch goes out just because of this!" exclaimed the president. "We'll kick their ass out of there! . . . But out their asses go! And then investigate the bastards. They're probably on the take."[72]

As the president's frustrations grew, Walters and his staff followed through on the White House's order to bring O'Brien in for an interview. When the IRS first scheduled an interview with O'Brien in early August, he failed to show up for the appointment. After Shultz alerted the White House about the no-show, Ehrlichman argued that the agency should issue a subpoena if the DNC chairman failed to show up for their next appointment. "George is very willing and he's the one that's doing it," said Ehrlichman to the president. At the same time, he also let Nixon know that the secretary was consistently pushing back on their requests. "He said to us, 'I don't like this cops and robbers business and all that.' I said, 'George, this is a major contribution you're going to make to this campaign.' "[73] Ehrlichman's plan to issue a subpoena was discussed by officials within the IRS as they continued to struggle to reach O'Brien to set up an official interview. However, John Hanlon later testified that his staff decided on August 10 that they would not aggressively pursue O'Brien through a subpoena. Ehrlichman's plan became a nonissue when the agents eventually heard from O'Brien and scheduled an interview for August 17.[74]

The White House remained unsatisfied, as Nixon and Ehrlichman still felt that the agency was not moving fast enough to catch their nemesis. "What is the situation briefly on the O'Brien thing? Anything been followed up with it?" asked the president on August 11. "The damn IRS did not do what we told them to do," complained Ehrlichman. He then informed Nixon that the IRS had scheduled an interview for August 17 and said, "I called Shultz and said that's too late and that I want it sooner." The conversation turned to Walters, whom Ehrlichman blamed for the delay. "Walters just completely, he blew their door, Walters, I have to assume it was Walters, just completely violated our instruction."[75] Without much direct access to the commissioner that summer, Ehrlichman increasingly labeled Walters as the White House's biggest obstacle to changing the IRS. Although Walters's resistance was controlled by Shultz, Nixon and his close confidants continued to view the IRS as their enemy. In a private conversation with his personal secretary Rose Mary Woods, Nixon repeated his frustrations with the IRS. Woods replied, "Of course we haven't had any control over the IRS," and suggested firing people who were disloyal to the president. After Nixon told Woods that they had one supporter in the IRS, she exclaimed, "They have the whole agency!"[76]

The president's obsession with the IRS kept the White House on the attack for the rest of the summer. When two IRS agents interviewed O'Brien at the Sheraton Park Hotel on the morning of August 17, the DNC chairman answered every one of their questions. O'Brien did not raise "any question of political implications during the interview," aside from asking the agents if they could delay the investigation until after the election. It was a request that they rejected. According to the agents, the interview produced "no real new information" about the Hughes case, refuting Ehrlichman's allegations.[77] Two days later, Haldeman told the president in a conversation at Camp David that O'Brien was "quite shook up about the whole thing," and that he left his records with the agents. Nixon made it clear to Haldeman that the interview was not good enough and that he was still interested in pursuing the investigation. "At least we've got a guy working on it like Barth who's not going to give it a cursory examination," said Nixon.[78] The following week, Haldeman wrote in his diary, "E's got to follow up on O'Brien, where that money went, so forth." Echoing the president's complaints about Shultz, he also wrote, "We need someone at Treasury who will talk politically and take the attack on this."[79]

The O'Brien case had also created much tension within the halls of the IRS as Walters became increasingly upset about Barth's conversations with Ehrlichman and others within the White House. On August 28, Walters scolded Barth about constantly going behind his back to talk to Ehrlichman. Barth wasted no time and met with Ehrlichman later that day to inform him about his confrontation with Walters. "This Walters, I don't know what he's been talking to the Secretary about," said Barth.[80] The very next day Barth was brought in to the phone conversation about the O'Brien investigation with Ehrlichman, Shultz, and the commissioner. The discussion primarily revolved around a common issue: Ehrlichman's feeling that the IRS was not doing enough to fully investigate O'Brien's past. After Walters told him that it would take the IRS at least a week to inspect four of O'Brien's returns, Ehrlichman proposed having the commissioner's assistant lead the project. "I would take it, if we give Roger nothing else to do, but go inspect those, that he would have all that done by tomorrow night." Walters countered, "John, you probably couldn't get it by tomorrow night . . . If we attempted to do it, we would have pie on our face." Ehrlichman replied, "I'm willing to take a little pie on my face, John, and I think you should too . . . This is very big stuff."

Before the commissioner could respond, Shultz interrupted him and insisted that the investigation had not uncovered anything about O'Brien. "As far as anyone can see, at this point, there's nothing wrong at all . . . There isn't any, there's nothing here that anyone can raise a question." After Shultz defended the IRS, Ehrlichman pressed on, "But there are a lot of unanswered questions that you won't have the answers to until you look at those four returns. I just want to give you a preeminent sense of urgency, Johnnie, and a week is too long!" Walters tried again to explain to Ehrlichman that the IRS was probably not going to find any dirt on O'Brien, and that it was not worth moving forward with an investigation that had already crossed several ethical boundaries. "John, let me ask you this, suppose we look at them today and find out that it wasn't. Then you still don't have anything you can use . . . The chances are 999 out of a 1,000 that this thing has been recorded properly . . . I can't believe it wasn't," stated Walters. "Well I can!" said Ehrlichman. Shultz took control of the conversation and tried to get the group to focus on the facts of the case. "There's no point in arguing about it . . . That is a fact. And that is something we can find out." He then reminded Ehrlichman that "so far, there's nothing wrong" with O'Brien tax returns. Summarizing the White House's battles with the IRS that summer, Ehrlichman replied, "I'm not quarreling with that. It's just attitudinal."[81]

The facts of the case were not all that important to the White House. The discovery of actual information that would hurt O'Brien and other Democrats would have been ideal for them, but the whole operation was a loyalty test. The two officials moved forward with investigating O'Brien during an election year, but their limited resistance meant that they could no longer be trusted, especially with future special projects that would involve targeting Nixon's enemies. Despite all his efforts to work with the White House, Nixon was especially disappointed in Shultz's performance throughout the O'Brien affair. "He screwed up the O'Brien thing," said the president to Ehrlichman on September 7. Ehrlichman, who had just received a report from Shultz that showed that O'Brien was in the clear, informed Nixon that Barth had concluded that the case was a "dry hole." Later on in the conversation, the president returned to his frustrations with Shultz, telling Ehrlichman, "I don't want George handling anything political, because he doesn't know his ass from first base."[82] Shultz met with the president that same day, but the O'Brien issue was never brought up during their meeting. The White House soon dropped the issue, and the O'Brien investigation was dead.[83]

The O'Brien case left several scars on Shultz and Walters, as they had participated, albeit unwillingly, in the White House's misdeeds. For Shultz, the case left him feeling frustrated about his inability to find a compromise that could work for both the IRS and the White House. Even though he had followed through on several of Ehrlichman's demands, his effort to protect Walters and the IRS from the White House placed him even further outside of Nixon's inner circle. In his interview with the Watergate Special Prosecution Force, he described the investigation as "an unpleasant, distasteful experience."[84] The O'Brien case also damaged Shultz's relationship with Walters; the investigation left the commissioner feeling bitter. "He did not protect the IRS the way he should have," wrote Walters in 2011. "In my view, Secretary Shultz liked to please the boss." According to him, Shultz should have blocked the White House's order after he was told that Mr. O'Brien had filed his returns in a proper manner. "That should have ended it but it did not," he wrote.[85]

WALTERS AND SHULTZ VS. THE ENEMIES LIST

Shultz and Walters's relationship may have been weakened by the O'Brien investigation, but the two would unite to resist the White House's large-scale enemies project. For more than a year and a half, Colson, Dean, and other White House officials had accumulated several different lists of political opponents, including hundreds of Democratic donors, antiwar activists, journalists, and other notable critics of the administration. In the summer of 1972, Colson and Dean developed two different lists, a short one with staff members for the McGovern campaign and a much longer one with major contributors to the Democratic Party. Dean received the finalized lists on September 7 and scheduled a meeting with Walters to discuss the White House's interest in moving forward on audits. Since Dean had become friends with Walters during their time at the Justice Department, he felt that he would have a better chance than others of convincing the commissioner to take action.[86]

Dean met with Walters on the afternoon of September 11 in the special counsel's office in Suite 106 of the Executive Office Building. After the two discussed old times at the Justice Department, Dean handed the two lists of the White House's enemies to Walters and told him that the White House wanted the IRS to begin audits. He also informed Walters that the order came from "the man he worked for," leaving the commissioner with the clear impression that he was referring to Ehrlichman. He also made sure to add that he hoped the IRS could use the list in a way that would "not cause ripples."[87] Walters took the two lists, but he also warned Dean that any further action would make Watergate look like a "Sunday School picnic."[88] The commissioner may have underestimated the overall impact of the Watergate break-in, but his evaluation of dangers of the enemies list was still correct. Walters felt that his best chance to get the White House to back off was not to make a moral argument, but to convince Dean that auditing political enemies would create problems for the president. He also asked him if he had talked about the two lists with Shultz, but Dean had not brought the request to the secretary.[89] Before he left the room, Walters let Dean know that he would inform Shultz of the request, and would recommend that the IRS should not take any further action.[90]

In the aftermath of the O'Brien investigation, Walters was left wary of Shultz's ability to stand up to the president. His meeting with Dean took place less than two weeks after he had nearly handed in his resignation, and he remained deeply skeptical of Shultz's motives. When he met with the secretary on September 13, Walters passionately argued, "Mr. Secretary, if we do this, this will ruin the tax system." While the two men were at odds over the O'Brien investigation, the secretary quickly agreed with the commissioner and supported his recommendation to defy the White House's order. Walters handed the two lists over to the secretary, who skimmed through them and told Walters to "do nothing."[91] According to Shultz, Walters then asked him what he should do if Dean asked for an update on the request. The secretary told him, "Tell him that you report to me. If he has a problem, he's got a problem with me." Shultz recalled, "It was an improper use of the IRS, and I wouldn't do it."[92] With the secretary firmly supporting him, Walters took the two lists back to his office, then placed them in a sealed envelope and locked them in a safe. For the next several months, no one else at the IRS knew about the existence of the lists; the envelope would remain in the locked safe until the following summer.[93]

Nixon and Haldeman met with Dean in the Oval Office on the evening of September 15 to discuss Watergate, but they also reviewed the current state of the IRS. Prior to Dean's arrival, Haldeman assured Nixon that the young lawyer was "moving ruthlessly on the investigation of McGovern people, Kennedy stuff, and all that too." He also referred to the enemies list when he informed the president, "Chuck has gone through, you know, has worked on the list, and Dean's working the, the thing through IRS." Haldeman praised Dean's efforts, as he told Nixon, "He turned out to be tougher than I thought he would," equating his masculinity with his willingness to attack their enemies. Soon after Dean walked in, the president brought up his expectations for the IRS during his second term. "Well, I look forward to the time when we have the engines of the Department of Justice and [the] IRS totally under our control after November 7," and repeated the accusation that previous administrations had used the IRS to unfairly target his returns. "The idea that you horse around with the IRS, my god, even when I was running for governor, and then of course in '68 when we (unintelligible) they pulled my file and I had nothing, of course . . . That's how it's done." The president asked Dean and Haldeman, "What the Christ is the matter with us? How come we haven't pulled [George] McGovern's file on his income tax?"

Without an answer that would have satisfied the president, Dean brought up his meeting with Walters. "Don't be surprised if George Shultz comes to see you in the next few days because I made a request of Johnnie Walters." Nixon was furious and asked, "On what grounds?" He added, "You mean George didn't want it? Let him see me. I'll throw him out of the office!" At one point, Nixon even stated that they should present the enemies list project as a direct order not just from Ehrlichman, but from the president. "Whoever it is, Shultz is to see that any order or list that he gets comes directly . . . you just be sure to tell him that!" The president had met with the secretary several times in the preceding weeks, but had never raised his issues with IRS. However, in his private meeting with Dean and Haldeman, he unleashed a tirade about his frustrations with Shultz. "Now, I don't want George Shultz ever raising a question like that . . . He should be thrown right out of the office . . . He didn't get secretary of treasury because he's got nice blue eyes and not for any other reason." Seeing the appointment as a favor, Nixon felt that he was owed one in return. "It was a goddamn big favor for him to get that job . . . He's gonna start repaying."

During the conversation, the three men also dissected the reasons behind their inability to control the IRS, and tried to come up with a plan to work around the agency. Haldeman suggested that the White House could take action to audit Democratic contributors and brush off any potential blowback. "I'd let the Democrats stand there and squeal, I mean just [say] 'Well, we've had as a result of the election campaign, we've had a lot of complaints and we've gotta check these things out,' and we just do it," he said. Nixon insisted that the White House should carry out the operation "artfully," so that "we don't create an issue by abusing the IRS." While the president seemed to have been recommending a less reckless approach to the project, he then suggested a break-in as an artful way to gain access to tax records. "And, there are ways to do it. Goddamn it, sneak in in the middle of the night."

Nixon also directed much of his rage toward Walters, arguing that the commissioner had failed to show what the president felt was a true sense of manliness. After insisting that the White House had to find a way to investigate their enemies, Nixon said, "Even if we've got to kick Walters' ass out first and get a man in there." He then exclaimed, "He's finished! He's finished! November the eighth believe me!" Haldeman agreed and argued, "We've just got to get a guy with guts in there." Going back to their discussions regarding Thrower's successor, he also blamed Mitchell for their current problems. "Now we forced Johnnie

FIGURE 2. As secretary of the treasury, George P. Shultz supported Johnnie Walters in his refusal to investigate the White House's enemies list and audit the president's political opponents. (From the Richard Nixon Presidential Library and Museum, MUG-S-272)

Walters on Connally. He didn't want Walters and we, we forced him because Mitchell said he was the guy who would cooperate." Nixon agreed and regretted trusting the judgment of the former attorney general. "Mitchell didn't know. Mitchell's a poor (unintelligible)." Instead of blaming one particular individual, Dean focused on the agency's bureaucracy. "You know there was no doubt that Walters would be cooperative. What's happened though, it happens in so many things is, that a person who appears to be loyal, (unintelligible) gets out and is captured immediately by the bureaucracy." The president and Haldeman were left impressed by Dean's actions and analysis; Nixon told his chief of staff the next day that he felt that his lawyer was "more steely than John [Mitchell] and he's meaner. You've got be steely and mean."[94]

Throughout the rest of the September 15 conversation, Nixon repeatedly stressed his desire to dramatically revamp the IRS through forcing out political appointees. The president especially emphasized Shultz's role in his plan for the agency. "He's got to know that the resignations of everybody—The point is, I want there to be no holdovers left. The whole goddamn bunch go out. And if he doesn't do it, he's out as secretary to the treasury." Nixon insisted that he was serious, telling Dean and Haldeman, "And that's the way it's going to be played. . . . We're not going to have a secretary to the treasury who doesn't do what we say." Toward the end of the conversation, the president reiterated his need for a major overhaul of not only the IRS, but the entire federal government. "It's time for a new team. Period . . . We didn't do it when we came in before, but now we have a mandate."[95]

Other segments of the recording of the September 15 meeting later played a key role in the Watergate investigation, as they directly linked Nixon to Dean's activities related to the Watergate cover-up. Aside from unveiling the true relationship between Nixon and Dean, the conversation also clearly showed that the president, and not just his staff, was actively involved in attempting to audit political enemies. Nixon was not only well aware of the details of both the O'Brien case and the enemies project, but he also repeatedly demanded that the White House press harder to take over the IRS as he prepared for what he envisioned to be his triumphant second term.

Meanwhile, the commissioner continued to carry out his day-to-day duties, while the two lists remained hidden in his safe. That fall, Walters repeatedly conveyed to Shultz that he was interested in resigning so that he could return to private practice. His confrontations with the White House were leading to an unhealthy amount of stress. "There were days, when it seemed all I could do was break down in my office and sob. That's how scary it was," remembered Walters of his last year as commissioner.[96] In addition to his frustrations with the White House, he was also interested in improving his family's financial standing. After living in Washington for nearly four years, and making less money that he would have as a private attorney, Walters was itching to leave the federal government.[97] The secretary understood Walters's reasons for wanting to leave, but convinced him to stay until the time was right to find a new commissioner.

Ten days after their first conversation about the enemies list, the commissioner talked to Dean over the phone about the request. With the backing of Shultz, Walters was even more adamant in his opposition, telling Dean that the project would be "inviting disaster," for the IRS and the White House. He also told Dean that he had already discussed the issue with the secretary and that the two agreed that the IRS would not participate in the project. Walters met with Shultz again on September 29, and the two agreed once more that the IRS would stand up to the White House and keep the two lists of enemies locked in the commissioner's safe.[98] In the weeks after Dean met with Walters, the president never once raised the issue with the secretary. "He never brought it up, so I didn't bring it up," said Shultz.[99] Although Shultz had previously caved on the O'Brien investigation, the enemies list crossed a line as it went against his deepest beliefs about civil service. With Walters consistently opposing the White House's efforts to politicize the IRS, Shultz knew that he had a commissioner who would stand with him in their refusal to carry out the president's vision for the agency.

NIXON'S LAST PLAY AND WATERGATE

Walters and Shultz's resistance to the enemies project did not deter Nixon, as their actions initially reinforced the president's belief that his team had to think even more boldly. While Dean backed away from the enemies list, Nixon reviewed the White House's past mistakes and continued to map out his future steps to transform the IRS during his second term. In the days before and after his landslide victory over McGovern, Nixon held a series of meetings with Haldeman and Ehrlichman that outlined the goals of the next four years. In the middle of these conversations, the president and his inner circle often brought up the IRS as a crucial component of their second term. According to Nixon, it was now time to "start screwing the bad guys" instead of their "good guys."[100] One idea that was proposed by Ehrlichman in a meeting with the president was for the White House to create an investigation group that would focus on left-wing organizations. Along with himself, Ehrlichman suggested the group would also include Dean and another White House lawyer, Dick Moore, and mentioned that Common Cause would be one of their initial targets.[101]

During a separate conversation in Camp David, Nixon repeated his desire to find a loyal commissioner to head up the IRS, someone who would not be "another Johnnie Walters." At one point, Ehrlichman even suggested campaign staffer Lyn Nofziger as a candidate, a former White House deputy assistant who had worked with Dean on the enemies list.[102] By November, the White House's preferred candidate became George D. Webster, a Washington lawyer and loyal supporter of the president who served as the director of the organization Lawyers for Nixon in 1968.[103] Webster was also closely connected to the White House's illegal activities. In 1971, he loaned Colson $5,000 for a secret operation that eventually became the burglary of the office of Fred Fielding, Daniel Ellsberg's psychiatrist.[104] Even before the Fielding office break-in, Colson had identified Webster as a valuable ally who deserved a spot in the administration. "He is a total political loyalist. I have used him on a number of outside assignments for us and he has always been effective and dependable."[105]

While Webster was eventually deemed to be too much of a political liability in 1971, Nixon's conversations about his candidacy in late 1972 showed that the president was considering taking a very different path in 1973. Colson was Webster's most vocal advocate, with the special counsel asserting in a phone conversation with the president that the tax lawyer was the "number one choice in the country." When Nixon asked him, "Would he do what we want?" Colson raved that Webster had personally complained about the IRS and encouraged Colson to find ways to control the agency. In order to further sell Webster to the president, he argued, "He's the only fellow who is as mean as I am."[106] The next day, Nixon and Colson met at Camp David to go over reorganization issues for the second term, and the subject of Webster as the next commissioner came up again. The president asked, "Are you sure he's programmed?" Before Colson could respond, Nixon reminded him, "You're responsible for him . . . I don't want him to get in there and act like Walters did. Mitchell put Walters in."[107]

Colson eventually convinced the White House that Webster would best serve the president, allowing Ehrlichman to call the lawyer on December 7, 1972, to prepare him for a meeting with Nixon. Whereas the White House had previously taken a more cautious approach when selecting a commissioner, Ehrlichman told Webster that they were now willing to push for a strong loyalist to head up the agency. "It's a fight we should have made four years ago," he said. During the conversation, Webster stated that he would take action, "anytime you see something you don't like." Ehrlichman insisted, "Don't worry, we're not bashful."[108] After Webster eventually met with Nixon, the president became even more committed to appointing him as the head of the IRS. "Webster is the man . . . [He] agreed with us on the tax matters," said Nixon in a meeting with Haldeman on December 13. Unlike Walters, Webster seemed to be prepared and all too willing to hand over control of the agency to the White

House. While Nixon was supportive of Webster, he still had a lingering suspicion that things would not work out for the White House. "We'll get someone stupid like Walters," said a skeptical Nixon.[109]

Nixon's suspicions proved to be partially correct when Webster's candidacy fell apart due to the combination of Shultz's opposition and the revelation of the lawyer's own murky financial history. Both factors eventually convinced the White House to go in a different direction in their search. Despite Webster's negatives, the president initially wanted to find a way to stick with his original choice. Soon after the White House discovered that Webster had committed tax violations in the past, Nixon asked Colson, "Should we stand by him or not?" Colson replied, "I would. Yes sir." The president later backed down on the issue to avoid negative publicity, but with Colson on the line, he remained defiant. "I told George Shultz that and all these assholes that want to run away from people."[110] As the White House learned more about Webster's tax problems, and it became clear that Shultz would not cave, Nixon and his aides reluctantly withdrew their support of his candidacy.

Several staff members of the White House later pushed to appoint Webster as the Treasury Department's general counsel so that he could still "provide oversight of the IRS."[111] Colson argued that the position was powerful enough to change the agency, telling the president, "You can control the IRS out of that office." The idea eventually stalled as Shultz believed that Webster's volatile relationship with organized labor would cause too many problems for the Treasury Department. The president met with Shultz in the Oval Office on February 8, 1973, and the two discussed the possibility of hiring Webster as general counsel. They had typically avoided sensitive issues in the past, but Shultz decided to raise the matter with the president. The secretary let Nixon know that he told Colson that appointing Webster was "a terrible idea" and that "it isn't going to work." He also told the president that Webster was "not respected" by many within the department and would face serious opposition from major labor unions. "He has a real problem with organized labor . . . [I] got a wild call from George Meany. I think for me to have him in the Treasury would be tough." Nixon was disappointed, but did not directly confront Shultz's arguments, choosing instead to focus on his broader frustrations with the IRS. "My main concern frankly with the IRS is that we have a man there who totally for once does what we want." Later on in the conversation, the two discussed alternative candidates who would be a good fit, but did not bring up Webster.[112] Days later, Nixon complained to Colson, "Shultz isn't the greatest picker," and asked if there was any chance they could still hire Webster. "I don't think I can sell Shultz. George just gets so . . .," answered Colson.[113]

The experience left Nixon worried that the White House would end up with another commissioner who would refuse to follow orders. "What they will come up with over in the IRS will be a well-qualified tax lawyer who will be just like Johnnie Walters . . . Who will kill our boys over there?" The president added, "You know, we struck out twice, right?" Haldeman agreed. "Yeah, sure thing. We struck out with Thrower and Walters both."[114] The president was pessimistic, but he was also determined to instill a heightened sense of loyalty across the administration. While the early years of Nixon's first term were shaped by a certain level of ideological diversity, the president was obsessed that his second term would bring what he referred to as "absolute loyalty." In a meeting with Haldeman and Malek, who was about to leave his post as special assistant to the president to become the deputy director of OMB, Nixon repeatedly stressed the importance of loyalty among his administration officials. "There must be absolute loyalty," said the president, who also argued that "there must be the ability that we speak out to this government; the damn government will start to pack."[115]

As the White House sought out more loyalists to fill positions across the administration, they continued to move forward with finding someone to replace Walters. Much like their previous searches, the White House asked for Roger Barth's opinion. In a memorandum sent to Ehrlichman, Tod Hullin wrote that Barth's "top recommendation" for the next commissioner was Don Alexander, a Republican tax lawyer who was based in Washington. Barth described the candidate "as very loyal, very tough, highly competent and capable of making the changes that are needed in the IRS."[116] Once the White House gave up on Webster, they zeroed in on Alexander as their new leading candidate in February. Although they were never as sure about his loyalty to the president as they were with Webster, Colson and Haldeman said that they were convinced that he would fully meet Nixon's expectations. In separate meetings on February 13, both tried to sell the president on Alexander as someone who could be very different from Walters. In a discussion with the president, Colson praised Alexander as a "good tough hard rock Republican."[117] Haldeman described Alexander as someone who "sounds awfully good," and made sure to let the president know that both Barth and Webster recommended him as an excellent candidate. "Colson described him as a clean Webster." Nixon was impressed and told his chief of staff, "Let's try him."[118] Weeks later, the president said to Haldeman that the IRS should take action against Congress as quickly as possible. "Now that we have our guy in IRS," there should be "a full examination of Congress's tax returns."[119]

In the end, the White House struck out again with their third appointee, as Alexander, like Walters and Thrower, refused to politicize the agency, albeit under different circumstances. With the president's standing among the public greatly weakened by Watergate in the summer of 1973, Alexander decided to shut down the Special Services Staff of the IRS. Alexander later wrote that he closed the unit because he felt that "political or social views" are irrelevant to taxation.[120] The move infuriated Nixon, who threatened to fire the new commissioner, but never did so for reasons that remain unclear. However, the growing Watergate scandal most likely played a role in keeping Alexander as commissioner for the rest of Nixon's time in office and beyond. He left the IRS in 1977.

The final few months of Walters's own tenure took place just as the American public began to pay greater attention to the details of the Watergate scandal. During this time period, the IRS continued its investigation into Howard Hughes's business interests and associates. Walters argued that the agency should investigate both Rebozo and Donald Nixon, but because of pressure from the White House, the cases were delayed until later in the year.[121] After a little more than a year and a half as commissioner, Walters submitted his official letter of resignation to Nixon on March 5, 1973. Shultz wrote back to Walters and praised him for demonstrating "sensitivity to public needs and an outstanding capability to assume new tasks." The secretary specifically cited the commissioner's decision to reintroduce the short form income tax return, 1040A, and his efforts to expand the agency's taxpayer service programs.[122] Walters was also responsible for bringing corporate returns up to date, after years of lagging behind on checking the tax records of big businesses. It was yet another sign of Walter's overwhelming need to take on a fair approach, even if it hurt the administration's allies and his own career. "As a result, I was an enemy to big corporations . . . And I never got much business from them later on," remembered Walters.[123]

After leaving the IRS, Walters wanted to return to South Carolina, but remained in Virginia so that his youngest child could finish high school there. He joined a law firm based in Richmond, and then five years later returned to his home state where he practiced law until the age of 77. Outside of his work as a tax lawyer, Walters also worked as a financial consultant until he was 85. His post-Nixon years may have been quiet compared to his time at the IRS, but they were also peaceful and allowed the former commissioner to improve his family's financial standing. When he died in 2014 at the age of 94, he received some media attention, including an obituary in the *New York Times* that described him as an "IRS Chief Who Resisted Nixon's Pressure."[124]

Aside from wrapping up his various responsibilities as commissioner in the spring of 1973, Walters also carried the moral weight of knowing that he was in possession of the two lists that Dean gave to him the previous fall. In his sworn affidavit to the House Judiciary Committee Impeachment Inquiry staff, Walters stated, "At no time did I furnish any name or names from the list to anyone, nor did I request any IRS employee or official to take any action with respect to the list." He also stated that on his last day as commissioner, he took the lists out of his office's safe, kept them in a sealed envelope, and locked them in his new private office.[125]

After both Dean and Ehrlichman testified that they gave the lists to the former commissioner, Walters decided to give the original documents to Laurence Woodworth, a friend who was also serving at the time as the executive director of the Joint Tax Committee. "I had known Larry for years and knew that he was totally honest and sound," Walters later wrote. When he handed the still-sealed envelope to Woodworth, Walters informed him of the contents inside the envelope, his meetings with Dean, and his refusal to carry out audits.[126] In addition to the two lists, he also handed over his handwritten notes of his September 11 meeting with Dean. Woodworth accepted the documents and immediately turned them over to the Joint Tax Committee.[127] For nearly a year, Walters had kept his heroic actions to himself in order to protect the IRS and its staff. Taking the enemies lists and locking them up in his safe may have forced him to deal with federal investigators, but it also gave him the opportunity to tell his story on the record.

The ex-commissioner's decision to tell the truth about the White House's enemies project eventually led to a wave of praise for both Walters and Shultz the following summer. With four lawyers from the Watergate Special Prosecution Force investigating Nixon's efforts to politicize the IRS, media outlets began to cover the important role that the two individuals played in defending the nation's tax system.[128] Even detailed accounts from figures such as Ehrlichman could not help but further bolster the public image of Shultz and Walters as heroic civil servants who stood up to a criminal president and his staff. "George Shultz wouldn't let me at him," said Ehrlichman to Senate investigators about his inability to meet with Walters. While Walters may have been more vocal in his resistance to the White House, Shultz also played an important, albeit more complex, role in protecting the IRS. Ehrlichman also bluntly stated that the August 29, 1972 conversation was "the first time I had a chance to tell the commissioner what a crappy job he had done."[129]

Despite all of the positive press, Shultz and Walters's efforts to defend the IRS from Nixon were overshadowed by the administration's improprieties. Their stories of resisting the president's orders were often brushed aside as new details about the White House's many misdeeds were uncovered by investigators. Over time, the many negative stories that came out of the Watergate scandal came to dominate most narratives about the entire administration. Placed alongside the public's general antipathy toward anything related to the Nixon administration, and the fact that the IRS was guilty of a certain level of politicizing their work, many took for granted the positive stories that involved good government Republicans. While the ethical standing of the agency was certainly hurt by certain elements of the SSS and the O'Brien case, Shultz and Walters's willingness to say no to the president protected the IRS from becoming a direct extension of the White House. Their actions stopped the IRS from further politicization and a dangerous new wave of abuses of power. The two men may have disagreed over how to deal with the White House in certain instances, but their shared adherence to keeping the IRS nonpartisan stopped Nixon's attempt to take over the agency.

. . .

Although they came from different backgrounds, Shultz and Walters were both independent figures who had displayed a strong sense of commitment to nonpartisanship throughout their respective careers. Their mutual resistance to the White House's attack on the IRS placed them at odds with the loyal men who surrounded the president. Unlike Nixon's closest aides, Shultz and Walters consistently sought to work with a wide range of figures across the federal government and beyond, and placed their professional duties above their politics. The order to audit the president's enemies was not only scandalous, but it clashed with the values of the more civil service–based Republicans within the Nixon administration. The two lists that Dean turned over to the commissioner were arguably the central component of Nixon's attempted takeover of the IRS. "I felt, and still feel that had IRS implemented the request it would have ruined our tax system for years to come," wrote Walters in his memoir.[130]

Shultz and Walters's acts of resistance were linked to a broader nonpartisan culture that had shaped much of the IRS. The IRS had in fact engaged in unethical investigations prior to and during the Nixon years, but the agency's institutional culture helped prevent it from fully embracing the Nixon White House's large-scale plans. Shultz and Walters both deserve respect for their individual acts, but it is important to acknowledge that they were partially the product of a longer history of nonpartisan service.

The White House tapes and numerous other records show that Nixon was fiercely determined to take over the IRS. The early years of Nixon's presidency laid the groundwork for his plans for the IRS, but the events of 1972 and 1973 truly showed that the White House was committed to a dangerous expansion of presidential power. Whether it was the countless memos that were circulated in the halls of the White House or the many recorded conversations that took place within the Oval Office, the contentious relationship between Nixon and the IRS highlights the role the agency played in the president's plans for the future. The fact that he did not succeed should not negate the seriousness of the threat that the president's plans posed to the nation's tax system and our democratic process.

Both as president and his later years, Nixon often cynically misrepresented the state of the White House's relationship with the IRS during his presidency. Nixon never fully admitted that he had attempted to politicize the IRS. "If our IRS study turns out as we hope and expect it to, this Administration has not used the IRS for political partisan purposes," wrote Nixon to Al Haig in the summer of 1973.[131] In an on-camera 1983 interview with his former aide Frank Gannon, Nixon stated that stories about his relationship with the IRS were overhyped and unfair. "They made a big hullabaloo about the fact that we had attempted to use the I.R.S. for political purposes. And then a few months later, Don Alexander, the head of the I.R.S., put out a report saying the I.R.S. had not audited anybody for political purposes, not one." He also argued, "We are charged with abusing the I.R.S. and abusing other people and using the I.R.S. for that purpose. We talked about it and so forth, but it did not happen." The former president never mentioned Johnnie Walters in his recollections of his relationship with the IRS.[132] The agency did not become a political weapon during the Nixon years, but it was in spite of the president's many attempts to dramatically reshape the agency. There were times when his own staff tried to either slow down or scale down his plans, but Nixon was always the driving force behind the White House's assault on the IRS.

Fortunately, the relationship between Nixon and the IRS was one that was ultimately defined not only by the White House's failures, but also by the ethical stands that were taken by Shultz and Walters. "My philosophy was and still is that the IRS is the very basis of our form of government. . . . By doing the job right, we were protecting our tax system and the tax laws and the taxpayers, and not the Administration, necessarily," said Walters in 2008. Without individuals such as Shultz and Walters, the IRS may have succumbed to becoming an extension of Nixon's darkest impulses. It was through the efforts of these Nixon appointees and other moderate Republicans that the IRS survived the Watergate era. In a 1973 Oval Office conversation about the IRS, Nixon remarked, "I don't want an independent son of a bitch over there." In Johnnie Walters and George Shultz, that's exactly what he got.[133]

2

"There's No Basis in Law to Carry Out This Order . . . and We're Not Going to Do It"

How the OMB Stopped Nixon's War on MIT

"Get me the information with regard to distribution of DOD [Department of Defense] research funds to major colleges and universities," said Richard Nixon to H. R. Haldeman during a May 13, 1970 conversation. "Two hundred million dollars I think is the total package. I would like a list of all colleges and universities that receive such funds with the amounts indicated. I would like this by noon today." In the days leading up to the order, the Nixon White House was facing rampant criticism over the invasion of Cambodia, the tragic shootings at Kent State University, and a new wave of antiwar protests. Shortly after recording his recollection of an impromptu early-morning meeting with young antiwar demonstrators at the Lincoln Memorial, he turned his attention to the future distribution of DOD funds to colleges and universities.[1] "I believe that no DOD funds for research be provided to any university, unless the faculty by a majority vote approves the receipt of those, receipt and use of the funds for those purposes," he argued. "I want the facts, but from now on, no funds go to any university, if the majority of the faculty opposes the receipt of such funds. Put the faculty, not the university presidents, on the spot." He then told Haldeman, "Give me a report on this." It was the president's first recorded mention of his desire to cut off federal funds to elite universities.[2]

Nixon and the antiwar movement were strangely in sync when it came to the distribution of defense grants to colleges and universities. Much like the students who were protesting the Vietnam War, Nixon had also become extremely critical of the Pentagon's relationship with the nation's elite schools. However, the president had very different motives from the typical campus protester of the early 1970s. While many students had serious concerns about the moral implications of their school's participation in the military industrial complex, the president wanted to find ways to punish colleges and universities for antiwar protests. Nixon was extremely anxious about the activities of antiwar college students and he directed much of his ire toward the university presidents, paying special attention to those from the Ivy League. With substantial protests across the Ivy League, the president believed that the university presidents were not doing enough to defend his administration's policies and combat the antiwar movement. Some of the university leaders tried to tranquilize protests through respectful negotiations and other forms of communication with student and faculty leaders; Nixon felt that they were doing nothing more than coddling young radicals. By refusing to show Nixon's version of "strength" when facing down campus protestors, the leaders of the Ivy League and other top-tier institutions became enemies of the White House.

The president's May 13, 1970 order did not lead to any immediate action either inside or outside the White House. While the president's interest waxed and waned over the next three years, he remained persistent in his belief that the White House could and should punish academic institutions that opposed the Vietnam War. Outside of the Ivy League, the president and his staff specifically set their sights on the Massachusetts Institute of Technology (MIT), the largest recipient of federal aid. Nixon was convinced that MIT's president Jerome Wiesner and the school's faculty were undermining his foreign policy in Vietnam. Following widespread antiwar protests on campus and faculty resolutions that strongly condemned the war, Nixon believed that he was under attack from what he often referred to as the "MIT Cabal."[3] With more than a hundred million dollars in grants from the federal government, and the majority of those funds coming from the Pentagon, Nixon placed MIT at the forefront of his efforts to reshape a central component of the nation's foreign policy establishment.[4] Starting in 1971, the president ordered White House aides to closely monitor the distribution of federal contracts to educational institutions, and MIT was at the top of the White House's targets. After the president ordered the bombing of Haiphong Harbor in the spring of 1972, and the subsequent campus protests, Nixon went beyond asking for reports and made a more concerted effort to cut off federal grants to MIT. While his own staff may have purposefully dragged their feet on the MIT request, Nixon never lost track of the order and took on a more active role in attempting to have his administration carry it out in 1972 and 1973. Nixon was the clear initiator and often at the center of his team's plan to further politicize the distribution of federal funds to universities.

The president's efforts were ultimately stopped not by the antiwar movement or university presidents, but by a group of Republicans within his administration. It was through the resistance of three assistant directors within the Office of Management and Budget (OMB), Kenneth W. Dam, William A. Morrill, and Paul H. O'Neill, that Nixon's plans were slowed down and eventually blocked. The three men saw no justification for the request and stated that they would resign if they were forced to carry it out. With the support of their former boss at OMB, Secretary of the Treasury George Shultz, they were able to stand their ground and keep their jobs. Prior to his move to the Treasury Department, Shultz had also resisted the plan to cut funds to MIT when he was the head of the OMB in 1972. A graduate and former faculty member of MIT, Shultz provided steady opposition at both of his posts and fully backed his former employees when they were confronted with Nixon's scheme. The secretary's decision to stand up yet again to the White House occurred just months after he had refused to pressure the IRS to audit political enemies. As he did with the enemies list, Shultz saw the danger in playing politics with the distribution of research funds, and did what he could to protect his former employees at OMB.

Together, the three assistant directors and Shultz not only rejected the MIT order, but they also never pursued any action to take away federal funds from any other university. Their collective opposition may not have immediately killed off the president's plan, but they provided an important roadblock to it. While other administration officials such as Caspar Weinberger moved forward with the request, Dam, Morrill, O'Neill, and Shultz made sure that they did not contribute to Nixon's war on the nation's premier colleges and universities.

That war was partially based on very real ideological differences between the president's handling of the Vietnam War and campus protestors, but it was also driven by cultural differences between Nixon and the nation's academic establishment. Nixon's resentment of the Ivy League and other top-tier institutions was well known among his staff, as it repeatedly came up in private discussions within the Oval Office. By the end of the first term, Nixon's distaste for elite universities was so well known among his staff that Haldeman once wrote in his daily diary, "He got into the Ivy League thing."[5] The president's "Ivy League thing" came to dominate much of his thinking about his enemies, whether they were in academia, the press, or the federal government. These groups were not just his political rivals, but had come from a different culture than the president. Nixon stressed those cultural differences and consistently placed himself firmly outside the nation's establishment, even during his presidency. During a meeting where Nixon and Kissinger discussed the upcoming Christmas Day bombings on December 14, 1972, Nixon lectured his national security advisor about their enemies. "The press is the enemy. The press is the enemy. The press is the enemy. The establishment is the enemy. The professors are the enemy. The professors are the enemy. Write that on a blackboard 100 times and never forget it," said the president. "Of course," replied Kissinger.[6]

Nixon's sometimes volatile relationship with Kissinger, his national security advisor and later secretary of state, was partially shaped by Nixon's animosity toward "the professors," particularly those from the Ivy League. Kissinger was a well-known product of the Ivy League, a Harvard graduate and former faculty member prior to joining the Nixon administration. As a result, Nixon often questioned Kissinger's cultural loyalties when he felt under attack.[7] Although Kissinger initially attempted to maintain communication with his former colleagues at Harvard, he eventually sided with the president and began to loathe the "establishment." In his recent book *Kissinger's Shadow*, Greg Grandin stresses that Kissinger "knew that his position depended entirely on melding himself to Nixon" when he shared the president's fixation on domestic politics. "I would be losing my only constituency," said Kissinger regarding the possibility of angering Nixon.[8] In order to mitigate the president's concerns about his Ivy League background, and maintain his influence over the administration's foreign policy, Kissinger joined the White House's war on his alma mater and other elite schools.

Throughout his time in office, Nixon repeatedly argued that the Ivy League presidents were representative of the moral decline of the country's leadership class. "The elite class in this country lacks character," he once told Colson.[9] According to the president, the nation's educational and foreign policy establishment had betrayed the White House and proven to be weak. During one of his many tirades about the state of American society, Nixon insisted that elite liberal academic types were a greater danger to the country than either the far right or the far left. When he specifically brought up the presidents of the Ivy League, the president referred to them as "flabby soft bastards" and concluded that "limousine libs are really a danger."[10]

His mindset was also likely influenced by his upbringing and his unfulfilled "dreams of going to college in the East." Even though a young Richard Nixon had received an award to attend Harvard, the effects of the Depression on his family and the costs of taking care of his sickly brother Harold forced him to stay in Southern California and attend Whittier College.[11] Most Nixon biographers agree that Nixon's working-class background, combined with his disappointment over his missed opportunity to go to Harvard, played a role in shaping his life-long resentment of academic elites. Since his arrival at the nation's capital as a congressman in 1947, Nixon was shunned by much of the more liberal-minded "Georgetown Set" for his crude anticommunism. Even as president, he never fully shook off the idea that he was at a clear disadvantage when compared to those in the DC establishment. It was that inner resentment that often bled through in his discussions about what he felt was the declining state of American culture and the establishment's permissiveness toward student radicals. Nixon truly believed he was in the middle of a divisive culture war that threatened to ruin the country and that the nation's elites were at the opposite end of his "Silent Majority."

Nixon's brand of populism primarily had a cultural bent. It relied heavily on the othering of the establishment, and encouraged voters to distrust those who ran many of the nation's liberal institutions. His deep-seated cultural populism had its limits, especially when it came to ideological battles, but it did much to shape his approach to the presidency. Nixon's culture war even extended to his battles with Republicans within his administration. The officials who refused to mix politics with their civil service were often lumped together with the more liberal establishment figures whom the president detested. If administrative officials did not completely fall in line with the White House's plans and appeared to be too close to their rivals, Nixon was quick to label them as being a part of the "Georgetown Set."[12] The president may have been open to ideological diversity within his administration, but he always abhorred the culture of Washington's elite social scene and how it overlapped with some of the more elite universities.

Nixon was especially leery of Shultz's background, particularly his strong ties to MIT. The president constantly viewed Shultz's academic credentials with great suspicion, and believed it was an obstacle to the White House's political goals. "George doesn't know politics from a can of shit," the president once said of Shultz in conversation with Haldeman and Ehrlichman.[13] As with his dealings with Shultz over the IRS, Nixon never fully confronted the secretary over his plan to cut federal funds to MIT, but the two men were both well aware of the deep discord. In a June 12, 1973 meeting with Shultz and several other advisers to talk about the president's economic plan, Nixon joked, "I'll stay away from such things as aid to MIT and other things George is for," leading everyone in the room to laugh awkwardly.[14] Nixon did not bring up the issue during the meeting, but the battle over MIT's federal funds proved to him that his suspicions about Shultz were correct—Shultz was not tough enough. When it came to playing politics with the distribution of federal funds, the president could not rely on him. The secretary, and his three former colleagues Dam, Morrill, and O'Neill, were not interested in becoming the president's men.

The men who resisted the order valued the federal government's relationship with various colleges and universities. They did not view academics as the enemy, and did not share the president's desire to dramatically change the nation's foreign policy establishment. Furthermore, they were government officials who did not adopt the president's bunker mentality in the wake of growing antiwar dissent. Dam, O'Neill, and Shultz were not mirror images of one another, but their collective refusal to play ball with the president kept federal research grants from being a part of Nixon's war on the establishment.

NIXON, THE CAMBODIA INVASION, AND THE IVY LEAGUE

In the days after the unveiling of the bombing of Cambodia in the spring of 1970, Nixon felt that the White House was under siege not only from a reinvigorated antiwar movement but also from educational elites. As hundreds of thousands of demonstrators descended on the nation's capital to protest the expansion of the war, the president surveyed the cultural landscape and felt betrayed by a lack of support from the nation's intellectuals. He increasingly looked to the country's universities as a bellwether for the mood of the liberal establishment. Although he constantly griped about academics and other intellectuals, he had brought several on board to join his administration in 1969 (Kissinger, Shultz, Daniel Patrick Moynihan, etc.), and cared about their opinions. Even though he often railed against intellectuals, the president also displayed a sincere interest in academia. During his presidency, Nixon consulted with Kissinger about the mood of the nation's campuses. He knew that his national security advisor had maintained his contacts at Harvard, and felt that he could provide more information about the influence of the antiwar movement on the country's universities.

Kissinger typically lambasted his former colleagues at Harvard, and sought to validate the president's complaints about intellectuals. Soon after Nixon learned about the shootings at Kent State, Kissinger told the president, "They'll blame it on us." After Nixon agreed, Kissinger also informed him that thirty-three university presidents were publicly appealing to him for a speedy withdrawal from Vietnam. Nixon initially brushed off Kissinger's report, but then later asked, "It's not new that the university presidents want us out, is it?" Kissinger reassured the president that it was not new, but the conversation still showed that Nixon had begun to worry about the White House's relationship with the academic community.[15]

While Kissinger told the president that there was nothing to fear, privately he was becoming increasingly anxious because his relationship with his former colleagues was quickly deteriorating. "I'm getting letters from angry academicians who want to run me out of academia," he once said to McGeorge Bundy during a May 5, 1970 conversation.[16] The very next day, he complained to Secretary of Defense Melvin Laird, "The whole academic community is descending on me."[17] In an attempt to calm the waters, Kissinger, along with other White House officials, met with student groups in the wake of the Kent State shootings. During the meetings, Kissinger explained the president's rationale behind the Cambodia bombings, but unsurprisingly failed at convincing the students. "I have been talking to student groups, but when the faculties are present, it is impossible," he told Secretary of State William Rogers. It would be a trope that Kissinger and later Nixon would repeat in subsequent conversations, as they believed that university leaders, and not student demonstrators, deserved the bulk of the blame for campus protests. Later in the conversation, Kissinger specifically brought up Wiesner and Yale's Kingman Brewster as two presidents who had lost control over their institutions. "MIT was ready to blow anyway," argued Kissinger, who also labeled Brewster "one of the most despicable people . . . This guy is a cheap grandstander."[18] Instead of trying to find ways to reach out to academics and other critics of the administration, Kissinger and the rest of the White House began to follow the president's lead in isolating themselves from the nation's establishment. "We will dig a moat," said Ehrlichman in a half-joking manner during a May

5, 1970 conversation with Kissinger just days before demonstrators arrived in DC. "Put piranha fish in it," replied Kissinger.[19]

The backlash over the Cambodia invasion was the moment at which the already fragile relationship between Nixon and the academic community collapsed. During that spring the president decided he would start to crack down on universities who opposed his policies. Following a tense meeting with the presidents of the Ivy League, Nixon let Kissinger know that he had threatened cutting defense funds to their schools. "What really shook him (Harvard president Nathan M. Pusey) was I said I don't think we should impose blood money on university professors who don't believe in national defense." He added, "These people were just cowering when they heard that." He then made sure to tell Kissinger that his previous place of employment would also be targeted. "Your friend (Pusey) isn't going to get any more blood money."[20] The president would not forget his threat as he recorded his thoughts about the Ivy League on his Dictabelt machine the very next day.

After the events of that spring, the White House's relationship with academia worsened as more professors began to publicly oppose the war. Kissinger was bombarded by letters and phone calls from colleges and universities, but he was most notably condemned by his former colleagues at Harvard. In a letter that was signed by sixty-eight faculty members who had worked alongside Kissinger in the Arts and Science Division, the professors stated, "We are convinced that the conduct of the war and its continuation in whatever form are profoundly immoral and violate basic human and national values." They concluded, "We must end the war, doing all we can to achieve a settlement that will avoid further bloodshed and allow the peoples of Indochina to rebuild their shattered societies." When it came to Kissinger's own role, they wrote, "We do not regard you as an immoral man. Yet you are one of the key architects and administrators of an immoral policy." Given that the letter came from Harvard, Kissinger felt compelled to reply and defended his position with a tepid offer to continue their discussions. "I believe that serious men can differ on what the moral issues are and can discuss their differences on the basis of mutual respect. No one has a monopoly on anguish over this war, or on moral insight. I would welcome a chance to talk these issues over personally with you."[21] The offer carried little weight, especially since the president had no intention of having anyone from the White House deal with Ivy League faculty members in a meaningful way. Instead, Nixon was taking his initial steps toward weakening the relationship between the federal government and the universities that he detested.

THE CREATION OF THE OMB

In order to enforce his plan, Nixon set his sights on using the Office of Management and Budget to punish certain academic institutions. Formerly the Bureau of the Budget, it was reorganized as the Office of Management and Budget in 1970 based on the recommendations of Roy Ash, the head of the president's Advisory Council on Executive Reorganization. The office was essentially given more power so that the White House could have greater control over the annual budget and provide more oversight of the day-to-day activities across the federal government. The OMB would give the president more power over his administration, without having to deal with the daily minutiae of the bureaucracy.

Months after the reorganization, Nixon appointed Shultz as the new head of the OMB, replacing Robert P. Mayo. With Shultz leading the OMB, the White House insisted that the office was "managerial" and "not ideological." In a memo that prepared Haldeman for any questions from the press about the reorganization in the summer of 1970, the White House highlighted Shultz's credentials along with his personal qualities. "He has earned his spurs by running probably the best-managed department in government, by being a forceful spokesman for his points of view, by being a team player once decisions have been made."[22] His experience as the head of the Labor Department showed that he was an extremely effective manager whom the White House could trust to deal with domestic issues. His background as a well-respected economist who was trained at MIT also gave the White House the public credibility it needed for its reconfigured office.

As the head of the OMB, Shultz was aided by a staff of able technocrats who valued efficiency over ideology. Three of the more notable staff members were Kenneth Dam, William Morrill, and Paul O'Neill. All three were assistant directors within the OMB, with each responsible for a different component of the office. Dam focused on the office's national security and international policy, Morrill concentrated on science and technology programs, and O'Neill led the human resources division. The three men would later have distinguished careers both in the public and private sectors, but in the 1960s and 1970s, they were busy establishing themselves within the academy and the federal bureaucracy.

Dam was born in Boston on August 10, 1932, but grew up in Marysville, Kansas, a small town in the northeast of the state near its border with Nebraska. Upon graduating from the University of Kansas in 1954, Dam moved on to the University of Chicago where he received his law degree in 1957. After a short stint as a law clerk for Supreme Court Justice Charles Whittaker, he was hired by the University of Chicago as a law professor in 1960. Dam remained at the university as a law professor until 1971 when he was hired by Shultz, a former colleague from Chicago.

Prior to hiring Dam, Shultz brought up the law professor to Nixon as a leading candidate in his search for a new assistant director at OMB. He described Dam as "a very able fellow," with a very strong law school ranking; the president was impressed and told Shultz, "Don't ever let [William] Rogers know that you have a man of that quality." Upon taking a closer look at his resume Nixon compared Dam's credentials to Elliot Richardson and said, "Gee, he's terrific!" Shultz also told Nixon that his soon-to-be employee was "a strong fellow . . . a young vigorous guy," using terms that he knew would appeal to the president. "If you are thinking about people for your second term. . ." Nixon was pleased by the selection, but told Shultz that he should make sure Dam would not become what he felt was a typical bureaucrat who would just "count numbers."[23]

Born in 1930, William A. Morrill grew up in Bronxville, New York. The son of a physician, Morrill was raised by a fairly strict family of Methodists. Morrill spent his college years at Wesleyan University, developing an interest in public service. His passion for civil service led him to enroll in the master's program in public administration in the Maxwell School at Syracuse University. After receiving his master's degree, he took a civilian job with the Air Force, where he was responsible for administrative and recruitment issues. In the early 1960s he joined the White House's Bureau of the Budget's atomic energy unit in the military division. It was there that Morrill, a registered independent, had the opportunity to work for five different presidents, from Kennedy to Ford.[24] At one point, he served as the bureau's liaison to the National Security Council, but later resigned in protest due to his opposition to the military's inefficient air war strategy. "I had little success in pursuing my views on nuclear programs and Vietnam War programs," remembered Morrill in a 2015 interview. "My particular angst with the administration was with tactical bombing. No one was listening to me."[25]

After taking a yearlong break from the federal government, Morrill returned to the Nixon administration when George Shultz brought him into the Office of Management and Budget. During his second stint in the administration, he played a key role in trying to pass the president's second health care reform proposal. Although he did not become as well known as some of his colleagues, he was still an important player within the OMB and developed a close working relationship with Shultz. "He was the best," said Morrill of his former boss. "I was given a lot of free rein. He left me to my own devices. But we could always meet with him when he had to raise something."[26]

Paul H. O'Neill was born on December 4, 1935, in St. Louis, but later lived on a military base with his family in Anchorage. Coming from a modest working-class background, O'Neill received an economics degree from Fresno State, continued his studies at Claremont Graduate University, and later received a master's degree in public administration from Indiana University. While working as a self-taught engineer in Claremont, O'Neill was inspired by President Kennedy's inaugural address and decided to find a job in the public sector. "It really appealed to my instinct for rational government." He got a job in the Veterans Administration after filling out an application for federal internships at the local post office. Out of more than 300,000 applicants, O'Neill was one of 300 who were offered jobs in 1961, officially beginning his career as a public servant.[27] He then moved on to the Bureau of Budget in 1966 and was eventually promoted to assistant director. O'Neill earned high marks as the head of the human resources division, which Elliot Richardson later referred to as "one of the best" run offices in the entire federal government.[28] Shultz quickly took a liking to O'Neill and even brought up his portfolio during a conversation with Nixon. "He's bright as he can be . . . Knowledgeable about these programs." Shultz added that he had checked O'Neill's registration and found out that he was a Republican, knowing that the information could quell any of the president's potential fears about his staff. "Isn't that nice? He's first class. Outstanding young fellow."[29]

Temperamentally, O'Neill was a perfect fit for civil service, as he was driven to find concrete solutions to problems within the government. As journalist Ron Suskind wrote in his 2004 profile on O'Neill, he was "a believer in the middle ground. Not in compromise, so much. Or horse trading. He was never much on any of that. It was the best, unaffiliated idea that enlivened him." O'Neill recognized that "These right answers fall indiscriminately, here and there, along the left/right political axis, or create new territory not yet charted."[30]

This approach to his work was shared by many others inside the OMB, including Dam, Morrill, and Shultz. The office may have been new, but it in many ways embodied the postwar technocratic culture that had dominated much of the federal bureaucracy of the era. In the early 1970s, the OMB became an exciting place for problem solvers within the government, especially given the dramatic expansion and elevated status of the office. Between 1970 and 1974, the office grew from 30 managers to 130. "I was fortunate to work in the BOB/OMB in its heyday," said Morrill. "There was a real appetite for analytic enterprises."[31] Staff members dealt with practically all of the major issues of the day and worked on coming up with detailed briefs that provided a list of potential choices and estimated outcomes for Nixon. O'Neill fondly remembered the process and believed that the briefs forced everyone to think about "the ideal of good government and how to get there." The briefs "weren't one pagers," but "were fully realized analyses of ten or so pages." He also commended the president for consistently challenging staff members to dissect all sides of an issue. "And pray God you didn't leave out some important point or counterpoint; Nixon would call you on the carpet. He forced us to not only collect the data, and be completely thorough about where all sides stood." O'Neill concluded that "for all his faults, he had an incredibly analytical mind."[32]

Despite the fact that the OMB became a place for moderate solution-oriented civil servants, Nixon and his advisers still sought to find ways to politicize the office as they neared a second term. The president felt that the office was doing an excellent job of overseeing the budget, but was not strong enough on the management side. The first major step was moving Shultz out of the OMB and over to the Treasury Department, and promoting the deputy director of the OMB, Caspar Weinberger, to replace him in the spring of 1972. A native of California, Weinberger began his political career as an assemblyman before serving as chairman of the state's Republican Party during Nixon's failed 1962 gubernatorial bid. As he rose through the ranks of California Republican Party politics, Weinberger built up a reputation as a budget cutter, especially while working for Governor Reagan as the state's director of finance. It was during this time that he earned the nickname "Cap the Knife" for his fiscal conservatism.

Weinberger was first brought to Washington in 1970 as head of the Federal Trade Commission before transferring to the OMB, where he served as a deputy director under Shultz. Shortly after Weinberger's promotion to director of the OMB, Ehrlichman sent him a memo regarding the office's reorganization and its mission. Echoing the president's views of the office, Ehrlichman recommended that Weinberger "properly staff it with loyal, highly political people," so that the office could become "one of the most important tools available to the President in wheeling the bureaucracy." In case there was any confusion, Ehrlichman explained that when he referred to "management" he meant "management in the get-the-Secretary-to-do-what-the-President-needs-and-wants-him-to-do-whether-he-likes-it-or-not sense." This would take some of the burden off of the White House's "political operators" and would help "strengthen the President's hand vs. the bureaucracy." In order to create such an office, Ehrlichman argued for two deputy directors at OMB, with one who would specifically focus on managing the federal bureaucracy. If Weinberger chose to stick with one deputy, Ehrlichman argued that he should pick "the strongest kind of management man you can find with the strongest kind of anti-bureaucracy biases obtainable, the strongest loyalties and the most astute political orientation imaginable." Based on his assessment of OMB's entire staff he concluded, "Frankly, I don't see that super-man on the present OMB personnel roster."[33]

The White House continued pushing for more changes within the OMB in the fall of 1972 when they were preparing for Weinberger's move to the Department of Health, Education, and Welfare (HEW). After selecting his personnel chief Fred Malek as the new deputy director of OMB, Nixon urged him to not "get bogged down in the goddamn budget" in his new position. "The OMB was set up in first instance, not as a glorified budget bureau which it has always been, but basically as a management bureau." He also let Malek know that he should not seek to model himself after Shultz's time at OMB since he believed that he "didn't do one damn thing on the management side."[34]

Shultz's refusal to follow through on the MIT order was one of the more notable examples where the president felt that the OMB was not focusing on "management" and helping the White House rein in the bureaucracy. Even though the president had first brought up the idea of taking away DOD funds from universities in the wake of the Cambodia protests, it was not until the summer of 1971 that the White House began to seriously investigate the issue. Weeks after the release of the Pentagon Papers and the president's increasing demands to punish his opponents, Ehrlichman's staff drafted a memo with the subject heading "Federal Funds for MIT and the University of California" that was delivered to the Oval Office. The note presented the total amount of funds that were distributed in 1969: MIT received $160.6 million and the entire UC system received $378 million. Nixon read the note and wrote down: "E[Ehrlichman]—I want the security clearances severely cut at all universities . . . People like Jerry Wiesner must not have a general security clearance."[35]

MIT AND THE ANTIWAR MOVEMENT

The high-level research that took place at MIT was the culmination of a nearly three-decade partnership with the federal government. MIT's relationship with the military began during World War II as the rapid development of science programs became a major objective for the federal government. Before World War II, MIT's operating budget came mostly from student fees. By 1940, defense contracts with MIT had a higher total than the previous year's annual budget. During the height of the war, MIT's budget reached $44.3 million, fourteen times the prewar figure. The Pentagon's contracts with MIT dramatically grew in the postwar period. By 1969, the major military research laboratories, the Instrumentation and Lincoln Laboratories, received more than $100 million in government funds. Together, the two laboratories added up to about one half of the total operating budget of the university. As detailed in Margaret O'Mara's *Cities of Knowledge: Cold War Science and the Search for the Next Silicon Valley*, MIT's development was connected to the government's broader effort to support "Cold War universities," but it was also in many ways an exceptional institution. Since both Harvard and MIT already had accumulated much prestige, O'Mara argued that they were able "to grow and prosper with relatively little effort." Unlike other Cold War universities, especially on the West Coast, Harvard and MIT were not connected to a large-scale development project in their area.[36] MIT was strengthened by the Cold War, but it was not a product of it. This meant that a school like MIT not only had more prestige than other research institutions, it also had stronger cultural ties to the nation's elites, including those within the federal government. Figures such as Shultz were products of MIT's Cold War development, and saw its links to the state as a necessity.

As the antiwar movement began to publicize the militarization of American campuses during the Vietnam era, both the White House and MIT's student body were increasingly questioning MIT's status as a Cold War university. Nixon's own growing obsession with MIT in the summer of 1971 followed more than two years of campus protests that placed an emphasis on connecting government-sponsored research with the realities of the Vietnam War. After several years of protests on campus there, students and faculty members began to focus more on MIT's military research labs in early 1969, and argued that the university was complicit in the atrocities that were being committed in Southeast Asia. Whereas previous demonstrations focused on Washington, demonstrators began to dissect the militarization of their own campus and many others across the nation. "Welcome to the Little Pentagon: The Military Institute of Technology," read one student pamphlet that summarized the school's role in developing American air war tactics in Vietnam.[37]

It did not take long for the MIT issue to reach the White House. Less than a week into the president's first term, a committee of faculty members and graduate students at MIT delivered a letter with 182 signatures to Lee DuBridge, the White House's main science advisor. The committee encouraged the Nixon administration to find ways to de-emphasize the ties between the scientific community and the Pentagon, and instead build strong ties between universities and federal agencies that focused on transportation, housing, and welfare. "Too many scientists and engineers spend their energies producing facilities to implement military policy . . . The urgency of neglected social and environmental problems now must claim the fullest attention of our intellectual and economic capabilities."[38] On March 4, 1969, MIT faculty members and students at MIT organized a symbolic research stoppage to protest the school's military labs. The protest received widespread publicity and showed that the campus's antiwar movement was expanding their critique of the war. On campus, the stoppage initiated a process whereby administrators negotiated with students and faculty members who were concerned about the laboratories.[39] Over the next three and a half years, MIT became a hotbed of antiwar activity, a place where an increasing number of students and faculty researchers began to demand an end to research that aided the military's efforts in Vietnam.

Following the March 4, 1969 research stoppage, campus protests continued the rest of the year. In the fall, the local chapter of the SDS (Students for a Democratic Society) disrupted an alumni officers' conference at MIT, with several students dancing around the dining area and chanting "Ho Ho Chi Minh!" in front of a group of university donors.[40] Faculty members also began to mobilize their opposition to the Instrumentation and Lincoln labs, the former having changed its name to Charles Stark Draper Laboratory in late 1969. At a December 1969 meeting, MIT's faculty drafted a statement that declared, "The faculty of MIT affirms its belief that the survival of our nation and the

FIGURE 3. MIT antiwar demonstration: Protesters, some with fists raised, by the Instrumentation Laboratory, February 1970. Three months later, Nixon began to discuss cutting federal funds to MIT. (Jeff Albertson Photograph Collection, Special Collections and University Archives, University of Massachusetts Amherst Libraries)

entire world are gravely threatened by the continued expansion of the strategic arms race." Two months later, MIT's faculty sent a list of recommendations regarding the two laboratories to the then president, Howard Wesley Johnson. The letter stated that a committee should be formed to make a recommendation on the "types of laboratories that are suitable to the educational and research objective of the Institute." They also recommended that "the President formulate plans by which the Institute can, in an orderly way, divest itself of the Draper and Lincoln Laboratories as now constituted."[41]

In response to the invasion of Cambodia, MIT's faculty voted to formally support the national student strike and cease all teaching and research during the rest of the semester. "We ask all our colleagues to respect this feeling, to allow maximum flexibility of academic schedule during the current crisis, and not penalize students academically for acts of consciences." With the approval of more than five hundred professors, the faculty committee called on the president to end the development of "high-accuracy MIRVS and to give the highest priority to negotiating an international agreement which should include a permanent ban on the development and deployment of these and other destabilizing weapons."[42]

In the face of growing protests, MIT's administrators sought to avoid a direct confrontation. In a May 4, 1970 note from the soon-to-be president Jerome Wiesner to MIT's faculty, the then provost wrote, "We encourage the faculty to be flexible about delayed assignments in view of the need for the redoubled efforts that so many of us feel the need to make."[43] Wiesner, a former member of President Kennedy's Science Advisory Committee, had been affiliated with MIT since the 1940s, first as a professor, then as a dean, and as provost starting in 1966. A critic of the use of the development of anti-ballistic missile systems, Wiesner was sympathetic toward the campus community's growing concerns about the Draper and Lincoln labs.

The pressure from the campus community to cut ties with the Pentagon eventually led to MIT's decision to begin the process to officially divest the Draper Laboratory, the main location for weapons-related research, from the MIT Corporation. On May 20, 1970, President Howard W. Johnson informed faculty that the Draper Laboratory would eventually become a not-for-profit laboratory that would no longer have an affiliation with the MIT Corporation. The process would take three years, but the Draper Laboratory was officially separated from MIT in 1973.[44] Regardless of the administration's efforts to distance itself from the Draper Laboratory, they did not quell the institute's antiwar movement. Instead of celebrating the divestment, students felt that the institute had just moved the lab in order to avoid a faculty-run committee that would provide more oversight of MIT's research for the Pentagon.[45] The divisions between students and administrators remained intact.

THE NIXON WHITE HOUSE TARGETS MIT

As MIT's administrators struggled to maintain good relations with their faculty and student body, the White House was working on cutting the security clearances for Wiesner, who had become president of the institute in 1971. In a July 3, 1971 memo to Ehrlichman, the president's special assistant and staff secretary Jon Huntsman Sr. wrote, "It was requested that security clearances be severely cut at all universities. A narrow security clearance area for the research involved by individuals may be necessary, but individuals like Jerry Weisman [Wiesner] must not have a general security clearance."[46] In addition to the security clearances, the White House also attempted to connect Daniel Ellsberg and the Pentagon Papers controversy to MIT. In a memo sent to Ehrlichman on July 8, White House speechwriter Pat Buchanan wrote, "If Ellsberg is from MIT, his connections with [MIT professor] Noam Chomsky might be explored."[47]

As White House staff members were slowly moving forward on the MIT issue, Nixon repeatedly reminded them to take more action. According to Ehrlichman's notes of a July 9 meeting with the president, Nixon brought up MIT along with the University of California. "MIT & Cal. Look into this," he wrote.[48] The president was not satisfied with staff reports about federal funding to MIT and other elite schools; he wanted his staff to move forward in punishing the universities. He would have to wait until the spring for any real progress to be made on his orders.

In April 1972, Nixon authorized the bombings of Hanoi and Haiphong, the first and third largest cities in North Vietnam, as a counter to the Easter Offensive by the North Vietnamese. They were the first major aerial attacks on the cities since 1968. Weeks later, the military began the mining of Haiphong Harbor in an effort to cut off supplies that were being delivered to communists in the south. Nixon also decided to put into place a blockade of the North Vietnamese coast, cutting off large ships from entering the harbor. Nixon's moves delivered a huge blow to the North Vietnamese's fuel supply, but were also responsible for numerous civilian casualties. On May 8, Nixon delivered a televised address where he defended his actions, arguing that they were necessary in order to bring the war to an end. The bombings sparked outrage across the nation and ignited a new wave of antiwar protests.

MIT's campus was beset by protests and sit-ins for a three-week period from late April to mid-May. Approximately 1,700 students called for the suspension of classes on May 4 to protest the recent bombings. These demonstrations included a large-scale march on May 11 that ended in campus police unleashing tear gas on a group of 400 protesters who blocked traffic at a railroad crossing a half-mile north of campus. Many students also participated in a sit-in at MIT's ROTC building on May 13 that led to MIT pressing charges against many of the demonstrators. During the school's graduation ceremony, graduate students wore red armbands to protest the bombings and took off their gowns before receiving their diplomas.[49]

Faculty members remained supportive of the students and passed a motion that called for "the immediate end to US involvement in Indochina and to the MIT projects which made the institute complicit in the Indochina war."[50] President Wiesner even publicly stated his support for giving students time off from classes in order to attend protests. "I am asking all Institute supervisors to apply as flexibly as possible within the existing framework of MIT personnel policies to such requests."[51] MIT's administrators and the school's student body may have been at odds with one another over the military research labs, but Wiesner tried to find ways to mitigate the deep divisions. As Nixon further insulated himself from any form of dissent, Wiesner tried to negotiate with faculty members and students who opposed the war.

Those very efforts to try to make peace with the antiwar movement exacerbated Nixon's feelings about MIT. "Where is the leader class?" Nixon pointedly asked his chief of staff. After complaining about the "sipping martini crowd" and their opposition to his policies, the president once again focused on MIT. "Why should I get up and lecture them and then give 50 million dollars to MIT, when the president of MIT comes out against the United States using his airpower against military targets to stop a communist invasion and doesn't say one goddamn word about the invasion!"[52] In a separate meeting with Haldeman and Kissinger, Nixon repeated his frustrations with Wiesner. He argued, that when the "quote worthwhile or respected colleges . . . come out strongly against the use of American airpower on military targets, and is totally silent with regard to massive Soviet bombers being used in a massive invasion . . . what the hell do you expect of those students?" When it was suggested that he make a speech to try to convince students to change their minds, he remained skeptical about its effect. "I could make that speech," but added that the opposition had "a drumbeat from the university presidents, from the university faculty, from the university associate professors, from the media, from the press lords, including the *Los Angeles Times*." It was clear that the president believed that Wiesner and MIT were only one piece of a conspiracy against his administration.[53]

Nixon's conspiratorial outlook drove him to refuse to meet with any major university administrators that spring. His refusal placed Kissinger in a tough bind, as his former colleagues pleaded for a meeting with the president. On May 11, Harvard president Derek Bok contacted Kissinger and tried to convince him to set up a meeting between Nixon and the Ivy League presidents. "I know how difficult that is and I see all the reasons but I felt I ought to," said Bok. "Well, particularly in the light of some of the public statements," replied Kissinger, who was particularly upset about a statement from the Ivy League that condemned the bombings without doing the same for the North Vietnamese. Bok was contrite during the conversation and tried to convince Kissinger that a meeting with the president could help lessen the tensions between

Nixon and the Ivy League. Knowing that the president was privately refusing to meet Bok or anyone else from the Ivy League, Kissinger offered to meet with the group. "It's essential that your main academic people remain in some sort of touch with us . . . And I would certainly do anything I can to maintain that contact."[54]

When the president found out that the university presidents met with Kissinger inside the White House on May 15, Nixon was furious. "No Ivy League Presidents. None of those, unless they change. I don't want to ever see them at the White House again! For anything! For anything!" said the president to Haldeman.[55] After the Haiphong Harbor bombing campaign, Nixon made sure that no one on his staff invited representatives from the Ivy League to the White House. He also repeatedly insisted that his staff cut off contact with the Ivy League, a subject that often came up in discussions with Kissinger.

Three days later, Nixon met with Kissinger at Camp David, at which time the national security advisor sheepishly admitted to the president that he met with the presidents of the Ivy League to discuss their concerns regarding the war. "I had the Ivy League presidents in yesterday," reported Kissinger, who before he could go any further was cut off by the president. "Bullshit! Sons of bitches! I wouldn't have seen them. They don't deserve it." After Kissinger said that the presidents asked for a meeting with the president, Nixon exclaimed, "They don't deserve it!" He added, "I won't let those sons of bitches ever in this White House again. Never, never, they're finished. The Ivy League schools are finished!" Kissinger agreed and said that the presidents had "embraced the program of the radicals," with their recent critiques of Nixon's foreign policy. "They said they want us to cut off military and economic aid . . . I'm amazed that leaders of an education institutions should take such a position on a moral issue." Nixon chastised Kissinger, "Henry, I would not have had them in. Don't ever do that . . . Don't ever go to any Ivy League school again."

The president then turned his attention back to the Ivies: "They don't know how bad they're going to be off, because I'm going to turn on those sons of bitches, finish those schools off to the extent that I can." Later on in the conversation, Nixon brought up the DOD funds to MIT and was once again adamant that they be cut. "They don't want to deal with the military, so I'm not going to give it to them. The hell with them. They're going to get it." He added, "When it's tough, they're not there. We don't want them." Kissinger's report on his meeting with the Ivy League presidents also brought out Nixon's ongoing frustrations with the number of Ivy Leaguers in his administration. "We've got to build a new establishment . . . It isn't going to come out of the Ivy League. You know there's never got to be another Harvard man hired in our staff, not any new ones. We've got too many already." The president conceded that they would miss out on some good men, but concluded that the Ivies had become too dangerous. "Why do we take people who have had their minds poisoned like that? Never ! Never! Never!"[56]

While the president was railing against the nation's academic elites that spring, administration officials were trying to find ways to cut off federal funds to MIT. From September 1971 to December 1972, Caspar Weinberger took brief notes of each of his meetings in his appointment diary. Although the notes do not provide many details of what was discussed during his meetings, they do document that the MIT order was passed down to both Shultz and Weinberger several times during the spring of 1972. They also suggest that in the two months preceding Shultz's move over to the Treasury Department, the White House began to look to Weinberger as their point person for the MIT order.

After an April 20, 1972 meeting with Ehrlichman, Weinberger jotted down, "Saw John Ehrlichman – re President's request to cut MIT funds." He also recorded that he met with each of the assistant directors at the OMB, but did not write down how they reacted to the order. "Saw Paul O'Neill – re above . . . Asst Directors meeting in Office . . . Morrill [illegible] re cutting MIT funds." Later in the day, he met with Dam and O'Neill again to continue their discussion about the MIT order. "Dam + O'Neill – in office – re MIT cuts." After another meeting with Ehrlichman, Weinberger met with Shultz regarding the President's request to cut MIT funds. The notes for that meeting mention that Shultz was "also unhappy about Pres desire to cut Ivy League colleges."[57] In the weeks following these meetings, Weinberger's appointment diary mentions the MIT order several more times. "Saw Ken Dam + Paul O'Neill – re addl data of NSC, NIH + AEC – on grants to college for President."[58] "Met with Ken Dam, Paul O'Neill, Jack Young + Bill Morrill – re cuts, MIT University research funds."[59] "Saw John Ehrlichman – re my MIT memo to President."[60] "Saw George Shultz – re Frank Davidson—MIT."[61]

With the help of the OMB's assistant directors, Weinberger sent a memorandum to the president on May 5 that listed the "options and probable consequences" of cutting funds to MIT and other elite universities. Under the heading of "Federal Support of MIT" Weinberger warned Nixon that direct cuts to MIT would "virtually guarantee front page attacks all over the country. It might be viewed as attack by you on MIT

FIGURE 4. Richard Nixon and George P. Shultz in the Executive Office Building, October 19, 1972. Shultz resisted Nixon's order to cut funds to MIT during his final months as director of the OMB and then again as secretary of the treasury. (From the Richard Nixon Presidential Library and Museum, WHPO-D0739–6a)

for personal reasons." Instead, Weinberger recommended that the president support his fourth option, a more modest plan that would "bring informal pressure on heads of some agencies—DOD, AEC and NAA—1 to cut back less critical work at MIT." He argued that "the advantages of this fourth option include some cuts at MIT with less visibility and desirable longer range reforms." Nixon checked off Weinberger's fourth option, but he would soon push for more aggressive cuts.[62]

Nothing was being done to punish MIT that spring, but Weinberger was slowly moving Nixon's order forward. Dam, Morrill, and O'Neill begrudgingly assisted in collecting data for Weinberger, but they did not support Nixon's plan. In his final months at OMB, Shultz stood his ground against the president and refused to participate with Nixon's request. "I believe that George sharpened his edges in that area," said Morrill of Shultz's opposition to Nixon's plan.[63]

As an academic who saw the value in maintaining a strong relationship with MIT, Shultz saw the truth behind the request. It was a clear attempt to turn the OMB into an office that would use the government to punish the president's enemies.

NIXON, WEINBERGER, AND THE FINAL PUSH

"I want those funds cut off, for that MIT," said Nixon to his chief of staff during a brief May 18, 1972 phone call from Camp David. The president had just finished haranguing Kissinger about meeting with the presidents of the Ivy League and demanded that his staff move faster with his MIT order. "Right, I know what you mean," replied Haldeman. The president had become impatient with the fact that Ehrlichman had not made any progress on getting Shultz to move forward with his order. "He was very distressed because he thinks E [Ehrlichman] is dragging his feet on the fund cutoff for MIT, and says now that Shultz is out of the budget bureau that he wants something done on this," wrote Haldeman in his diary. With Shultz out, the president's plan was to turn to Caspar Weinberger, the next director of the OMB. "Now . . . All right. You get ahold of Weinberger and say, 'I want the Goddamn funds, and I want them to know it now.' Get it done."[64]

The May 18 conversation set off a new wave of activity and raised the level of urgency within the White House. While the president's aides previously gathered reports on the subject, Nixon's repeated tirades in May 1972 led to more substantial attempts to cut off federal funds to MIT. The backlash over the Haiphong Harbor bombings marked a significant turning point, with the president concluding that he had to push harder to attack MIT. Although Nixon was at the center of the plan, Weinberger played a key role in moving forward with the president's order as the head of OMB. As a more conservative and more loyal member of the administration than Shultz, he became Nixon's man for the job.

The day after his phone call with Haldeman, Nixon met with Ehrlichman to discuss Weinberger's promotion and the MIT order. According to Ehrlichman, "Cap" [Weinberger] had already developed a plan to quietly cut off the funds. The plan was based around a formula that would gradually cut down the contracts with MIT in a way that would not attract much attention. "I mean the money dries up but we don't make a big show of it. We don't let them pin it on you as retribution. And what we do is we quietly pass the word to the agencies that those contracts are not to be renewed," said Ehrlichman. "I mean, do it!" declared Nixon, officially authorizing his staff to go after MIT.[65]

Weeks before Weinberger was officially promoted to succeed Shultz, Nixon met with the two of them in the Oval Office to discuss the transition and his expectations for the OMB. "Everyone will know that we've unleashed Weinberger now," said the president, who told the new director that he expected him to be "tough" and "political." With Shultz in the room, Nixon complained about the White House business council, which he described as having "no guts." He added, "It's an incestuous inbred group. Have as much steel and character as a college president at an Ivy League college."[66] The comment may not have been overtly directed at Shultz, but it still captured the tensions between the president and the outgoing director of the OMB. For Nixon, Weinberger was the man the White House could trust to punish their political enemies, including those at MIT.

Weinberger initially attempted to cut around the edges rather than directly taking away funds from MIT. Perhaps recognizing the potential implications of Nixon's order, Weinberger tried to focus on smaller ways to divest federal funds to MIT. In an Oval Office conversation that mostly focused on the federal budget, Nixon brought up his MIT order. "Like for example, your cutbacks on those damn universities, cut a little bit more down. Cut as much as you can." After Weinberger reported that they had already begun to make deep cuts, Nixon asked, "Have they squealed yet?" Weinberger replied, "No." Instead of focusing on the defense contracts, Weinberger then brought up a plan to target HEW grants to universities. The total amount of the grants paled in comparison to the DOD contracts, but Weinberger tried to keep the president focused on eliminating HEW's grants. He explained, "The way to get is to change those advisory committees . . . HEW lets all these grants be awarded by advisory committees and the advisory committees were appointed sometimes two administrations ago . . . We have a full exercise going on trying to get control of the budget." While Weinberger did not specifically address Nixon's order, the president was interested and said, "If there's any discretion, stop the grants. You know what I mean?" Weinberger replied, "Yes."[67]

On August 25, 1972, Weinberger sent Nixon a memorandum with a heading that simply read, "MIT." In the note, the OMB director reported on the progress he had made over the summer on cutting funds to MIT. "You asked me to take this action to cut back Federal funding at MIT. This is a report of progress." Weinberger proceeded to update the president on how he had paid close attention to the continued separation of the Draper Laboratory from MIT. He also claimed that he was looking into ways to also cut off the Lincoln Laboratory from MIT. "The separation of these laboratories from the University should, in addition to its intrinsic value, reduce overhead costs now going to the University."

Taking the two together, he concluded that "Federal funding going to or through the University should be reduced significantly eventually." Weinberger also wrote that he was working with James R. Schlesinger from the Atomic Energy Commission and Jim Fletcher at NASA to "reduce University funding as part of the very necessary 1973 and 1974 budget restrictions." He added, "I will keep you advised of the results." In another instance of officially documenting his interest in the plan to attack MIT, Nixon jotted down, "Good—Keep it up," on the memo.[68]

After his reelection, Nixon decided to move Weinberger out of OMB so that he could replace Elliot Richardson as the head of the Department of Health, Education, and Welfare (HEW). The president was satisfied with Weinberger's performance at OMB, but he believed he needed to have a fiscal conservative lead the more liberal-minded HEW. Despite the move, Nixon still looked to Weinberger as the White House's attack dog, as someone who could get involved in special projects for the White House. In mid-November, the president asked Weinberger to find a way to cut off all government contracts to the Brookings Institution. Nixon recounted the conversation in a November 19 meeting with Chuck Colson and sounded confident that Weinberger would get the job done.[69]

Nixon's distrust of MIT, the Ivy League, and the nation's academic elites did not lessen in the weeks and months after his reelection. Instead, his victory further emboldened him. He was convinced that his administration needed to take on an even more aggressive tone when dealing with their enemies. Nixon even argued that the administration should avoid bringing in moderate-minded technocrats. "You can't defeat left radicalism with bland professionalism," specifically pointing to his outgoing Secretary of Housing and Urban Development George Romney and George Shultz as examples.[70] Nixon's views of the "bland professionals" like Shultz were directly tied to his deep distrust of the culture of the nation's top-tier universities. Anyone who was remotely associated with the Ivy League or was too closely affiliated with the elite social networks of Washington was under suspicion. Those who avoided blatant partisanship and chose to follow a technocratic approach to their work were not a part of Nixon's broader vision of his second term. The president wanted a new culture within his administration, one that excluded Republicans such as Shultz.

When plotting out his next four years, the president often returned to his theories on the decline of the "leader class," arguing that the elite universities were at the heart of the country's problems. "Where is the American establishment?" asked Nixon during a May 5, 1972 cabinet meeting and vented that the leaders of the elite universities had abandoned him. Describing the American elite as a "source of national weakness," he lamented the fact that the most prestigious universities were having a negative impact on "those that publish the great magazines, those that run the great communications media, those that run the great universities." He added, "The more you see the educational process (unintelligible), you find very great erosion in the leader class in this country."[71] In his discussions about the nation's leader class, Nixon mostly focused on those from the Northeast, but also included other regions of the country. "The South isn't poisoned by bad universities," said Nixon in an October 14 meeting with his staff. They are "weak and soft in educated America," he argued, pointing to New York, Chicago, and Los Angeles as prime examples. As always, weakness was directly tied to opposing his policies—he later complained to his staff about the lack of support he received from the major universities after the Haiphong Harbor bombings. "Did you see any educators? Not one. Not one college president called me. Not one of those assholes. They're sitting it out because they have no guts and no character."[72]

Nixon also targeted academics over their ability to lead an organization, claiming that they were not men of action. In a meeting with one of his administration's resident academics, Daniel Patrick Moynihan, Nixon argued, "The difficulty with many people, with intellectuals, really great at telling you what's wrong . . . But when you ask him to do something, good god he screws it up. He can't run a university, how the hell could he run a department." The president later backtracked and cited the intellectuals on his staff including Moynihan and Shultz, describing both as "smart as hell." Moments later, he bragged to the future New York senator that he had recently banned the Ivy League presidents from the White House.[73]

Months after his reelection, Nixon met with Shultz, along with Haldeman, Ehrlichman, and Roy Ash, to talk about his expectations for his second term. The president complained that his administration was dominated by managers who were "cold and efficient." He told both Ash and Shultz that they should seek to be more like Robert F. Kennedy and add more warmth and excitement to their presentations. Soon after his lecture on public speaking, he also delivered a rant about the Ivy League and the broader changes of the 1960s. "Deep down, you have to realize there's something in the country today that wasn't here in the 50s, it developed in the 60s, it will probably be with us for the rest of our times. And that is the poison that the younger classes get from universities." According to Nixon, the universities were responsible for a loss of faith in the nation. "They frankly hate the country. They think that it's corrupt, that it's prejudiced." With Shultz sitting just a few feet away from him, Nixon then dissected the intellectual as an individual. He argued that "individual is a very unstable person," but added, "We can all talk this way, because we are all intellectuals," in a half-hearted attempted to soothe any uneasiness over his comments. He continued, "The intellectual is high-strung, emotionally unstable. That's why law firms are so bad. Half these guys are on the couch."[74]

Nixon's deep-seated anxiety over the influence of the nation's more prominent academics and other intellectuals led to the White House coming up with a list of people the president could talk to "on the philosophical side." The list was developed by Haldeman's aide, Larry Higby, and included conservative intellectuals such as Robert Bork, William Buckley, Lionel Trilling, and James Q. Wilson.[75] Taken as a whole, the list was a sign that the White House was turning away from its more moderate and liberal voices and moving toward building a more conservative intellectual establishment. Nixon's conception of a new establishment may have been somewhat amorphous, but it was clear in its determination to move the country toward the right. Nixon's obsession with the presence of Ivy Leaguers and the creation of a new establishment within his administration led to a conversation with Haldeman on November 24, 1972, where the two men went over the alma maters of each of the cabinet members. When Nixon and Haldeman came to Shultz's time at Princeton and MIT, Nixon exclaimed, "Oh shit!"[76] The president must have had already known about Shultz's academic background, but the conversation reminded him that the secretary had deep ties to MIT. For the president, Shultz's relationship to MIT gave him an even better understanding of the secretary's opposition to cutting off funds to the institute. It also gave Nixon even more of a reason to be suspicious of Shultz, especially in lieu of his recent refusal to pressure the IRS to audit political enemies. "George has the fundamental liberal's belief that all people are nice people," concluded Colson in a meeting with the president.[77]

While the White House was planning for an ambitious second term, antiwar demonstrations continued at MIT during the fall of 1972. More than two years after the announcement to divest the Draper Laboratory from MIT, a large number of students continued to oppose the school's military-based research. In mid-October 1972, a bomb was set off in a bathroom on the fourth floor of MIT's Grover M. Hermann building shortly after an anonymous caller warned that the detonation was imminent. The area was cleared and no one was hurt, but the bombing resulted in approximately $35,000 in damages. The incident took place a year after a group that called itself the Proud Eagle Tribe took credit for the bombing of the Harvard Center for International Affairs. The group said their target was the former assistant secretary of state William Bundy—their intent was to "punish him for the role he played in the Vietnam War," and to call attention to the universities that "have these murderers as professors."[78]

As 1972 came to a close, the president was weeks away from bringing the American war in Vietnam to an end, but he showed no intention of giving up on his battle with MIT. In a December 28, 1972 memo to Ehrlichman and his assistant Kenneth Cole, Nixon expressed his disappointment over the lack of progress that had been made to punish the institute. He wrote, "Both of you know how I feel better about the huge subsidies for higher education," referring to his desire to cut the amount of money given to prestigious schools. Nixon also explicitly pitted himself against Shultz and other administration officials who disagreed with his plan. "I know this is a sacred cow in HEW and in the educational committee. I know too that virtually everybody on the Domestic Council staff and in the HEW and OMB bureaucracy, as well as George Shultz, completely disagree with my convictions on this issue."[79]

The president even became frustrated with Weinberger's lack of progress when it came to cutting defense funds to MIT. "I thought, Bob, that I made it so clear beyond belief that I wanted MIT and other schools like that, the entire government's research programs, grants, everything we could possibly imagined examined and (inaudible) so they could be cut," he said to Haldeman on January 4, 1973. "We've got to get at that, goddamn it, there's 100 million dollars around some place that I didn't know about. I mean, I want the whole Defense Department budget . . . and a study made of the direct and indirect subsidy of higher education by this government." He added, "When I saw Cap, now that I recall, it was only from HEW." Nixon was no longer satisfied with Weinberger's plan; now the president wanted his staff to find ways to cut the school's defense contracts, not just the smaller grants from HEW.[80]

Nixon was impatient and demanded that immediate action be taken to come up with a better plan to go after MIT. "I want that done within 24 hours. Is that clear?" He also began to question Weinberger's loyalty for not going after the school's defense contracts. "All they gave me was HEW. That's all Weinberger gave me when I asked for a report. Now, that is a dishonest answer. It really is, because I didn't ask him about HEW." The president then requested that Haldeman look into the details of how Weinberger and James Schlesinger could actually carry out the order, and speculated about the influence of Weinberger's staff. "And if maybe Weinberger hasn't had the chance to get down to the bowels of it. He probably has a second man who is a graduate of MIT. No really. That's the way it works."[81]

Later that day Haldeman tried to settle the president's concerns about Weinberger. "I talked to Cap about that. He's moving on it. He had talked to Schlesinger." According to Haldeman, Weinberger conceded that he had not gone after the defense contracts. He also admitted that he had not made the progress that he wanted with the HEW grants, but argued that his efforts had already started the process that would subsequently lead to more drastic cuts. With the HEW grants, Weinberger blamed his inability to take action on the agency's advisory committees that controlled the grants to colleges and universities across the nation. "A lot of the people are left over from Johnson and before," said Haldeman to Nixon, who replied, "Maybe change . . . They're not quite well." Haldeman reported that Weinberger agreed, but that he wanted to focus on stopping the grants before making a big play to get rid of the more liberal committee members.

When it came to the defense contracts, Haldeman said about Weinberger: "He completely agrees there ought to be crash effort at MIT and he had already talked to Schlesinger about it, before [soon-to-be secretary of defense] Elliot [Richardson] gets over there." Nixon repeated his argument about the distribution of defense funds to universities that opposed his foreign policy. "My view about that is that it's not because it's MIT, but because I do not think that the Defense Department should give contracts to individuals who are against Defense. That's what it's all about."

The president seemed somewhat satisfied by Haldeman's report, but was still frustrated that his order had not yet been carried out. Upon looking back on the lack of progress on his order over the previous eight months, Nixon placed much of the blame on Shultz. "Of course we didn't do it, Shultz torpedoed the goddamn thing because George is (Haldeman laughs), well, basically, everybody is thinking of what he was previously."[82] For Nixon, the culture of MIT, of the establishment, had proven to be too strong of an influence on Shultz. The president could not see Shultz's resistance to the order outside of his own distrust of the nation's academic elites.

While Shultz was viewed as a lost cause, the White House continued to put pressure on Weinberger to carry out the MIT order. As the new head of HEW, Weinberger began to respond to the president's demand for more

FIGURE 5. While serving as director of OMB and secretary of HEW, Caspar Weinberger tried to find ways to follow through on Nixon's request to cut funds to MIT. (From the Richard Nixon Presidential Library and Museum, MUG-W-316)

action in January and February 1973. During a meeting with Haldeman and Ehrlichman to discuss the president's upcoming speech on the federal budget, Nixon debated whether or not he should include a mention of his desire to reduce the amount of money that went to colleges and universities. "God, I think it's such a waste. I really think it's a waste. Subsidizing professors who are against war with defense money, it's gotta stop." Both Haldeman and Ehrlichman ignored the suggestion to put the issue in the speech, but brought up Weinberger's decision to shift federal grants away from educational institutions to students. "And they [the universities] are going to scream and scream and scream." Nixon asked, "They don't like that?" to which Ehrlichman replied, "Oh they hate that, hate that. It's a marketplace approach to education . . . Weinberger is for it."[83] Four days later, Weinberger wrote down in his appointment diary, "Ken Rush – he'll join Bill Clements in trying to block MIT contracts." Rush was the outgoing deputy secretary of defense and Clements was his successor.[84]

In mid-February, the president received a detailed memo from Weinberger with the subject heading, "Federal Aid to Higher Education – Response to Your Questions of February 10." Attached to the memo was a note to Haldeman that read, "At SC [San Clemente] yesterday, the President asked to have this report on his desk this morning. A copy has gone to John Ehrlichman and to Gen. [Brent] Scowcroft through who he originally placed the request." He added, "I would appreciate it if you could move as rapidly as possible on this one so we can comply with the President's request," showing that he was interested in taking more aggressive action on the issue.[85] In his report, Weinberger laid out the updated statistics on the amount of federal aid that went to higher education: $3.4 billion in the 1973 budget with a plan to reduce spending to $2.8 billion in 1974. That total included tens of millions of dollars to MIT, the Ivy League, and some of the more prominent state schools. Responding to the president's repeated requests to take federal funds away from elite schools in the Northeast, Weinberger noted that when it came to the National Institutes of Health's funds for heart and cancer research, he would try to identify "mid-western and far-western State schools" that "are moving to develop capacity on their own. We will take positive steps to see that they are involved in the expanded heart and cancer research effort." Nixon approved of the plan to politicize funds for cancer research and wrote on the report, "Cap – good. Keep up the move away from the haves to the have nots."

Throughout the rest of the report, Weinberger listed the various initiatives he had taken up over the previous eight months to cut down on federal funds to universities. He mentioned that he was working with officials within the Pentagon who were "enthusiastic" about the project, and noted that he was also working with Schlesinger to see if they could move funds away from MIT and the University of California. He concluded, "We have adopted a policy, which is reflected in 1973 and 1974 budgets and will be continued, of increasing HEW support for the so-called developing institutions and decreasing aid elsewhere."[86] In a February 15 memo that was sent to Weinberger, the president's staff wrote that Nixon had reviewed the report and "noted that it was a good response."[87]

Although Weinberger had not accomplished everything the president wanted, his plan to restructure certain federal grants to universities attracted attention from academics across the nation. In a January 1973 issue of *Higher Education and National Affairs,* it was reported that the Nixon administration would begin to end many federal education grants in the 1974 fiscal year budget. The piece stated, "No funds for grants or direct loans for construction of academic facilities, new fellowships, foreign language and area studies, the university community services." The journal also noted that "President Nixon has disclosed that Caspar W. Weinberger and two other Cabinet officers will be given added responsibilities over Federal domestic programs in his second term."[88] University administrators were unaware of Nixon's private conversations, but the proposed budget for 1974 and Weinberger's elevated status within the administration sent a clear signal that the White House was prepared to take a more conservative approach toward subsidizing higher education.

THE OMB ASSISTANT DIRECTORS SAY NO

Around the same time that Weinberger was seeking to find ways to appease the president, Nixon's MIT order was also delivered to the assistant directors of the OMB: Dam, Morrill, and O'Neill. The three men had developed a deep respect for the president, but were troubled by his plan to politicize federal funds. In a 2007 Oral History interview with the Nixon Library, O'Neill remembered that although he "never saw the ugly side of Nixon personally . . . there was a time when we got an order." He recalled that Haldeman's office told them that they were to "cut off all funding to universities, all research funding to universities where there were campus protests against the Vietnamese War." He added, "Particularly those terrible people at MIT. Don't let those people have any more federal money."[89] For O'Neill, there was little doubt that the order had come from Nixon or was at least representative of something he had said to Haldeman. Morrill also documented the incident in his 2013 memoir as he wrote that he felt that the order was driven by Nixon's desire to go after Wiesner. "My own rumor mill indicated that Nixon wanted to do damage to the MIT contracts of Jerry Wiesner . . . I'd heard that Nixon adviser Bob Haldeman had been told by the president more than once that he wanted to punish Wiesner."[90]

Faced with Nixon's MIT order, the three managers decided to turn to their former boss, George Shultz, who was now the secretary of the treasury. According to O'Neill, they told Shultz that they would resign if they were forced to carry out the president's request. "There's no basis in law to carry out this order," said O'Neill. He also argued, "And the Congress established eligibility for federal grant funds, and the authority vested in the departments and agencies receive the funds. We have no authority in the executive office to overrule it and we're not going to do it." Morrill also remembered planning to resign in protest, and was so disgusted that he considered going to the press. "I was going to pick up my pen for public consumption."[91] After the three men threatened their resignations from the OMB, Shultz told them not to worry about the issue. "And George said, leave it with me. And you know, the next day we were told, stand down, you don't have to do that, you don't have to resign," remembered O'Neill. Morrill's version of the MIT incident matches up with O'Neill's, as he wrote, "George listened to my story and said, 'don't worry, I'll take care of it.' And I never heard further about the matter. I hope that neither did he."[92]

The meeting between the secretary and his former employees was an important one for solidifying opposition to the MIT order, but it was also a curious one given that Shultz was no longer their boss. O'Neill explained, "George was a really important influence. And it's apparent now in retrospect in what one sees in the Nixon tapes, he didn't get called into every event, but when he got called in, he stood up. And he prevailed." When asked why they met with Shultz instead of discussing the issue with either Ash or Weinberger, O'Neill said it was because they saw Shultz as the person who could make a difference. "He was still assistant to the president on economic affairs and he had a little cubbyhole office in the White House . . . He was still sitting up there . . . Roy [Ash] was the director of OMB. We needed to talk to somebody who had some influence." According to O'Neill, he never heard anything that suggested that either Ash or the OMB's new deputy director Fred Malek was upset about their meeting with Shultz.

The issue may have never been brought up outside of private meetings within the White House, but it was clear that the three assistant directors viewed Shultz as someone they could trust to stand up to the president. Over the previous four years in the Nixon administration, Shultz had proven that he was willing to protect the integrity of the OMB and fight back against attempts to politicize the office. Unlike Ash, Weinberger, or Malek, Shultz had shown the ability to maintain his independence in the face of great pressure, and because of that, he inspired great confidence in the people who worked for him in the federal government. "He was our godfather or something," said O'Neill.[93] It was through his steady support that O'Neill, Dam, and Morrill were able to keep their jobs and stop Nixon's MIT order from being fully carried out.

Their collective refusal to cut federal funds to universities limited what the White House and Weinberger could do with the president's plan. If the three assistant directors of the OMB went along with the order, Nixon would have had more institutional support to punish MIT, the Ivy League, and possibly many other schools across the nation. Without their support, the White House was forced to rely heavily on Weinberger's efforts, which had been somewhat cautious since the previous spring. Their threat to resign from their prestigious positions within the OMB provided the necessary counterweight to Weinberger's decision to follow through on Nixon's demands.

Despite the resistance he faced within his own administration, and the growing political pressures of the Watergate scandal, Nixon did not completely give up on his plan. "The ones I really wanted to cut are at MIT," said Nixon to Ehrlichman during a March 20, 1973 conversation about health research. "The defense grants, John, the defense grants that's the real gravy train . . . I want one more crack at that." Ehrlichman was mostly silent during the discussion, perhaps because he knew that the order was unlikely to go anywhere; nonetheless, he dutifully replied, "I'll get a report on that."[94] During a March 13 meeting with administration officials to discuss the president's revenue sharing plan, Nixon insisted that they needed "a new approach" to subsidizing universities. Using grants to universities as an example of how the federal government had mishandled subsidies, Nixon stated he wanted to "cut out all of the money for MIT and Cal Tech and Harvard and all of the rest." He then awkwardly brought up his own academic background, "I was the only one on my staff who didn't go to Harvard (room laughs)," and complained about how left wing the nation's top universities had become in recent years. "Eighty percent of the faculty is totally against the administration."[95]

Even after the resignations of Haldeman and Ehrlichman on April 30, 1973, and the public's growing awareness of the Watergate scandal, the president did not fully abandon his MIT plan. In a June 14, 1973 meeting with Shultz in the Oval Office, the president complained about the distribution of federal funds to universities, arguing that the government should not give most of its research money to MIT, Stanford, and the University of Chicago.[96] Shultz remained silent throughout that portion of their discussion. During the meeting, Nixon never gave Shultz a direct order on MIT or any other university. He knew that Shultz would not listen. Nevertheless, he tried one last time to make his case to the secretary who had blocked his plan.

The president's plot to politicize the distribution of federal funds to colleges and universities never came to fruition. With the exception of Weinberger's efforts to make across-the-board cuts on the federal government's grants to universities and other education programs, the president failed to punish his enemies at MIT, the Ivy League, and other elite schools. What little momentum Weinberger built up to follow through on Nixon's plan in his time at HEW and beyond faded away once Watergate became a national scandal in the spring of 1973. There is no evidence that Weinberger or any other administration official worked any further on the president's plan after February 1973.

Aside from acting as a hindrance to the president's MIT plan, the growing effects of the Watergate scandal on the White House also led Nixon to give up on producing compelling policy plans with OMB. Paul O'Neill's biographer, Ron Suskind, noted that the OMB was running much of the government by default in the final year of the Nixon presidency.[97] Although they were located in the White House, much of the office became disconnected from the president. A year after its three assistant directors opposed the president's MIT order, the office was both more powerful and more independent of Nixon's influence.

. . .

In 1974, O'Neill was promoted to deputy director of OMB, a position he held through the end of the Ford administration. During that time he helped design the structure for Medicare financing and provided semi-regular briefings for President Ford on the federal budget.[98] He left the public sector in 1977 to take a job with International Paper, where he was vice president until 1985 and then president until 1987. O'Neill continued his career in the private sector in Pittsburgh as the CEO of Alcoa, one of the world's largest producers of aluminum. He ended his run as CEO in 1999, and then retired as chairman of the company in 2000 to become secretary of the treasury for George W. Bush. Although O'Neill had been officially out of the federal government for more than two decades, he had maintained his contacts from the Nixon/Ford years and played an influential role in the first Bush administration. He even served on the elder Bush's advisory group on education and advised the president to raise taxes to deal with the deficit. His time in George W. Bush's administration was marked by his criticisms of the president's ideologically driven fiscal and environmental policies. While he previously felt at home among the moderates in the Nixon, Ford, and first Bush administrations, O'Neill was now one of the few solution-oriented technocrats in an administration dominated by domestic and foreign policy ideologues who were determined to cut taxes and invade Iraq. After a little less than two years on the job, he resigned in December 2002 and later worked with Ron Suskind on his biting account of his time in the Bush administration.

Although O'Neill later became more aware of Nixon's dark side through his exposure to the tapes, he still maintained fond memories of working for the president. "One might say I saw the president with the public policy veneer." It was clear that his opposition to Nixon's MIT order was not driven by any personal animosity toward the thirty-seventh president. He added, "I saw the unbelievably intelligent person that was in that body too. You can maybe argue that there were quite a few people in that body, but there was a thoughtful intellectual person in there."[99]

Kenneth Dam left the OMB in 1973 to become the executive director of the White House's Council on Economic Policy. From 1980 to 1982 he served as the provost of his alma mater, the University of Chicago. During the Reagan years, Dam reunited with Shultz when he served as his deputy at the State Department from 1982 to 1985. He later worked for IBM, was the CEO of the United Way of America, and was a member of the board of Alcoa with his former colleague O'Neill. The two also worked together at the Treasury Department during the Bush years, as Dam served as O'Neill's deputy, before leaving the administration in 2003.

Soon after the MIT incident, William Morrill moved out of the OMB and over to HEW to work with his former boss, Caspar Weinberger. While Morrill recalled that their "political convictions differed," he still developed a friendly and productive working relationship with Weinberger that led to him being brought over to HEW. "He periodically said to me that 'we could disagree without being disagreeable,'" he wrote of Weinberger.[100] "Cap was a strong supporter of civil servants," said Morrill, who recalled that Weinberger supported him whenever the White House would complain about his disloyalty. Still, Morrill did not deny Weinberger's role in trying to push forward Nixon's MIT plan. "Cap was involved in it. Cap had a penchant for being loyal to his president." However, he also believed that Weinberger never fully supported the president's plan to punish MIT. He added, "I think that Cap was stalling and hoped that it would go away. It was a common tactic."[101]

At HEW, Morrill helped push through Title XX of the Social Security Act, which developed block grants for social services through the states. When he left the federal government in 1977, Morrill stayed active in the promotion of public policy organizations that received funding from the private sector. While he maintained respect for Nixon's accomplishments, his personal experiences with his flaws shaped his final judgment. "While his contributions cannot be overlooked, his flaws poisoned his presidency."[102]

George Shultz left the Nixon administration just months before the president's own resignation. Upon leaving the administration, he joined the Bechtel Group, where he eventually became the president of the engineering company. Shultz returned to the public sector when President Reagan appointed him secretary of state in 1982, replacing Alexander Haig. As the head of the State Department for seven years, he earned high marks for his diplomatic efforts with the Soviet Union. His steady support for arms control negotiations with the Soviets often pitted him against the then secretary of defense Caspar Weinberger, who advocated a more aggressive posture toward the Russians. Shultz became noticeably more conservative in his later years, especially in his hawkish defense of George W. Bush' foreign policy, but he also wrote pieces in favor of the legalization of recreational drugs and the normalization of relations with Cuba. When discussing Nixon, Shultz consistently maintained a respectful outlook on the thirty-seventh president's legacy and rarely talked about his negative interactions with Nixon. While he proudly discussed his refusal to use the IRS to punish those on the enemies list, he has never publicly discussed or written about his resistance to Nixon's MIT order.

After Nixon's resignation, Weinberger stayed on as the head of HEW until 1975, when he moved back to his native California with his family. Over the next five years he worked with Shultz as the vice president of Bechtel, before returning to the federal government in 1981 as secretary of defense. While leading the Pentagon, Weinberger became entangled in the Iran-Contra scandal by participating in the transfer of weapons to Iran. He subsequently resigned in the fall of 1987 because of his wife's deteriorating health. In 1992, he was indicted on felony charges, including obstruction of justice, for his role in Iran-Contra; investigators accused him of hiding evidence and participating in a cover-up. Weinberger was pardoned by outgoing President George H. W. Bush in late 1992 and denied the charges that were leveled at him for the rest of his life.

In addition to the Iran-Contra scandal, Weinberger also batted away what were then accusations that he carried out Nixon's order to cut funds to MIT. Shortly after a batch of transcripts of Nixon White House tapes were released in 1993, the *New York Times* interviewed Weinberger about the president's May 18 conversation with Haldeman concerning the MIT order. When asked why the president and the chief of staff brought up his name as someone who would punish MIT, Weinberger dismissed the conversation as just one of Nixon's rants. "People were always furious with somebody over at the White House," he said. "It's absurd that anybody called me and asked me to come up with a plan to punish MIT."[103] In the more than twenty years since his denial, we now know, through the release of additional tapes and other materials, that Weinberger lied about his participation in Nixon's MIT plan. The president's May 18 order was not a single tirade, but one of many conversations that showed that Nixon was fiercely determined to attack MIT. Weinberger may not have carried out the order to Nixon's desired end point, but the records clearly show that he still cooperated with the president in trying to find ways to punish colleges and universities for their antiwar activities.

With the help of Weinberger and his inner circle at the White House, Nixon developed a plan to dramatically weaken the influence of MIT, the Ivy League, and other educational institutions. Nixon's plan was a part of the White House's broader effort to create a new establishment, one that would be significantly more conservative and would defend Nixon's foreign policy. Although there were a wide range of misdeeds that were connected to Nixon's desire to reshape the federal government, his MIT order perfectly captured his resentment toward the cultural elites. The president's differences with academia were certainly ideologically driven, but they were largely shaped by his polemical understanding of the nation's culture wars. Nixon's efforts to cut funds to MIT were a dangerous attempt to conflate policy with his cultural and political battles.

Nixon's plan only failed because of the individuals within the OMB who refused to carry out his orders. As with the IRS, it was the moderate-minded Republicans within the OMB who provided the most important roadblock to the president's plans. Led by their former boss George Shultz, the three managers within the OMB refused to cave to the White House's demands to politicize their work. In doing so, they prevented the federal government from taking punitive measures against several colleges and universities. Despite the fact that they faced serious pressure, they did not view the presence of antiwar protests as grounds for taking away federal funds from a university. Unlike Nixon, they valued civil service over their political loyalties and objective analysis over everything else. It was those values that shaped their decision to stand up to the White House and kept the nation's top universities safe from the president.

3

"Get Him the Hell Out of HEW"

Elliot Richardson's Quiet Battles
with President Nixon

In one of the many meetings that focused on their goals for a second term in the weeks following Nixon's reelection, Haldeman, Ehrlichman, and the president sat down for over two and a half hours to discuss the strengths and weaknesses of different members in their cabinet. In a previously unpublished conversation, they specifically placed an emphasis on each individual's loyalty to the president and their ability to follow the White House's lead on policy issues. When the three men came to Elliot Richardson, the then head of the Department of Health, Education, and Welfare (HEW), Nixon expressed his discomfort with keeping him in that position. "I just don't know," said the president, who brought up his disagreements with Richardson over busing and health care that had led to hushed battles between the White House and HEW. "He will always move to the left of you," argued Ehrlichman, "As the night to day." Despite his concerns over their policy differences, Nixon quickly conceded that for political purposes, Richardson should remain in the cabinet. "I suppose you've got to keep one person in the goddamned government that's considered to be sort of interested in the people. You see he has that."[1]

While the president's remarks may have been somewhat facetious, the conversation encapsulated his thoughts on Richardson. The president saw the value in keeping a well-respected moderate such as Richardson in his cabinet. Richardson had also proven to be loyal during several of the administration's toughest moments, most notably after the invasion of Cambodia. Although some of Richardson's staff at the State Department resigned in protest, the then undersecretary brushed aside his private concerns and chose to publicly support the president. Despite Richardson's loyalty, Nixon saw him as a person whom he could never fully trust. Richardson was an effective manager who often followed the White House's instructions, but he also had an independent streak that at times pitted him against the president. In various conversations, Nixon and his advisers often labeled Richardson as not tough enough with regard to foreign policy, too liberal on domestic issues, and too soft on dealing with the administration's opponents. "He's more of a willow type. He waves in the wind," said Ehrlichman in a separate meeting during which the president was frustrated over Richardson's inability to clamp down on HEW's liberal staff.[2] As with other moderates within the administration, Nixon and his advisers were all too willing to disparage Richardson's character whenever they were confronted with resistance from their prized asset. Whether it was his sense of loyalty or his masculinity that was being questioned by the president, Richardson was someone who was firmly outside of his plans for the development of his new establishment.

After many conversations, Nixon decided to move Richardson out of HEW and over to the Pentagon as his new secretary of defense in January 1973. This was a position that caused fewer political problems for the White House because the Pentagon's staff was considered to be more in line with the president's goals than HEW. The president passed legislation during his first term that was decidedly liberal, but he had no interest in expanding on these accomplishments in his second term. He was now interested in putting a cap on the work of the liberal bureaucracy at HEW. For Nixon, the Pentagon was a better place for Richardson

By late April, new developments in the Watergate scandal forced Nixon to ask for the resignations of Haldeman, Ehrlichman, and John Dean due to their roles in the cover-up. The president had also decided to ask for the resignation of the current attorney general, Richard Kleindienst. In the days leading up to the resignations, close advisers to the president such as Chuck Colson and William Rogers convinced Nixon that Richardson was the best man to replace Kleindienst. Even though Nixon never saw Richardson as a part of his inner circle, the president felt that he had shown what was then the necessary combination of loyalty and credibility that he desperately needed that spring. Critics of the White House would be hard-pressed to depict the new attorney general as a Nixon stooge. Nixon and Richardson met at Camp David on April

29, and the president officially offered him the job. It was one of only a few face-to-face conversations between the two men, a remarkable fact that underlined their tense relationship. In November, Nixon had gone back and forth on whether or not there was a place for the then head of HEW within the administration. The president now felt that he had to put Richardson in charge of an investigation that could potentially bring down his presidency. This was the moment when he had to appeal to the establishment, including the influential moderate wing of the GOP.

The very next day, Nixon delivered his first televised speech on Watergate where he announced his decision to name Richardson the next attorney general of the United States. A few hours after the speech, the president took phone calls late into the night, from various administration figures and friends. Richardson had just watched the speech with several other Pentagon officials in the middle of a dinner party that he was hosting at his house. When Richardson called, he told Nixon that he felt that the speech "was really great," and that he would not let the president down in his new position. Nixon, whose speech was noticeably slurred, replied, "Do your job, boy, and it may take you all the way," implying perhaps that the investigation could elevate Richardson's career to the White House in 1976. Richardson said, "I have the feeling that I think I can do it right." Nixon agreed, but then pivoted to the possibility of the Senate pressuring him to name a special prosecutor. "The point is I'm not sure you should have one. I'm not sure . . ." Avoiding any details about his future plans, Richardson only told him that he was "thinking about" the possibility of a special prosecutor, and that he met with Assistant Attorney General Henry Petersen earlier that day to discuss the issue. Instead of diving into the specifics of the potential special prosecutor position, Nixon backtracked and reiterated his support. "Do what you want and I'll back you to the hilt. I don't give a damn what you do, I am for you. Do you understand? Get to the bottom of this son-of-a-bitch." Richardson replied, "I do."[3]

Less than six months later, Richardson and his deputy, William Ruckelshaus, would both refuse to fire the Watergate special prosecutor, Archibald Cox, and resign in what came to be known as the Saturday Night Massacre. It was the moment where Richardson could no longer say yes to the president. He was no longer a loyal soldier. In retrospect, the conversations between Nixon and Richardson that took place in late April foreshadowed what would later transpire—what was left unsaid led to a full-blown confrontation. Within the context of the spring of 1973, the hope that both figures had for a common solution for the Watergate investigation was not completely irrational. While Richardson was never a particularly close adviser to Nixon, many in the White House considered him to be an independent, who was also a manageable and effective administrator. "Nixon saw in Richardson a highly intelligent man that could continue to add luster to the Nixon administration," said John Thomas (J. T.) Smith, an adviser to Elliot Richardson at three different departments, during a 2013 interview. Although Nixon never felt comfortable with Richardson, he had a history with the man that showed that the reward often outweighed the risk of working with an "establishment type."[4] For more than four years, Richardson had added luster to the administration, and despite pressure from friends and former colleagues who opposed Nixon, he did little to publicize his disagreements with the White House.

The Saturday Night Massacre was the culmination of Richardson's behind-the-scenes battles with the White House, dating back to 1969. Underlying those battles were the cultural divisions between the president and Richardson. Nixon may have respected Richardson for his intelligence and managerial skills, but he always viewed Richardson as the archetypical figure of the old guard that he railed against throughout his political career. Richardson's upper-class upbringing, Ivy League education, calm disposition, and emphasis on openness put him directly at odds with Nixon's own upbringing, leadership style, and visions of a new type of an establishment. His good looks, dark-rimmed glasses, and aloof demeanor led some to compare Richardson to Superman's alter-ego, Clark Kent. The *New York Times* once even described Richardson as "looking like a banker contemplating a loan," a description that only slightly exaggerated his appearance.[5] On a policy level, his many connections to systems analysis foreign policy types and comparatively more liberal approach to domestic affairs also put him at odds with the White House. For Nixon, his suspicions about Richardson and what he saw as the elite class proved to be true. Following the Saturday Night Massacre, the president jotted down his thoughts about the "Richardson incident" and who he felt the White House should trust. He wrote that "Establishment types like Richardson simply won't stand with us when [the] chips are down and they have to choose between their political ambitions and standing by the President who made it possible for them to hold the high positions from which they were now resigning."[6] The beleaguered president clearly saw the resignations of Richardson and Ruckelshaus as an act of betrayal—two men who were more loyal to the establishment than his presidency. Nixon did not regret the decision to fire Cox, but forever regretted his decision to select an establishment figure such as Richardson to be his attorney general in the tumultuous spring of 1973. In his memoirs, Nixon concluded, "The first major mistake was the appointment of Richardson as Attorney General." Returning to the issue of strength, he added, "Richardson's weakness, which came to light during the Cox firing, should have been apparent."[7]

While Nixon may have never been able to dissociate Richardson's actions from his upbringing, it is clear that the Saturday Night Massacre was much more than just another battle between the president and the "Eastern Establishment." Looking at the history of Richardson's relationship with Nixon, dating back to the Eisenhower years, it becomes evident that Richardson had consistently worked hard to avoid confrontations with the president. Their differing views on democracy, politics, the role of the government, and subsequently the role of the Watergate special prosecutor are what led them to the Saturday Night Massacre. Even though his natural instinct as a pragmatist was to seek a compromise with the president, Richardson's idealism and willingness to quietly oppose the White House often made him an uneasy fit within the administration. His clean-cut reputation made him a valuable cabinet member that Nixon needed at various points in his presidency, but it also eventually made him an enemy of the White House. Much like other moderates within the administration, Richardson was viewed by Nixon with great suspicion, and Nixon constantly worried about Richardson's loyalty to his presidency.

ELLIOT RICHARDSON'S PATH TO THE NIXON ADMINISTRATION

Born on July 20, 1920, Elliot Lee Richardson was raised in the affluent Back Bay neighborhood of Boston. Even in his youth, Richardson was serious about his work, as he graduated at the top of his class from Milton Academy in 1937.[8] After his graduation, he chose to attend Harvard, where he once again excelled as a student. Soon after enrolling in Harvard Law, he enlisted in the Army and fought during World War II. After his unit landed on Omaha Beach, Elliot risked his life by crossing a minefield to rescue a wounded soldier who was lying in a patch of barbed wire. "He was in agonizing pain. Somebody had to get him. I stepped carefully across the barbed wire, picked up the wounded soldier, and retraced my steps. All I could do was put down one foot after the other, hoping each time that nothing would go off," wrote

Richardson, whose actions earned him a Bronze Star and two Purple Hearts. Years later, Richardson stressed the importance of his meticulous approach to the rescue, and later compared the experience to the week leading up to the Saturday Night Massacre.[9]

After the war, Richardson resumed his studies at Harvard Law and eventually became editor and president of the *Harvard Law Review*. Upon receiving his degree, he moved to work as a clerk for Judge Learned Hand of the U.S. Court of Appeals and then Supreme Court Justice Felix Frankfurter. Early on in his career, Richardson was already known for his self-assuredness, especially after he asked for an uninterrupted hour every morning to read poetry. Regardless of how others viewed his demands, Richardson impressed Frankfurter, who later recommended that his former clerk be named president of Harvard in 1953.[10] Toward the end of his first stay in Washington, he even received a job offer from Secretary of State Dean Acheson to work at the State Department. While considering the job, Richardson reached out to his former law professor Archibald Cox, who told him to decline the offer and go back to Boston to work as a private attorney. "When I was in Washington, I always thought it important to come from somewhere," said Cox. Richardson took the advice, moved back to Boston, and later remembered the conversation as a turning point for his career. "I can't imagine what a different life I would have had, if I had stayed in Washington."[11]

During the early 1950s, Richardson beefed up his law credentials, participated in many local meetings in his hometown, and became more connected to the state's Republican Party, especially when Senator Leverett Saltonstall hired him as a political adviser. While working as an aide to the senator, Richardson had his first, albeit brief, encounter with Richard Nixon at the 1956 Republican National Convention. The two were introduced when Richardson delivered a speech he had drafted for Governor Herter that would be used to officially nominate the then vice president for a second term. They later developed somewhat of a working relationship when Richardson became the assistant secretary of HEW for legislation during Eisenhower's second term. The position meant that he was third in line at HEW, but Richardson served as acting secretary for a short period of time.[12] In meetings with Eisenhower and his other advisers, Nixon and Richardson bonded over their shared frustrations regarding how the administration handled certain domestic policy initiatives. Richardson later recalled that there were times when the vice president grew frustrated during cabinet meetings and would become "so tense that beads of sweat were standing out on his brow." At one cabinet meeting that Richardson attended, Nixon refused to stay silent and stood up for an HEW-backed bill that provided federal subsidies for bonds funding the expansion of higher education. Once he spoke up, Nixon convinced everyone at the meeting to support the bill, including Eisenhower. Richardson, who was close to resigning over the cabinet's initial opposition to the bill, respected Nixon for his ability to build up the needed support for the bill. "He had won the bill almost single-handed, and I was extremely grateful to him since I was saved from the need to resign. Quite an irony, when you consider what happened to me in 1973."[13] Over the next several years, the two remained friendly acquaintances as Nixon selected Richardson to be a part of his informal kitchen cabinet for his first presidential campaign.[14]

During the late 1950s, Richardson once again moved back to Boston where he was appointed the U.S. district attorney for Massachusetts in 1959. Over the next decade, Richardson climbed to the rank of lieutenant governor of Massachusetts in 1965, and then two years later, became the state's attorney general. With his star rising within the GOP, Richardson developed a reputation for being a tough investigator who fought corruption across party lines in Massachusetts.[15]

By 1968, Richardson had not only earned notoriety for his prosecutorial skills, but also for his devotion to objective analysis, a characteristic that kept him deeply connected with other moderate and liberal establishment figures of the era. Adelberg Ames, a Boston doctor asked by reporters to describe his longtime friend, chose to emphasize Richardson's broader views on problem solving. "He really believes that problems are amenable to analysis, and it doesn't really matter what the problem is as long as you have the technique for analyzing it." One of Richardson's closest advisers, Jonathan Moore, a like-minded moderate Republican from Massachusetts, shared many of Elliot's views on civil service and governance. Moore first became acquainted with Richardson during the Eisenhower years as an aide to Senator Saltonstall. Richardson saw great value in Moore, especially when it came to his decision-making process, as he later wrote that he enjoyed Moore's "readiness to take me on."[16] In addition to his work for Richardson, Moore had also worked as a foreign policy adviser for the presidential campaigns of George Romney and Nelson Rockefeller in 1967 and 1968. After both campaigns failed to win the nomination, he turned down an offer to work with the Nixon campaign. "I didn't want to be responsible for getting Nixon elected president," remembered Moore in a 2012 interview. His distaste for Nixon was partially rooted in his own father's experience with Nixon during the Eisenhower years. Charles F. Moore, a speechwriter for Eisenhower's presidential campaigns, was one of several Republican party figures who tried to convince the president to dump Nixon from the ticket in 1956.[17]

While Moore and Richardson did not work with each other in 1968, the two often socialized since Richardson lived just across the bay from Moore's family's house in Cape Cod. When Richardson was brought back to Washington to serve in the Nixon administration, Moore joined him and the two worked together until the Saturday Night Massacre. The young aide would play a valuable role within Richardson's staff, especially during their confrontations with the White House.

Soon after Nixon's victory in 1968, Richardson was offered to work for the administration as the deputy secretary at HEW, but turned the position down to remain in Massachusetts. A second offer from soon-to-be secretary of state William Rogers piqued Richardson's interest. Rogers, who had known Richardson through their respective posts in the Eisenhower administration, wanted him as his undersecretary, the number two position within the department. Although Richardson was originally hesitant due to his lack of foreign policy experience, Rogers convinced him that he was the right man for the job. When he was announced as the new undersecretary of state, Rogers introduced his new deputy as his "alter ego," and stressed that the two would share leadership responsibilities within the department.[18]

THE STATE DEPARTMENT AND THE CAMBODIA INVASION

As undersecretary, one of Richardson's main duties was to work directly with Henry Kissinger, especially since Rogers's relationship with the national security advisor was almost always either contentious or nonexistent. Richardson met with Kissinger almost every Thursday for lunch to discuss foreign affairs and departmental issues. Richardson, who was well aware of the tensions between the department and the White House, sometimes came back from his lunches with Kissinger more optimistic about his influence on the White House. Moore, who had previously butted heads with Kissinger when both worked on the Rockefeller campaign, remembered that he would often temper his boss's expectations. According to Moore, Richardson excitedly believed that "he brought the conversations to a more elevated place." Moore countered, "That's fine, Elliot, but he's screwing you."[19]

Richardson was also put in charge of handling personnel issues in the department, a role that occasionally put him at odds with the White House. Since the department included many holdovers from the Johnson years, Nixon and his advisers attempted to pressure Richardson to fire liberal Democrats and replace them with Nixon loyalists. Most of the orders came from Peter Flanigan and Harry Fleming, two of the president's assistants who were consultants on personnel issues across the federal government. Moore documented one attempt to influence Richardson in a March 1, 1969 memo. Beginning with a section entitled "White House Transition Pressure," Moore wrote that there had been "efforts" from "White House staffers" to "force resignations and appointments in the political categories."[20] Just a few months later, Flanigan asked Richardson to remind administrators that there was a need to replace certain people within the Agency for International Development (AID) "with Republicans." He added, "The faster they do it the happier the WH will be." Richardson replied that he would follow through on the reminder, but there is no evidence that he took any action on the order.

Throughout the rest of his tenure at the State Department, Richardson and his staff continued to deal with numerous phone calls, memos, and other attempts to place more pro-Nixon figures within the State Department. Richardson's frustrations with the White House never exploded into a full-blown confrontation, but they did continue to simmer as can be seen in a dictated memo that was written soon after one of his weekly lunches with Kissinger. "ELR on the President at staff debriefing after HAK lunch, he makes adjustments to change but not adjustments to attitudes."[21]

Amidst the ongoing battles over personnel issues, Richardson continued to be a skilled manager. A *New York Times* profile on Richardson claimed that the undersecretary was arguably "the most effective administrator at Foggy Bottom in the last decade," and had earned high marks from many employees for being "a tough minded realist," who was also "immune to the Administration's own propaganda."[22] While many respected Richardson for his ability to stand up to the administration in certain cases, the undersecretary chose to remain loyal to the president, especially during the spring of 1970.

When Nixon decided to invade Cambodia, his undersecretary of state was overseas. Just like Rogers, Secretary of Defense Mel Laird, and Kissinger's own NSA staff, Richardson was left out of the entire decision-making process. Outside of Nixon and Kissinger, most of the administration's foreign policy officials found out about the decision only a few days before the public watched the president address the nation on April 30. Once the State Department was told about the invasion, Richardson flew back to Washington, met with various officials, and briefly talked to Kissinger the night before the president's speech. Richardson began the telephone conversation by saying, "You have had a busy time." Kissinger responded by joking, "Without the restraining influence of these Thursday lunches—this is what happens when you go out of town." After the two awkwardly swapped jokes about the planning of the invasion, Richardson informed Kissinger that the reason he had called was because he had received information that Congress was planning to take action on limiting the president's future actions in Southeast Asia.[23]

If Richardson was insulted by the decision-making process of the Nixon White House, he kept it to himself and continued to carry on as a dutiful official. The day after the president's speech, Richardson was sent to the Capitol to brief members of Congress on Nixon's recent actions.[24] His public defense of the invasion was incredibly important for the White House because Rogers, who had previously stated his opposition to any sort of incursion into Cambodia, remained mostly silent on the subject. Richardson's performance was closely monitored by Kissinger, who brought up the undersecretary in a conversation with Nixon, the day after he briefed Congress on Cambodia. "He [Richardson] didn't do well at the Congressional briefing. I will pump him up," said Kissinger.[25] It was an extremely humbling situation for the undersecretary, given his and his department's lack of influence in shaping policy. However, he showed no signs of opposition, and defended the invasion as a way to end the war in Vietnam.

As Richardson continued to speak in favor of the invasion, opposition broke out all across the country. Antiwar protests led to the shutdown of hundreds of college campuses. On May 4, 1970, the Ohio National Guard shot into a crowd of antiwar demonstrators at Kent State University. Four students were killed by the gunfire. Days later, hundreds of thousands of protestors descended on the nation's capital to voice their opposition to the war. Antiwar dissent had even seeped into the administration, with several members of Kissinger's own NSA staff resigning in protest. The wave of resignations also spread to Richardson's staff as Moore, who was the head of a State Department committee on Southeast Asia, resigned based on his opposition to the invasion. Although Moore and Richardson may have differed in their public stances on

Cambodia, the latter never tried to convince the former to change his mind. "He was clearly sympathetic," said Moore of Richardson.[26] Aside from his staff, Richardson also directly dealt with opposition to Cambodia through correspondence and meetings with friends and colleagues, especially from his alma mater. A delegation of antiwar Harvard faculty members visited Richardson and Kissinger, forcing the undersecretary to align himself with one of the architects of the invasion.[27] Richardson also received numerous letters from different academics who were disappointed in his decision to support the invasion. Herbert Feis, a historian, was especially critical of Richardson's willingness to go along with the White House. In the letter, Feis argued for "a quick and announced decision on withdrawal of our combat forces in Cambodia and Vietnam," and asked, "How much longer will the State Department allow that drafter of options named Kissinger to influence policy?"[28]

Despite the various resignations, protests, and complaints from friends and colleagues, Richardson continued to publicly defend the president on the Sunday morning talk shows. After he was asked by one reporter on how his current support of the president jibed with his reported prior misgivings about the invasion, Richardson danced around the question and claimed that his reservations were only a part of the broader advising process. When he was asked about whether or not he was able to report his misgivings directly to the president, Richardson admitted that his role was only "within the Department of State" and that Secretary Rogers was "in direct communication" with the White House.[29] Previously ignored by the White House, Richardson was now not only forced to defend the invasion, but also the White House's decision-making process. That same week, Richardson attended a meeting with the Soviets at the United Nations, where the undersecretary unveiled a new plan to prevent future local skirmishes from becoming major military conflicts. Just days after the beginning of the invasion of Cambodia, Richardson's presentation of the peace-making plan rang hollow as U.S. planes were bombing Cambodia.[30] For all of his efforts, Nixon called Richardson and thanked him on May 11. The president began the conversation by letting Richardson know that he did not see him on television, but that his "spies" told him that he did "an excellent job on TV yesterday."[31]

If the White House was auditioning Richardson throughout the Cambodia crisis for a promotion, he passed their test. Despite being surrounded by friends and colleagues who opposed the decision to invade Cambodia, Richardson proved to be a loyal member of the administration and was rewarded with a cabinet-level position as the head of HEW. The move over to HEW was not just a step up for Richardson, but was also beneficial for the White House. Under the leadership of Robert Finch, a moderate Republican and previously the lieutenant governor of California, HEW was in a state of chaos. Described by Finch as "a political minefield," HEW had grown exponentially during the Johnson years, and by 1970 it employed 107,000 people who were responsible for 270 federal programs.[32] Aside from the department's rapid growth during the Great Society, much of the department was at odds with the White House on most key issues, ranging from civil rights to Vietnam.

RICHARDSON AT HEW: TESTING THE WHITE HOUSE'S TOLERANCE FOR LIBERAL REFORM

In early 1970, the department's director of the Office of Civil Rights, Leon Panetta, was forced to resign after causing problems for the White House. Panetta, a then liberal Republican from California, was often vocal in his disagreement with southern conservatives, and consistently endorsed a more rapid desegregation process than what Nixon favored. The firing of Panetta was met with outrage across HEW as more than a hundred Office of Civil Rights employees signed an open letter of protest to the president. Another 1,800 HEW employees signed a petition that pleaded for an open meeting with Finch to explain the administration's positions on civil rights.[33] The drama surrounding Panetta's resignation was soon followed by the firing of HEW's education commissioner, James E. Allen Jr., due to his public opposition to the invasion of Cambodia.[34] The department's headquarters even became the site of a chaotic demonstration by the National Welfare Rights Organization, with some demonstrators urinating on a portrait of Nixon. Instead of stopping the demonstrators, the mostly sympathetic HEW staff later collected money to post bail for those who had been arrested.[35] In the middle of the chaos of 1969–70, Finch proved to be an ineffective manager who did little to open up the department's decision-making process, alienating both his liberal staff and even many conservative Nixon supporters.

Nixon selected Richardson to head up HEW based on the reputation the latter had built up as an efficient manager at Foggy Bottom, as well as the real sense of loyalty he had shown to the president during the Cambodia invasion. Richardson, like Finch, was a moderate Republican whose liberal outlook on domestic issues did not automatically alienate him from many of HEW's liberal staff members. He was in many ways the ideal candidate for the job. The president did not want to directly deal with domestic issues on a regular basis, but was also concerned that without steady leadership, HEW would move too far to the left. Moore, who was brought back into the Nixon administration to work with his former boss at HEW, attended Richardson's swearing-in ceremony with his high school friend and former colleague in the offices of Senator Salt-onstall, Chuck Colson. Before the ceremony, he asked Colson about the reasoning behind Richardson's promotion. Moore recalled Colson's response in an interview with the Nixon Library in 2008:

> He's appointing him head of HEW so today he can say: Elliot, thank you so much for taking on this extraordinarily important responsibility . . . because I know you will do it brilliantly . . . And that two and a half years later . . . the president can then say to Elliot: Elliot, thank you so much for everything that you've done to . . . keep HEW under wraps . . . and having never seen him or having had to talk to him in between.[36]

Whatever Nixon's motives may have been in promoting Richardson, it was clear that he considered him to be a valuable figure within the administration. Even if he was never a close adviser, Richardson was still viewed by Nixon as someone the White House could keep in mind for various prestigious positions. In late 1971, Nixon thought so highly of Richardson that he even mentioned him as someone who could be the chief justice of the Supreme Court. In a conversation with Haldeman, he argued that since he had selected two conservatives for the Supreme Court, "he would be willing to go to a middle of the road guy," and if anything happened to Burger, he would "keep Richardson in mind, because he thinks he would be a towering, historic Chief Justice."[37] The White House strongly felt that they could use Richardson's squeaky clean reputation to calm the stormy waters within HEW. It would create yet another complex balancing act for Richardson, who now had to find a way to satisfy both the White House and HEW's staff.

Still, Richardson continued to push the boundaries of his unspoken arrangement with the White House as the head of HEW. Instead of trying to clamp down on dissent, he attempted to create a department that was more open to debating different proposals and significantly more transparent. Years later, Richardson remembered that when he first came to HEW, he was met with "a markedly sour atmosphere," mainly as a result of his predecessor restricting "the policy-making process to a small insider group." Richardson lamented that this often led to decisions being made "without any clear explanation of how they had been reached." In order to improve morale, he encouraged each of his bureau chiefs to bring any employee to high-level meetings at which their work was to be discussed. "This made for a pretty crowded conference room, but it assured that the staffers who had participated in preparing their boss's case would get direct exposure to the opposing arguments," recalled Richardson.[38] The strategy was successful in improving morale and calming dissent; within six months, many began to notice that HEW was becoming a more stable department. A story that appeared in the *New York Times* in November 1970 described "the atmosphere" around the department as "calm," and even featured praise for Richardson from some of the department's younger staff members.[39]

In addition to making a concerted effort to open up the department's decision-making process, Richardson also consistently crafted policy plans that attempted to push the administration to a more progressive position. Weeks after moving over to HEW, he vowed to make a major push toward desegregating schools in the South, warning schools that government funds could be cut off if they did not comply with court orders.[40] Richardson's stance on desegregation created tensions with the White House over major policy differences, as the president sought to avoid alienating southern whites. Nixon expressed his uneasiness about HEW's approach to civil rights in an April 1971 meeting at which the president ordered Ehrlichman "to get Richardson in" and "tell HEW to not do anything except what is specifically required by the law."[41]

Nixon's and Richardson's differences over civil rights reached a boiling point in August 1971 when the president publicly disavowed HEW's ambitious proposal for crosstown school busing in Austin, Texas. Nixon's rejection of the plan was a major reversal from the White House's prior interpretation of court rulings, and forced Richardson to publicly distance himself from a plan he had previously supported.[42] Although there were reports that Richardson considered resigning over the issue, he publicly denied those rumors after meeting with the president in San Clemente on September 1. Richardson told the press that he now disavowed his department's proposal. Much like Cambodia, Richardson offered some resistance behind the scenes, but ultimately decided to remain loyal to Nixon. In a January 1972 meeting with Ehrlichman, Nixon said, "get legislation or a const. amendment [prohibiting busing] ready as an option as soon as possible," adding, "I reject the advice of Richardson, Garment, et al. To relax & enjoy it."[43]

Along with his defeats on civil rights, Richardson also lost several other policy battles with the White House. This was especially true of his failed push for the Family Assistance Plan (FAP), an initiative that sought to reform welfare while also instituting a guaranteed income for poor families. Richardson and many staff members within HEW were enthusiastic about the plan, but the bill failed to gain enough support in Congress. While Nixon publicly backed the plan, he privately reversed course and became interested in making sure the bill would not succeed. Haldeman recorded in his daily diary that the president "wants to be sure it's [Family Assistance Plan] killed by Democrats and that we make big play for it, but don't let it pass, can't afford it."[44] Nixon became frustrated with Richardson when he found out that Richardson was trying to rally support for the FAP among liberal Democrats and even proposed more liberal alternatives to the plan itself. Despite HEW's efforts, the FAP died in 1971, and Richardson was once again forced to remain silent in his opposition.

Less than a year later, the White House rejected an HEW-backed childcare bill that would have established free daycare for children from low-income families. When details of the bill became public, conservative activists mobilized against what they felt was an attack on the American family. Within the White House, Pat Buchanan led the charge against HEW's childcare plan and compared it to what he had saw during his recent trip to the Soviet Union. "I had been in the USSR for eighteen days in November and had been exposed to the 'Young Pioneers,' where children were indoctrinated in communism and sang songs to Lenin."[45] In the end, Nixon concluded that the plan was "bad politics," and that it was "legislation which might take children away from their mothers."[46]

By 1971, Nixon had become increasingly suspicious of Richardson's actions at HEW, and at one point attempted to reel him back in line by hinting at a Supreme Court seat. According to Ehrlichman, Nixon once sent him to give a message to Richardson at a time when Ehrlichman remembered that the president "suspected him [Richardson] of disloyalty." Ehrlichman did in fact bring the message to Richardson, telling him that "if he was a faithful team player, his next move might be to the Court," which he "received without a blink."[47]

While there were many disappointments during Richardson's time at HEW, his efforts to open up the department's decision-making process were still successful in improving the department's morale. John Thomas "J. T." Smith, the son of Gerard C. Smith, a diplomat who helped lead the negotiating team for the Strategic Arms Limitation Talks (SALT), joined HEW as the special assistant to the comptroller in 1971. "The environment was quite exciting at the time," recalled Smith, who was in his late 20s when he was brought into HEW. After a stint at the CIA, Smith was drawn to HEW because of the department's ability "to bring systems analysis to the domestic side." After a year at HEW, he was brought into Richardson's inner circle as an adviser until the Saturday Night Massacre. "I was an idealistic youngster, and I had admired Richardson before I even worked with him," remembered Smith. "There was high morale and the department was aided by Richardson being a high-brained power" who "didn't isolate himself" from the rest of the staff.[48]

Richardson also sought to expand the department's communication with liberal and progressive activist groups at the same time the White House was closing itself off from those very same organizations. During his time at HEW, Richardson made it a priority to regularly meet with high school and college groups so that he could include them in discussions related to HEW's programs.[49] The department also improved its communication with civil rights organizations despite tensions over Nixon's stance on busing. "We had civil rights organizers and activists in there all the time. Talking with them, not doing everything they wanted but maintaining communications. Richardson was like this, he was able to do that kind of thing," said Moore.[50] Aside from improving the department's outreach efforts, Richardson was able to fight back against the White House's proposed budget cuts.[51] HEW won a few policy victories, especially when it came to education. Through Richardson's efforts, HEW helped increase federal aid to black colleges, distributing approximately $29 million in funds to those institutions during the 1970 fiscal year.[52]

Nixon was appreciative of certain aspects of Richardson's time at HEW, but he also became increasingly uneasy about the latter's loyalty to the White House as he began to plot a major reorganizational effort for his second term. As with other members of his administration who caused problems for him, Nixon regularly complained about Richardson's background, his inability to stand up to bureaucrats, and even his dullness in many taped conversations in the fall of 1972. During a conversation with Ehrlichman in October 1972, the president brought up Richardson and his concerns over how he was handling HEW's bureaucracy. Nixon asked Ehrlichman, "What is it? Is it the bureaucracy over there?" Ehrlichman, who had praised Richardson in other conversations, chose instead to appeal to the president's instincts and latch on to Nixon's frustrations with Richardson. "Well . . . it's that basically he's liberal . . . he's not a rock." The president replied that they had to get "him out of that goddamned job. He's not fit for that." Ehrlichman argued that Richardson would not want to leave HEW, but Nixon ignored the advice and pushed on: "I'd like to change the agency," although he admitted that Richardson was "doing a hell of a job . . . keeping the thing flowing." He concluded that he had to make a change at HEW. "He's got to realize this is a political decision," said Nixon.[53]

Nixon's concerns about HEW persisted after winning a second term; he had decided that he could no longer trust Richardson to be in charge of the department. However, despite all of their complaints about Richardson, Nixon and his advisers continued to see the advantages of keeping him in the administration. When Nixon finally decided to make a change at HEW, he figured out a way to keep Richardson in his cabinet that would not cause any problems for the White House. Instead of cutting Richardson loose, the president chose to name Richardson his next secretary of defense, replacing Mel Laird, and appoint William Clements, a hawkish conservative who had made a fortune in the oil industry, as his deputy. Nixon bragged about this move as his "big play." It was a change that would allow the administration to keep Richardson and his prestige while also diminishing the threat of his political views. On November 16, 1972, Nixon told Haldeman and Ehrlichman about his plan, arguing that they could not afford to leave Richardson at HEW. "Get him the hell out of HEW!" exclaimed Nixon, who said he was "sick of Family Assistance and busing!" He then focused on Clements, whom he described as a "tough son of a bitch."[54] Nixon clearly felt that Richardson's liberal tendencies could be controlled at Defense, especially with Clements as the deputy secretary. In a conversation with Colson, Nixon once again focused on Clements's masculinity, describing him as a "tough mean bastard." Later on in the conversation, Nixon also argued, "Elliot will work with Henry on defense."[55] Just as when Richardson was at the State Department, Nixon recognized that the other check on his new secretary of defense could be found in Kissinger. While Nixon acknowledged that it was rare to find someone who could work with Kissinger, he also knew that he could use their relationship to tighten his control over Richardson.

In other conversations regarding his new secretary of defense, the president focused on Richardson's connections to the establishment as a way of explaining his lack of toughness. That winter, the president often described Clements in ways that emphasized his masculinity. In contrast, Nixon described Richardson's Ivy League credentials as a source of weakness. In a dictated memorandum, Nixon acknowledged that

Richardson followed directions, but also stated that he could not fully trust him because he was "simply a member of the establishment . . . and he can't bear up to think of moving some of these establishment people out." He added, "And if we had left him at HEW, he of course couldn't possibly bear cutting some of the establishment programs like education, higher education."[56] In a separate conversation with Haldeman, Nixon argued that they should "get the hell out of the Ivy League!" when staffing his new administration and instead "go after southerners," so that they could bring in more "color and creativity." In the same conversation, Nixon brought up Richardson as an example, describing him as "always dull as dish wash."[57] Richardson's lack of charisma was another recurring theme for Nixon and his advisers, as Ehrlichman complained to the president that he once fell asleep during a conversation with the secretary. "You know you get these evening calls from Elliot and he will go on for hours. I once fell asleep. Literally, fell asleep."[58] Whether it was his perceived weakness when it came to confronting bureaucrats or his long-windedness, Nixon continued to see Richardson as a stuffy elitist who did not fit within the overall direction of his second term.

Nixon's decision to replace Richardson with Caspar Weinberger at HEW also spoke volumes about how the president viewed the department, Richardson's leadership, and the next four years of his presidency. Weinberger later wrote that the president's decision was motivated by his desire to institute a more conservative agenda at HEW for his second term. "The President said he thought it would be an interesting twist to send a budget cutter to HEW and a big spender to the Pentagon," remembered Weinberger. "Indeed, he felt I was better suited to HEW and shared many of his general goals for the department, such as reining in a runaway budget and devolving a good deal of power back to the states and the private sector."[59] Unlike Richardson, Weinberger was someone who could be trusted to battle the department's bureaucracy. In a December 1972 meeting between Nixon and Ehrlichman, the two recapped the major changes that had been made to the administration for their second term. When the two brought up HEW, the president remarked, "Richardson's gone. That's good."[60]

MOVING TO THE DEFENSE DEPARTMENT AND THE ATTACKS ON RICHARDSON'S STAFF

Nixon's fears about Richardson may have been diminished, but they did not disappear. In the days after the "big play" was first brought up, the president wanted to know who Richardson would bring with him to the Pentagon. Over the next two months, his concerns eventually turned into a concerted effort to stop Jonathan Moore from working at the Pentagon. The White House's attempt to block Richardson's most trusted adviser further demonstrated Nixon's own anxieties about the Ivy League establishment and the presence of opposing views in his administration. During a conversation with Colson in the weeks after his reelection, Nixon brought up his concerns regarding Richardson's staff. "Henry says he's [Richardson] awful close to the Brookings, McNamara, system analysis type, and for example Elliot is taking with him over to Defense Larry Lynn (the then assistant secretary for planning and evaluation at HEW) and uh and uh, also Jonathan Moore."[61] The conversation was shaped by a few interesting dimensions, considering that both Colson and Kissinger had worked with Richardson's assistant in the past. While Colson had maintained his friendship, albeit one filled with tension, with Moore, Kissinger despised his former colleague. In addition to Colson and Kissinger's past associations with Richardson's assistant, Nixon knew that Moore had resigned in protest after the Cambodia invasion. The president was also keenly aware that Moore was the son of Charles Moore, and did not forget the speechwriter's attempt to convince Eisenhower to cut him loose in 1956. Whatever the primary motivations may have been, Moore became the focal point of Nixon's uneasiness about Richardson that winter.

Less than a month later, Nixon brought up the Moore issue during a meeting with Haldeman when the two discussed their plans for the second term. Haldeman told the president that he had said to Richardson that neither Lynn nor Moore was acceptable at Defense. Lynn, who had previously worked under Kissinger in the National Security Council, also resigned after Cambodia with several of his other colleagues. Although Lynn and Moore had resigned under slightly different circumstances, the two were grouped together as being too connected to the systems analysis school of foreign policy.[62] In a meeting with Senator Henry "Scoop" Jackson, a hawkish Democrat from the state of Washington, Nixon discussed his fears about Richardson's staff. Jackson, who knew Moore through his work at the Institute of Politics at the Kennedy School of Government, warned the president that Richardson's adviser was "bad news." He added that Moore had "Jerry Wiesner [president of MIT] syndrome . . . They're not loyal to you, Mr. President." Nixon replied, "Elliot does come from that community unfortunately." The president then went on to complain yet again about the number of Ivy

Leaguers who worked at the Pentagon. Jackson agreed with the president and argued that Richardson's staff could be a real threat. "The only thing I'm worried about is that Elliot brings in a lot of these soft-headed guys and subconsciously they will influence him."[63]

Although Nixon's main source of information was Kissinger, the issue still worried the president—Moore was representative of everything that he disliked not only in Richardson, but in his administration. Just minutes before the president talked to Kissinger about Richardson's staff on January 4, 1973, he mentioned his order to cut MIT's funds. "I mean I'm seeing this Richardson today and it's a reminder that I'm not going to raise it with him," said Nixon, who knew that his new secretary of defense would not follow the MIT plan. Soon after the reminder, Kissinger walked in and told Nixon that Richardson was going to keep on fighting for Moore to join as the assistant secretary of defense for International Security Affairs. "We cannot have that," said Kissinger. "Oh shit! He's a dove!" exclaimed Nixon. Kissinger then claimed that "Jonathan Moore leaks," as the conversation turned to Moore's resignation after Cambodia. Nixon vented, "He opposed us on Cambodia and Elliot said, 'Well, so did I.' I said I don't care, Elliot . . . I'm appointing you, I'm not appointing Moore!"[64]

When pressure from the White House became more than just another of the president's rants, Richardson fought for Moore to come with him to the Pentagon. In a memo to the president, Richardson wrote that while Larry Lynn would not be joining him at DOD, he was planning on bringing Moore with him to the Pentagon. Richardson also stated that Nixon's fears about Moore's background were completely unfounded, writing that "Moore had never worked closely with Sec. McNamara in Systems Analysis or anywhere else." At the end of the memo, Richardson stated that Moore was his "most valued and trusted assistant as well as my close personal friend," and that "If you intended Bob Haldeman's express mention of Jonathan at Camp David to constitute a condition on my own acceptability for Defense, I, of course, accept the consequences."[65]

Nixon and Haldeman discussed the issue again later that week, after the latter had met with Richardson. While Haldeman had agreed with the president about Moore in previous meetings, he now believed that the issue had been greatly exaggerated by Kissinger. Haldeman, who had always been suspicious of Kissinger's motives, told Nixon that Richardson had no interest in bringing Lynn over to the Pentagon. He then informed him that Richardson had written a memo that appealed the Moore decision, but that he had also been investigating the issue. "It turns out that Colson is a very strong advocate for Jonathan Moore," said Haldeman. "Colson?" asked a surprised Nixon. "Yes sir. Says he's getting a totally bum rap from Henry. The reason he is, is that he worked for Rockefeller on Henry's staff . . . and challenged Henry on several things, which Henry very much resented," said Haldeman. The president then reminded Haldeman, "Henry says he's a dove," to which the chief of staff responded, "What's his name says he's not, Colson. And Richardson says he's not." When it came to Kissinger's allegation that Moore was a leaker, Haldeman stated that he could not find anything to prove the claim. Nixon, who still did not trust Moore, began to focus on Kissinger's manipulation of the facts. "Henry is like a woman. He's vindictive as hell, anybody that fights him. He doesn't want any space between him and the president."[66]

The president never brought up Moore during his conversations with Richardson, and the issue was brushed aside by mid-January. Richardson was sworn in as the new secretary of defense at the end of the month, and Moore joined him as an assistant. Richardson had originally planned to have Moore work as an assistant secretary, but because Moore was so frustrated by the White House's actions, he instead decided to take a position where he did not have to work with Kissinger. The battle with the White House received enough attention that when Moore left HEW, his coworkers presented him with two doves at a going-away party as a reference to his stance on Vietnam. Moore jokingly promised to release the doves during his swearing-in ceremony, but instead chose to keep them as family pets. Weeks later, Nixon invited both Richardson and Moore to a very different gathering, a small luncheon with Pentagon officials to commemorate the beginning of his second term. After Nixon and the dozen or so Pentagon officials had lunch, the president thanked the group for their service and took photographs with each of the individuals. Moore, who was last one in line, remembered that the president slowed down before approaching him to shake his hand. Nixon then looked him in the eye and said in a voice that could be heard by everybody in the room, "It has been my great honor to work with the father, and now it's a privilege for me to meet the son." The comment amused Moore, who remembered, "He was saying to me with his eyes, you and I are the only people in this room who know that I'm lying through my teeth."[67]

Regardless of how Nixon continued to view Moore and others who worked at the Pentagon, the experience showed that Richardson was able to stand up to the White House. It also demonstrated that Richardson saw the value in surrounding himself with advisers who were willing to take on the president. "Elliot had confidence in me that I would say no," said Moore.[68] This was especially crucial at Defense, where Richardson was now dealing with a department that was much more connected to the White House's daily operations than HEW had been. While Nixon had always attempted to control Richardson, his grip at the Pentagon was significantly tighter. Richardson's awareness of how the president viewed his role within the administration could be seen in a Christmas card that he drew himself in December 1972. The card depicted Santa Claus luring in a reindeer with an apple, but behind its back, he was holding a bridle to rein in the animal.[69]

NIXON SETTLES ON RICHARDSON AS ATTORNEY GENERAL

As Richardson and his staff were settling into their new positions at the Pentagon, the investigation into the Watergate break-in was beginning to gain more attention in the mainstream media. On March 19, one of the Watergate burglars, James McCord, sent a letter to U.S. District Judge John Sirica stating that he had lied under oath and was pressured by the White House to do so. By April, the scandal had escalated to the point where the president was forced to ask for Haldeman and Ehrlichman's resignations for their roles in the cover-up. Nixon also chose to ask Attorney General Richard Kleindienst for his resignation. The president knew he had to replace Kleindienst with someone who was nonpartisan, had experience as a prosecutor, and whose reputation garnered trust with the American public. The president's later actions demonstrated that he had always hoped to limit the investigation, especially when it came to his own records, but the events of that spring pressured him into selecting someone like Richardson to be his next attorney general.

Nixon's suspicions of his then secretary of defense partially explained why Richardson was not his automatic first choice. Instead, the president first suggested John Connally, the former secretary of treasury, as his lead candidate during a meeting with Haldeman on April 26, but the idea did not go anywhere since Connally was viewed as too close to Nixon.[70] Two days later, Nixon told Ron Ziegler that he needed to pick a well-respected figure to be his next attorney general, mentioning William Rogers. The president then expressed serious doubts about whether Rogers would take the job. "If he won't do it, maybe I'll make Richardson."[71]

Unlike Connally or Rogers, Richardson was always kept outside of the president's inner circle. Nixon even acknowledged this in a conversation with his speechwriter, Ray Price, when he explained that he could not select Rogers as attorney general because "everyone will think he's a Nixon crony." He then predicted that Richardson would work because "no one will figure he's a friend," and that most people saw him as "Mr. Integrity" or "Mr. Clean." Later on he also described Richardson as "a little tortuous," but also as "a hell of a fellow" who would be "infinitely trusted."[72] In a separate conversation with Kissinger, Nixon described Richardson as someone who would be trusted by "the so-called damned establishment."[73] Along with the optics of the selection, the president also embraced the idea of moving Richardson out of the Pentagon and replacing him with someone who was more hawkish. In a conversation with his new chief of staff, Al Haig, the president described his incoming secretary of defense, James Schlesinger, as someone who was "more hardline" and "more tough" than Richardson. "He'll cut the fat off, but he won't cut the muscle. Richardson will cut the muscle," argued Nixon.[74] This was another one of the president's "double plays," fulfilling two needs with one transition, but it was one that placed a figure he did not have full confidence in as the head of the Watergate investigation. During his first televised address on Watergate, Nixon told the American public that Richardson would "assume full responsibility and authority for coordinating all Federal agencies in uncovering the whole truth about this matter," and that he would have "total support from me in getting this job done."[75] In Nixon's mind, it was his only option to combat the growing attacks on his administration.

When Richardson was first told that Nixon wanted him to lead the Justice Department, he was disappointed. He even called Kissinger and joked, "Have you heard what's happened to me? I should have gotten you to block it."[76] Richardson was frustrated by the unfinished work at the Defense Department and was also hesitant to leave because he had developed a strong passion for dealing with foreign affairs. "He really liked being involved in large national security stuff," said J.T. Smith, who would move to the Justice Department as one of Richardson's executive assistants. Richardson was also reluctant to take the position because he did not think of himself as an expert on Watergate. According to Smith, other than reading the headlines of the major newspapers, Richardson and his staff were "not terribly familiar" with the developing scandal. "Richardson probably knew even less than I did," said

Smith.[77] Upon being told that the president had picked him to be the next attorney general, Richardson talked to his wife and the two agreed that if he could, he should avoid the position. For a brief moment, Richardson thought it might be better for an outsider to fill the role, but concluded that it was impossible under the current circumstances to avoid the position.[78]

His feelings were also compounded by his awareness of Nixon's flaws and how they had contributed to their working relationship. "He thought there was darkness in Nixon and it was unnecessary," said Moore.[79] In his memoir, Richardson later wrote that he "caught glimpses of a suspicious and manipulative streak in him [Nixon]," but that he had "no way of knowing how deep it ran or how much it widened out below the surface," prior to becoming attorney general. Although he did not know the full extent of the president's dark side, Richardson was skeptical enough of Nixon's character that he once wrote in a note to himself, "the more I think about it, the more the job seems to be one of real danger and risk." In the same memo, he expressed doubts about the president's innocence, as he asked, "What if the President did know about it?" and "Do you have the stomach for it?"[80]

On Sunday, April 29, Richardson looked down at the Maryland countryside from a helicopter and took in the "gentle and serene" scenery. It was, as he later remembered, "a beautiful spring day," but the calm, peaceful setting offered up a contrast to the turmoil inside Camp David. The president was waiting to officially offer him his new position. When Richardson walked into the president's office, he noticed that the president seemed strained and depressed over having to ask Haldeman and Ehrlichman for their resignations, describing it as the toughest thing he had ever done in his life. The president then told him that that he was "more needed at Justice than at Defense." Despite his serious concerns about the job, Richardson agreed and accepted the offer. Nixon then brought up Watergate, insisting that his new attorney general would have "full control" over the investigation and that "anybody who is guilty must be prosecuted, no matter who it hurts." He also added, "above all, protect the presidency, not the President."

Richardson brought up a point he had made directly to different White House staff members, but never to the president himself. He had repeatedly compromised with the White House when it came to policy. He was unwilling to do the same when it came to ethics. "I hope you will respond to the crisis of confidence that Watergate has created by opening up your administration and reaching out to people in a more magnanimous spirit," said Richardson. Although Richardson had been loyal to Nixon and maintained a high level of respect for the man, he had long been bothered, and at times directly affected, by Nixon's isolation and paranoia. Hoping to become a calming influence on the president, Richardson pleaded with him to adopt a less conspiratorial view of his political adversaries. "I believe your real problem is that you have somehow been unable to realize that you have won, not only won, but been reelected by a tremendous margin." He added, "You are the President of all the people of the United States. There is no 'they' out there—nobody trying to destroy you." As Richardson spoke, the president's expression did not change. When his soon-to-be attorney general finished, Nixon simply stared at Richardson and did not say anything in response.[81]

. . .

The new attorney general may not have had a close or even a positive relationship with Nixon, but he chose to take him at his word when it came to Watergate. His respect for the office of the presidency and the man who selected him for three cabinet-level positions made him deeply hesitant to conclude that Nixon was guilty. While he was wary of Nixon's dark side, he still remained supportive of the president as he prepared to become the next attorney general.

The combination of Richardson's inner fears and public support of the president in the spring of 1973 was representative of his uneasy role within the administration. His loyalty may have kept him in the administration, but it did not buy him much influence within the White House. For more than four years, Nixon praised Richardson's work at the State Department, HEW, and the Defense Department, but also closely monitored his actions and reined him in whenever necessary. Richardson may not have been a part of his new establishment, but he was also a figure who would play ball, and could be used in certain positions to build up credibility for the White House. Nixon valued Richardson's popularity among liberals, moderates, and other establishment figures, but he kept his distance from him for the very same reasons. No matter how many times Richardson reluctantly sided with the White House, Nixon was skeptical about his loyalties.

Nixon's concerns only grew after naming Richardson attorney general, but they were deeply rooted in his first term. By protecting his employees from unethical attacks and battling the president over domestic and foreign policy, Richardson's actions had garnered Nixon's distrust. Over the previous four years, Nixon had often said Richardson had become dull, proved to be weak, and was too connected to the liberal bureaucracy that he held in contempt. Listening to the president's taped conversations about Richardson, his decision to name him attorney general is stunning. Watergate created the conditions for the appointment, and it also led to the Saturday Night Massacre.

4

"He's Going to Have to Prove He's the White Knight"

Elliot Richardson and the
Saturday Night Massacre

The day after Nixon publicly announced the appointment of his new attorney general, it became painfully clear that Richardson's dedication to support a credible investigation would collide with the president's desire to conceal damaging evidence. Richardson, along with then acting FBI director William Ruckelshaus and Nixon's special counsel Leonard Garment, agreed to place under the protection of the FBI all of the files of the outgoing White House staff members: Ehrlichman, Haldeman, and Dean.[1] The decision to protect the records seemed to be a routine measure to reassure the public, but Nixon was livid when he saw FBI agents standing just outside of the Oval Office. According to Al Haig, the president slammed one of the guards against the wall, before apologizing for his behavior. As his "first act as Chief of Staff," Haig immediately called Richardson and ordered that the agents be removed. Richardson agreed to the order, without an argument.[2]

Even though a few staff members insisted that the FBI's presence was only a protective measure, Nixon vented about the incident for the rest of the day, arguing that his former advisers should not have been treated like criminals. He was especially disappointed in Garment, telling Ziegler, "That son of a bitch, I'm gonna fire him tomorrow . . . goddamn his Jewish soul."[3] The incident foreshadowed the White House's later confrontations with the Justice Department—Nixon was already refusing to budge on his control of the White House's records. In a meeting with Garment on May 3, the president, who was in the middle of scolding his counsel, exclaimed, "I'm not going to allow Elliot Richardson or you to look at those papers."[4]

When Nixon talked to the soon-to-be attorney general later that day, he chose to keep his emotions to himself as he once again emphasized Richardson's independence. "If you want to name somebody, that's your prerogative," said Nixon on naming a special prosecutor. Richardson replied that his "present thinking is that I should name somebody," but that he would not "abdicate responsibility" for the broader investigation. The two avoided a final decision on a special prosecutor as Nixon politely argued that Richardson did not need one, but also insisted that he would not interfere in the process. With no major confrontation, the two continued to have a fraught relationship that was shaped by an underlying tension over their competing visions of what constituted a proper investigation. Richardson's loyalty to the president allowed him to become attorney general, but his careful approach to the investigation made him a problem for the White House. Nixon needed Richardson for his credibility, but whenever the moderate Republican attempted to maintain the integrity of the investigation, the president was quick to conclude that his new attorney general was a disloyal ingrate.

The White House's early frustrations with Richardson's performance often echoed the president's prior concerns about the longtime cabinet member. Although Nixon publicly extolled the attorney general's credentials, privately he and his advisers quickly fell back to their lingering concerns about his character. Within days, the White House had begun to view Richardson's attempts to maintain his independence from the White House as yet another sign of his innate weakness. A day after FBI agents were outside his office, Nixon vented about Richardson's actions to Kissinger, describing the decision to place guards in the White House as "a gimmick" for the press. Kissinger replied, "Elliot worries me, he's going to be very ambitious . . . Elliot is out for himself." While Nixon shared Kissinger's concerns, he attempted to reassure himself in the conversation and insisted that "Elliot is a team player."[5] Weeks later the president and Haig were annoyed that his nominee told the Senate during his confirmation hearings that he felt "betrayed by the shoddy standards of morals" in the White House.[6] Haig warned Nixon that the statement was a sign that Richardson was disloyal due to his political ambitions. "He wants to come out of this as Mr. Clean. . . I don't trust the son of a bitch."[7]

RICHARDSON SELECTS A WATERGATE SPECIAL PROSECUTOR

Richardson's statements during his confirmation hearings and later on to the press were signs not of his political aspirations, but of a necessary determination to work with a Democratic Senate. The most significant product of the hearings was not only a promise of a Watergate special prosecutor, but that the position would have complete independence. Before the hearings, Richardson announced that he would choose a special prosecutor for the case, adding that he would give him "all the independence, authority, and staff support needed to carry out the tasks entrusted to him."[8] Even after the statement, there were debates over the independence of the position. When Richardson argued that he should have final authority over the investigation, he was challenged by several Democratic senators who were afraid that he would try to limit the investigation on behalf of the White House. In order to save his nomination, Richardson then began to come up with a set of guidelines that gave the position much more independence from any sort of potential interference from the attorney general or the White House.

The political pressure that was exerted on Richardson during the hearings convinced him that in order to become attorney general, he had to find a special prosecutor who would gain the complete confidence of Senate Democrats. The eventual selection of Richardson's former law professor Archibald Cox assuaged the Senate's fears about Richardson trying to limit the investigation on behalf of the White House. Much like Richardson, Cox, a former solicitor general during the Kennedy years, had built up much goodwill through his public service. He had specifically received much praise for his skills as an arbiter during the 1967 New York City teacher strike and as an investigator of student protests at Columbia University in 1968. Later in his life, Richardson wrote that he felt that Cox had demonstrated "unfailing fairness and firmness" throughout his career, and that his reputation as a tough but fair investigator would make him a perfect candidate to become the Watergate special prosecutor. On Cox's background as a Kennedy Democrat, Richardson wrote, "I regarded the circumstances that he was identified as a Democrat and had been appointed Solicitor General by President Kennedy as unimportant except to the extent that they precluded the questions that might have been asked had I, a Republican, appointed another Republican."[9]

Richardson's admiration for the professor was undeniable, but the reason that Cox was selected was primarily because many others had refused to take the job. From the moment he was named attorney general, Richardson wanted someone who had prosecutorial experience, credibility among the public, and preferably a Democrat who had no ties to the administration. He began the search process by taking recommendations from staff members, former colleagues, and even outside experts. Cox was absent from most of the lists that were sent to Richardson in early May.[10] Soon after announcing that he would appoint a special prosecutor, Richardson sent a list of prospective nominees to the Senate.[11] The list of candidates who were under "active consideration" by the department included prestigious lawyers and civil servants such as former deputy attorney general Warren Christopher, renowned lawyer and future Watergate special prosecutor Leon Jaworski, Judge of the United States Court of Appeals for the Second Circuit Edward Lumbard, U. S. District Judge for the Southern District of New York Harold Tyler, former deputy secretary of defense Cy Vance, but not Archibald Cox.[12] In another list, Richardson provided his top eight candidates, with Lumbard first. At one point, Richardson's staff even drafted a press release that would have announced Tyler as the special prosecutor, before the offer was eventually turned down by the judge.[13]

Tyler was not the first person to turn down the job, as Richardson's offer had already been declined by Lumbard, Christopher, retired appellate court judge David Peck of New York, and Justice William H. Erickson of the Colorado Supreme Court.[14] His staff also convinced him to cross off a few of the candidates, including Cy Vance, whom they felt was too close to Richardson.[15] There was a similar fear about Cox, who had been somewhat of a mentor to a young Richardson during his time at Harvard Law. The truth of their relationship was that they were more acquaintances than true friends, and according to Cox were not "in any sense intimate."[16] The two larger concerns about Cox were his strong connections to the Kennedy family and his lack of formal prosecutorial experience, as both made several members of Richardson's own staff uneasy about settling on the law professor.

Despite the lack of unanimous support from his staff, Richardson, who was running out of options, decided to offer the position to Cox in mid-May. Richardson knew that he could trust Cox to take on the position and maintain an open dialogue between the Justice Department and the soon-to-be-created Watergate Special Prosecution Force (WSPF). Cox, who knew that several people had turned down the job, was fully aware of the potential risks of the position. Despite his serious concerns, he was comforted by a charter that guaranteed real independence. One vital part of the charter gave Cox the authority to investigate issues outside of the Watergate break-in, including all other allegations of wrongdoing by the White House. With an ambitious charter that was supplemented by the trust that he had in his former student, Cox became convinced that he could lead a credible investigation.

Surprisingly, Richardson received no resistance from the White House when it came to selecting Cox. Years after the Saturday Night Massacre, Cox asked Richardson why Nixon approved his appointment to Watergate special prosecutor. Richardson responded, "Well that's easy, I didn't consult him."[17] Aside from Richardson's lack of communication with the president, the White House, well aware of the current political climate, was also hesitant to pressure their soon-to-be attorney general to choose one of their preferred candidates. On May 8, the president asked Haig, "Has Richardson gotten any word of special counsel yet?" Haig replied, "Well, he knows quietly that he's to appoint no one without checking," showing that the White House wanted to play a role in choosing a prosecutor, but one that was discreet.[18] Nixon's desire to influence the selection faded away when he became concerned about Richardson's confirmation; on May 15, Haig warned him that there was a chance that the nomination was in jeopardy. The president concluded that Richardson needed to choose a prosecutor as soon as possible, telling Haig, "Why don't we find a tactic to get an independent prosecutor or a special prosecutor named here? And name [Judge Harold R.] Tyler . . . I don't care who the Christ does that. I really don't."[19] When the White House got Cox instead of Tyler, Nixon and his advisors were not enraged, but were instead relieved and even dismissive of the law professor. In one meeting, the president described Cox as "not very smart" but also "reasonably decent." Although he admitted that Cox was "of course a Kennedy man," Nixon did not sound overly concerned about the selection.[20]

Nixon still hoped that his new attorney general could restore the administration's credibility and help blunt the impact of the Watergate scandal. Richardson's swearing-in ceremony took place in the White House's East Room on May 25, and it began with the president reaping praise on "one of the ablest men ever to hold the office of Attorney General of the United States." After announcing that Richardson would also serve as a member of the National Security Council, the president playfully joked that the new attorney general had managed to do something that he had never accomplished in his political career. "He has carried Massachusetts twice." When Richardson stood in front of the podium,

FIGURE 6. Richard Nixon and Elliot Richardson at the latter's swearing-in ceremony to become attorney general on May 25, 1973. They are joined by Chief Justice Warren Burger and Elliot's wife, Anne Richardson. The Saturday Night Massacre occurred less than five months later. (From the Richard Nixon Presidential Library and Museum, WHPO-E0861–6a)

he argued to an increasingly cynical public that the structure of our government "is sound and it is strong and it will endure." He added, "If there are flaws, they are in ourselves and our task must be one therefore not of re-design, but of renewal, of reaffirmation."[21] Richardson's statement was echoed in many conversations he had with colleagues as he often hoped that he could find a way to restore the public's confidence. His main problem was that his goal was at odds with the White House's cynical approach to the investigation. While Nixon may have publicly supported Richardson and Cox, he also consistently tried to find ways to limit their investigation. Nixon and his aides were persistent in trying to appeal to the attorney general's ever-present desire to find a compromise. Soon, Richardson became a referee that the White House could and would manipulate whenever Cox's investigation would venture onto uncomfortable grounds.

The night before the swearing-in ceremony, Nixon shared his concerns about Richardson to Haig, calling him "sort of a weak reed." He added, "See, Richardson's in the spot where, as you know, he's going to have to prove that he's the white knight and all that bull."[22] The president naturally kept his thoughts to himself when he met with Richardson the next day, but made sure to apply some pressure on him when discussing executive privilege. Nixon insisted to Richardson that he had "complete support," and that he could "talk in total confidence," an amusing statement considering the two were being taped in the Oval Office. Later on, Richardson praised the president for his recent decision that "executive privilege would not be invoked" during the investigation. Nixon quickly corrected the attorney general, arguing that executive privilege could not "be revoked with regards to the President's papers," and made it clear that he would never allow him or Cox access to his papers. "Because, you see . . . if you ever break into the President's papers, Elliot, we'd have a hell of a problem here." The president then awkwardly transitioned to Richardson's future as he said, "you never know when somebody's going to die . . . you know . . . by that I mean I'm speaking of the Supreme Court." Nixon even encouraged Richardson to spend some time with then chief justice Warren Burger, hinting in a less than subtle manner that he could become a Supreme Court justice if he followed orders. Richardson did not respond to the bribe, but instead chose to praise Cox. "I think he'll be good . . . He's certainly fair and honorable, scrupulous and so on." The two ended the meeting with a discussion of their concerns over investigating materials related to the Plumbers, with the president warning Richardson to be extremely mindful of national security.[23]

When it came to the national security issue, Richardson chose to trust Nixon, admitting years later that he "half believed him" whenever it was raised by the president. By late May, Richardson had already interviewed Egil "Bud" Krogh, the former head of the White House's Special Investigations Unit, about his role in approving the break-in of the office of Daniel Ellsberg's psychiatrist, and had learned that Kissinger had placed wiretaps on several members of his own staff. These two new developments placed alongside stories about the Plumbers led several within Richardson's staff to begin to question the president's innocence. "It went from political shenanigans to real abuse of power," said J. T. Smith about the discovery of the Ellsberg break-in and the Kissinger wiretaps. Faced with new damaging evidence against the White House, Richardson still viewed national security as a legitimate concern when dealing with Watergate. Others around Richardson became more skeptical about Nixon's claims, but the attorney general's background in foreign affairs and his tendency to see the best in people contributed to being overly sympathetic to arguments about national security. "He liked to see the good Nixon, instead of the bad Nixon," explained Smith.[24] Although Richardson would sometimes let his trust in the president get the best of him, the attorney general was self-aware enough to recognize his tendency to be loyal to his superiors. Looking back at the beginning of his tenure as head of the Justice Department, Richardson wrote that he knew himself to be "a person in whom loyalty runs deep" and that "the struggle to preserve my independence would be painful."[25]

RICHARDSON STRUGGLES TO FIND A MIDDLE GROUND

Richardson's struggle to temper his loyalty with his independence became even more painful after the White House quickly turned against Cox. Just a few hours after Richardson became attorney general, Cox's significantly smaller ceremony in the solicitor general's office set off Nixon's suspicions due to the presence of both Senator Ted Kennedy and his sister-in-law, Ethel. Cox, already labeled a "Kennedy man" by the president, personally invited the two to the ceremony because they were his friends. For Nixon, this was a clear sign that the special prosecutor was determined to embark on a witch hunt.[26] When Cox hired mostly Democratic lawyers from the Ivy League to work in his office on K Street, the president became he even more convinced that he could not trust the special prosecutor or his staff. During a conversation with Rogers a few days after the swearing-in ceremony, Nixon exclaimed, "I don't know if anyone in this chair has taken so much shit." He later called Cox a "Kennedy man, McGovern man," and added that "all of the assistants are!"[27] When Cox mentioned to reporters in June that he could subpoena the president, Nixon was furious and ordered Haig to call Richardson to complain about the statement. "The whole thing is blatantly partisan," said Haig of Cox's comments to the press. Kissinger, who knew Cox through his time at Harvard, was also encouraging the president's paranoia. "Cox will come after you, I don't doubt it," said Kissinger. "He's a fanatic liberal Democrat and all of his associates are fanatics." The president's increasingly antagonistic approach to Cox continued to grow each week as it became more apparent to the White House that they would not be able to fully control the developing investigation into Watergate. Later that summer, Haig called Richardson again to complain about wiretapping questionnaires that Cox's staff had sent to several agencies, telling the attorney general to get rid of the questionnaires. "If Cox does not agree, we get rid of Cox," said Haig.[28] While Cox was well aware of the White House's complaints, Richardson made sure to never tell his friend that the president was threatening to fire him.

Nixon's anger was also often pointed directly at Richardson. At one point, Richardson told the press that if a conflict arose between the special prosecutor and the White House, the president could not rely on him for legal advice. Haig called Richardson to confront him on his statement. Richardson argued that he could best serve the president if he created more distance between the White House and himself. Following the conversation, Haig informed the president of Richardson's argument and his own efforts to rebuke it. "I'll be goddamned if we have to put up with that crap," said Haig. Nixon agreed and said, "By god, the Attorney General of the United States is one of the President's top legal advisers, now doggone it!"[29] For Richardson, it had become apparent that Nixon "had not clearly grasped the new relationships."[30] Whenever the attorney general attempted to exert his independence from the White House, Nixon became enraged over the perceived disloyalty. "Incidentally, I have not been pleased with Richardson . . . Not at all," said Nixon in a meeting with Colson on June 13. He argued, "And I know you've been very high on him, but I thought his saying the President oughta himself be his own personal lawyer . . . very disturbing to me." Later in the conversation Nixon also brought up another friend of Colson's, Jonathan Moore, and his influence on Richardson. "Goddamnit, Elliot's over there with Jonathan Moore, what the hell do you think they've come up with?" Colson insisted that his old friend from Massachusetts would fight for the president, but Nixon remained skeptical. "Well, he better start fighting for me or he's gonna be out. I want him to do right, but he must not cut the President!"[31]

Throughout the summer, Richardson rapidly became an enemy of the White House. The characteristics that once made Richardson the object of an occasional joke were now used as proof of Richardson's weaknesses. The credentials that made Richardson such a strong selection in late April were now the sources of Nixon's absolute scorn. The president, Haig, and others within the White House often specifically targeted Richardson's ties to the Ivy League when discussing their collective frustration with the attorney general. In a meeting with the embattled Spiro Agnew, Nixon referred to his attorney general as "that little Ivy League pipsqueak s.o.b."[32] In yet another conversation, the president raised another common concern about Richardson—the influence of his staff. After Nixon told Haig to put more pressure on the Justice Department to make sure they were on the same page as the White House, the president vented about Richardson's "little boys" who "run in that social set."[33]

Nixon was referring to Jonathan Moore, J.T. Smith, and Dick Darman, a thirty-year-old deputy assistant secretary who had previously conducted public policy analysis at HEW. Together, the three assistants became a crucial part of Richardson's decision-making process at the Justice Department, while also encouraging their boss to become more suspicious of the White House's actions. Over time, the three were referred to as "Richardson's mafia" for their ability to protect the attorney general, especially during their tenure at the Justice Department.[34] While Richardson greatly valued the roles that each of his advisers played in his office, Nixon and Haig only saw them as negative influences on the attorney general.

The already tumultuous relationship between the White House and the Justice Department took a turn for the worse when reports that members of Cox's staff were investigating the purchase of the president's home in San Clemente, California, were picked up by the media.[35] Several of the stories suggested that there were questions about whether campaign funds and/or donations from outside sources were used toward improving Nixon's ocean-view vacation property. The president was furious, directing most of his anger toward Richardson for selecting Cox. "The San Clemente property—what the hell is he [Cox] getting [into] that for? What the hell has Elliot done here, uh?" asked Nixon in a meeting with Haig, Ziegler, and J. Fred Buzhardt, Nixon's counsel for Watergate.[36] Later in the day, he began to further question Richardson's judgment. "Elliot knows the President's not guilty of anything, doesn't he?" asked Nixon as Haig attempted to reassure his boss, "He knows it. He knows it."[37] Haig soon ordered Richardson to put a stop to any sort of investigation into Nixon's vacation home. The president's fears about the reports were overblown; when Richardson went to Cox to confront him about the rumored investigation, the special prosecutor explained that he was only collecting press clippings because the subject had been brought up at a recent press conference. Richardson then went back to Haig and explained Cox's side of the story, but Haig did not relent, telling him that Nixon was considering firing Cox. As a compromise, Richardson agreed to tell Cox to issue a statement that informed the public that he was not investigating Nixon's homes. Although Cox was annoyed by the command, he agreed to write up a statement as a favor to Richardson. When the White House received the first draft, Haig and Nixon called Richardson to tell him that the statement was inadequate and demanded a new statement within the hour or else they would fire Cox.[38] Richardson and Cox soon delivered a new draft that the White House deemed appropriate, and a potential conflict between the two sides was avoided.

The attorney general prevented the situation from escalating at that point, but the San Clemente incident forced him to accept that Nixon had come to despise Cox and his staff. Inside the White House, the president and his advisers regularly ranted about Cox and Richardson into the final days of the secret taping system. In a July 11 conversation with the president about a recent meeting between Richardson and Cox, Haig bluntly stated, "I just don't trust either of them . . . We need to watch them like a hawk."[39] Later that day, Nixon exclaimed to Ziegler, "I should give them a kick in the ass now and then. That son of a bitch Cox." After Ziegler brought up the possibility of firing the special prosecutor, the president's press secretary boldly predicted that "Archibald Cox will not be remembered."[40] Days later, Alexander Butterfield's testimony before the Senate Watergate Committee revealed that President Nixon had ordered the installation of a secret voice activated taping system in the White House in early 1971. The revelation guaranteed that tensions between Cox and the president would remain unresolved, as the special prosecutor could not avoid seeking access to the tapes. The collection was a must-have for any serious prosecutor, and they immediately became the center of the battle between Cox and the White House.

The same morning that the White House turned down Cox's request for access to the tapes, Haig told Richardson that they would not budge on the issue and repeated Nixon's threat to fire Cox. "The president is uptight about Cox. He wants a tight line drawn. No further mistakes, or we'll get rid of Cox," said Haig. Richardson met with Cox later in the day, summarized his conversation with Haig, but once again, never mentioned the threat from Nixon.[41] With the two sides at odds over access to the tapes, Richardson attempted to craft a statement that would avoid taking a side. When he delivered his first draft to the White House, Haig rejected it. Even though Richardson was cautious in his initial draft, claiming that he believed that both Cox and the president had sound arguments, Haig objected to a line which called for a compromise that would make "material portions available." "What you have said in your last sentence is that the President would make the material available, and there's no way he will do that," said Haig. Richardson took out the line and replaced it with a vague substitute that Haig approved. "In the interest of justice, it seems to me important to try to work out some practical means of reconciling the competing public interests at stake."[42]

Watergate was not the only issue on Richardson's plate that summer, as the U.S. Attorney's Office in Maryland began to uncover evidence that Spiro Agnew accepted bribes as governor and later as vice president. By October, the investigation led to formal charges against Agnew for accepting more than $100,000 in bribes. During the Justice Department's negotiations with Agnew, Richardson was determined to find a way to get the vice president to resign, a desired outcome that was also shared by the White House due to their mutual fear of a double impeachment. In the end, Richardson succeeded after Agnew agreed to plead no contest to a single charge of tax evasion on the condition that he resign. Agnew was disbarred from the state of Maryland, fined $10,000, and put on probation for three years.

While Nixon and his aides were relieved that Agnew resigned, the initial investigation into the vice president's wrongdoing further contributed to the president's belief that Richardson was out to get the White House. Nixon may have never relied on Agnew as a real adviser, but he valued his popularity among conservatives and initially saw Richardson's investigation as a possible attempt to bring down a political rival. It was known among Republicans that Richardson was one of several moderates who attempted to organize a protest vote for George Romney in order to block Agnew's nomination in 1968.[43] Along with Richardson's disapproval of Agnew's nomination, the two were often at odd with one another in policy council meetings, especially during the former's time at HEW. It was also known that Agnew and Richardson were each considering a run for the presidency in 1976. Throughout the final months of his political career, Agnew was convinced that the attorney general's investigation was purely political and according to Haig, Nixon did not completely disagree. " 'Elliot,' the President was fond of saying, 'wants to be in the Oval Office,' " wrote Haig.[44]

Nixon's frustrations with Richardson's performance overlooked the fact that the attorney general was fairly cooperative with the White House when dealing with Watergate. Despite the heavy workload, Richardson positioned himself as "the lawyer for the situation," a favorite phrase of his that described his attempt to objectively represent the interests of both Cox and Nixon. Richardson knew that his relationship with the president had deteriorated, as he had practically been cut off from having direct access to Nixon, but he still refused to turn against the White House. Instead, he occasionally reached out to Nixon and pushed for a more positive approach to Watergate. In a memo that was written to the president in late August, Richardson encouraged

Nixon to be "forward looking" and propose legislation to set up a nonpartisan commission on federal election reform. "The important thing, it seems to me, is to communicate to the public . . . the seriousness of your view that the future to which you would have the public turn must not include the abuse of the past," wrote Richardson.

Richardson also continued to meet with Cox on a regular basis, as the two tried to find a way to make peace with the White House. In his notes from a meeting with Cox on September 6, Richardson jotted down, "Subpoena case—thinking down the road—one has to give a little thought to [question] of avoiding a constitutional crisis. If time ever comes when important to try to find a way out, would be glad to explore."[45] As he did with the White House, Richardson attempted to be the lawyer for the situation when dealing with Cox. This meant that Richardson adopted a strategy where he would both push Cox to be more aggressive but also take up the White House's arguments about the tapes. Richardson's approach to Cox has been disputed by various figures who either worked for him or in the WSPF. Cox's own deputy, Henry Ruth, recalled that he grew impatient with the attorney general, especially when he argued to Cox in several conversations that the WSPF did not need the tapes. "He was sincerely arguing that executive privilege applied. I never understood that argument," remembered Ruth.[46] His frustrations with Richardson may have been justified, but they also failed to capture the full scope of the meetings. According to Moore, Richardson had much less tolerance for the White House's arguments about national security than Cox. "He [Richardson] would encourage him to keep pressing. It was the opposite of what most people thought."[47] The truth was a mixture of both accounts, as Richardson felt that he could best serve the investigation by supporting Cox while also playing the devil's advocate. Richardson was firmly a part of the technocratic culture that had dominated the postwar bureaucracy. As a faithful empiricist, he strongly believed that a nuanced and neutral approach would best serve the country.

A neutral approach became more difficult as the courts began to apply more pressure on the White House to turn over several of the tapes. In late August, John Sirica, chief judge for the U.S. District Court of the District of Columbia, ordered Nixon to turn over nine of the tapes so that they could be reviewed. By October 12, the U.S. Appeals Court ordered the president to turn over the tapes that were related to Watergate, giving the White House a week to officially respond. On the same day, Richardson met with Cox to discuss the ruling and its implications on the investigation. In his notes from the meeting, Richardson wrote, "Nat. Sec. Doesn't justify superior interest."[48] Richardson had concluded that even if a compromise was reached, there would have to be some outside access to the tapes. Even though he had previously attempted to argue that the tapes were not necessary for the investigation, Richardson recognized that the court's ruling was something that could not be ignored in future negotiations.

RUCKELSHAUS JOINS THE JUSTICE DEPARTMENT

As the courts were ruling against the White House, Richardson was assisted by his most prominent adviser, William Ruckelshaus, who was sworn in as deputy attorney general just weeks before the October 12 ruling. As deputy, the former administrator of the Environmental Protection Agency (EPA) and the FBI played a brief but important role in helping Richardson manage his battles with the White House. Ruckelshaus was a similar figure to Richardson, in that he was a moderate Republican, a product of the Ivy League, and also a former student of Archibald Cox. Ruckelshaus also had serious reservations about Nixon's character, especially when it came to the president's penchant for dividing the nation into friends and enemies.[49] Much like the attorney general, Ruckelshaus was loyal to the president, but also had serious disagreements with the White House, especially over the administration's environmental policies. While there were many similarities between the two, there were also some differences, most noticeably in their personalities. Compared to the attorney general, Ruckelshaus was looser, funnier, and was less likely to speak in full paragraphs when addressing a simple question. Richardson was certainly a more complex figure than the stuffy Brahmin caricature that defined his public persona, but he was never as affable as Ruckelshaus. One reporter wrote, "One immediately respected Richardson, but one immediately liked Ruckelshaus."[50]

Ruckelshaus began his political career as the deputy attorney general of Indiana in 1960 and later served in the state's House of Representatives. After losing his bid for a Senate seat in 1968, he was brought into the Nixon administration as an assistant attorney general in the Civil Division of the Justice Department. In 1970, Ruckelshaus was named the head of the newly created EPA. As with Richardson's tenure at HEW, the president gradually became uncomfortable with Ruckelshaus's leadership. Nixon often described Ruckelshaus in similar terms to the attorney general when evaluating his leadership. As with Richardson, Nixon was suspicious of Ruckelshaus's intentions, but also

FIGURE 7. William Ruckelshaus at a White House press briefing, April 27, 1973. Prior to his role in the Saturday Night Massacre, Ruckelshaus served as the first EPA administrator and interim director of the FBI before he became deputy attorney general. (From the Richard Nixon Presidential Library and Museum, WHPO-E0714–6a)

valued the credibility he brought to the administration. "All Ruckelshaus does is act like a candidate for the United States Senate," the president said in a conversation with Ehrlichman, who reminded Nixon, "He's got credibility with the damn environmental movement, and that's important."[51]

Richardson and Ruckelshaus became inextricably linked during the Watergate investigation. The latter became the acting director of the FBI the very same day the president announced that the former would be selected as his next attorney general. During his two months at the FBI, Ruckelshaus worked closely with Richardson to coordinate different elements of the ongoing Watergate investigation. When moving over to the Justice Department, Richardson and his staff were concerned that the White House had filled many positions within the department with political appointments, and felt that they needed a strong deputy to replace the outgoing Joseph Sneed.[52] With his past experience at the

Justice Department, Ruckelshaus was more than qualified to provide strong support for the attorney general. His arrival also filled somewhat of a void in the department because he had developed a much deeper understanding of Watergate during his time at the FBI than anyone else on Richardson's staff. His exposure to the agency's investigation had even convinced him that Nixon was in some way involved in the Watergate cover-up. Although Richardson felt it was too early to reach the same conclusion, he valued Ruckelshaus's knowledge about the case and decided to bring him into the department. Even though the White House had grown weary of Richardson, they inexplicably approved of Ruckelshaus without ever asking him about his own thoughts regarding the president's innocence. By late September, Ruckelshaus was sworn in as the deputy attorney general and moved into an office that was a floor below Richardson's, with a private elevator that connected the two.

Earlier that year, Robert Bork, a conservative legal scholar from Yale, also joined the Justice Department as the solicitor general. Prior to joining the department, Bork had become a favorite scholar among many in the White House, including Nixon, for his conservative views. In a conversation with Haldeman, the president praised Bork, and argued that he would be a good fit for attorney general, describing him as a "tough guy." From Nixon's vantage point, Richardson represented what Nixon felt were the worst elements of the Ivy League establishment. By comparison, Bork was an exceptional figure. "How is it Bork came out of that?" he asked Haldeman in December 1972.[53] When the president decided to select Bork as his next solicitor general, he made sure to let the professor know about his distaste for the Ivy League, joking that it was too bad that he had graduated from Yale. When Bork corrected the president and told him that he actually had graduated from the University of Chicago, the president exclaimed, "That's almost as bad!"[54] Regardless of Nixon's suspicions about certain universities, Bork remained a person the White House felt that they could trust. At one point, Bork was even offered the opportunity to become Nixon's chief defense counsel for Watergate. Bork politely declined so that he could remain at the Justice Department.[55]

Bork and Richardson may have differed in how they were perceived by the president, but they worked well together while at the Justice Department. Despite their political differences, the two shared a mutual respect for one another that carried through the Agnew and Watergate investigations. Bork even prepared the department's position combating the Agnew brief in early October, playing a key role in the vice president's eventual resignation.[56] Although he may have been more sympathetic to the White House's frustrations with Cox, his views about the ongoing investigation never affected his relationship with the attorney general. While the president, and many liberal critics of the solicitor general, viewed Bork as the White House's ally within the department, his actual role within Justice was more complicated. He was not a part of Richardson's inner circle, but he was still an important part of Richardson's team of advisers that fall.

THE STENNIS COMPROMISE

Richardson relied heavily on that team in October, as the president sought a way to get rid of Cox and the WSPF. By mid-October, war had broken out in the Middle East (the Yom Kippur War), the vice president of the United States had resigned in disgrace, and two courts had ordered the president to turn over the White House tapes. Richardson and his staff were dealing with a chain of events that taken together were unprecedented in the nation's history. The day after Agnew resigned, Richardson brought Darman and Smith to one of his favorite French restaurants for a celebratory lunch. During the lunch Richardson pointed to a painting of a bullfight that was on one of the walls, and compared himself to the matador. "The trouble with being a matador," he said, "is that you have to face a new bull every Sunday."[57]

Richardson was even more disturbed about the investigation's future after he met with the president following Agnew's resignation. Toward the end of the discussion, Nixon told the attorney general, "Now that we have disposed of that matter, we can go ahead and get rid of Cox."[58] Nixon had been considering the possibility of firing Cox for months, but the October 12 ruling, along with the Yom Kippur War, convinced him that he had to come up with a plan to force Cox out. Emboldened by his actions in the Middle East and his decision to nominate Gerald Ford as Agnew's successor, the president felt that it was time to take a strong stance on the tapes issue. The White House's efforts to fire the special prosecutor began on Sunday, October 14, when Nixon reached out to Senator John Stennis after he joined the president for one of the White House's weekly worship services. The two discussed a plan that would have the conservative Democrat from Mississippi listen to the White House tapes and then report on its contents. The selection of Stennis was yet another attempt to limit the investigation and block any real access to the tapes. Earlier that year, the seventy-two-year-old senator was shot by a mugger outside of his home. Aside from his near-fatal injuries, Stennis was also known for his poor hearing, an obvious hindrance to any listener of the tapes. While the senator was respected by many Democrats and Republicans, he was also a friend of the White House whose hawkish views made him a prime candidate to be overly sympathetic to arguments regarding national security. After the worship service, Nixon brought up the plan to Stennis and the senator agreed to participate. Although their plan was now in place, Nixon remained suspicious of the role that the attorney general would play during the negotiations. He told Haig, "You know Elliot. If Elliot feels that he has to go with his Harvard boy, then that's it." The president added, "Either Cox takes it or Cox is out . . . There is no negotiation with Cox."[59]

On Monday morning, Richardson met with Haig and Buzhardt at the White House, as the president's legal team began its attempt to gain Richardson's support for the Stennis plan. Throughout that tumultuous week, the attorney general would have no direct communication with the president until his resignation, even when he was inside of the White House to meet with Nixon's legal team. In addition to cutting Richardson off from the president, Haig also made sure that Richardson went to the White House meeting alone, falling into the chief of staff's strategy of outnumbering the attorney general whenever there was an important discussion on Watergate. Haig knew how to stroke Richardson's ego before delivering bad news as he began the meeting with a discussion of the Middle East, appealing to Richardson's desire to play a role in the president's decision-making process. It soon became obvious that the reason he had brought Richardson to the White House had little to do with foreign policy. Haig told him that Nixon had agreed to a plan where he would prepare a version of nine tapes for the courts, but that he would also fire Cox. Upon hearing the proposal, Richardson argued that it was completely unacceptable, and that if it was carried out, he would resign.

The offer was either a test or a part of the White House's often-used strategy to present the worst-case scenario before presenting an actual proposal. Hours later, Haig called Richardson and for the first time presented the Stennis plan. Richardson told Haig that the plan "had merit." Haig then said he would try his best to convince the president it was a fair proposal, without telling Richardson that it had already been discussed with Nixon and Stennis. Later that day, Haig called Richardson back and said that the president agreed, but that "this was it" when it came to allowing access to presidential materials. Richardson agreed to work with the Stennis part of the plan, but never consented to anything else that the president mentioned. He never agreed with the White House's threat to bar Cox from requesting any additional materials.[60]

That afternoon, Richardson presented what eventually came to be known as the "Stennis compromise" to Cox. During the meeting, Richardson never mentioned the White House's earlier plan to stop the special prosecutor from gaining access to other materials or their threat to fire Cox. The two talked about the basic contours of the proposal that evening and again the next morning. The morning meeting concluded with Richardson agreeing to Cox's request to put the plan in writing so that he could study it and show the details to his staff. Cox was not exactly thrilled by the basic outline of the plan, but was open to the general idea of having a third party listen to the nine tapes so that his team could have some sort of access to the materials.

Among the attorney general's staff, the plan was often derided as the "gospel according to St. John," but Richardson sincerely hoped that the plan was a starting point to a more productive agreement.[61] Despite his serious reservations about the White House's motives, Richardson felt it was his last chance to save the country from a constitutional crisis. The attorney general's optimism about the proposal was not shared by others in the Justice Department, including his inner circle. "My belief is that he had a somewhat elevated if not inflated view of his own influence to resolve this situation," said Moore.[62] Richardson may have been hopeful, but he was also not completely naïve about his chances. Upon returning from a lunch meeting with Kissinger, where he was told that the president had a strong desire to fire Cox, Richardson told his Catholic secretary, "If you ever lighted candles, now is the time to do it."[63]

With only three days until the court's deadline, Richardson began to work on a draft of the proposal on his way back from New York City, where he had attended the dedication of the police department's new headquarters. A notoriously slow and careful writer, Richardson completed the draft the next morning and sent it over to Buzhardt for approval. The draft included major concessions to the White House, such as an agreement that "Any continuous portion not relating to Watergate matters at all would be omitted," and that "Any reference to national defense or foreign relations matter whose disclosure would, in the judgment of the Reporter, do real harm" would be left out from the summary. Buzhardt approved most of the draft, but made a few suggestions, including cutting out a section entitled, "Other Tapes and Documents," which he labeled "redundant." Richardson agreed and took the paragraph out of the proposal. The section stated that the "proposed arrangement would undertake to cover only the tapes heretofore subpoenaed by the Watergate grand jury at the request of the special prosecutor."[64] The removal of the section further contributed to the White House's strategy of avoiding details and opened the door to more miscommunication. Richardson turned in the final draft of the proposal to Cox late Wednesday afternoon, without any mention of how the proposal would affect his ability to request other materials. The lack of clarity regarding future requests shaped the rest of the week's negotiations, and their eventual breakdown.

That evening, the attorney general held a dinner party at his house to celebrate Ruckelshaus's recent confirmation. Along with the deputy attorney general and his wife, the dinner party guest list also included Robert Bork, his wife, and several other friends of the Richardson family. While Richardson led a discussion on the role of government and morality, skimming the broader surface of the ongoing negotiations over the tapes, neither he nor anyone else made any specific references to current events. "Given what was going on that week, the innocuous conversation wasn't nearly as telling as the absence of a conversation that should have been going on," remembered Bork.[65]

Cox and his staff went over the details of the Stennis compromise that same evening, without knowing about Nixon's refusal to negotiate any further on the tapes issue. Although Cox knew that the summaries would be useless as a form of evidence in any court, he was willing to agree to most of the major components of the proposal, including the deletion of conversations related to national security, the lack of direct access to the tapes, and the use of a third party to produce summaries. The only item he objected to was the use of a single person to serve in the third-party position. In his comments on the Stennis proposal, he argued, "The public cannot be fairly asked to confide so difficult and responsible a task to any one man operating in secrecy, consulting only with the White House." Cox proposed that an independent panel, picked by the courts, could verify transcripts of the tapes. Cox sensed that the White House would not receive his feedback warmly, but he also made sure to leave the door open for future negotiations. "I am glad to sit down with anyone in order to work out a solution if we can."[66]

Cox's comments were delivered to Richardson on Thursday afternoon, who then brought them to a meeting with the president's legal team: Haig, Buzhardt, Garment, and Charles Alan Wright. When it came to Cox's suggestions to improve the proposal, Richardson was met with staunch resistance from the White House. According to his notes from the meeting, the president's lawyers viewed the special prosecutor's letter "as a rejection of the proposal." Every single person at the meeting, with the exception of Richardson, "agreed that if Cox failed to accept the proposal, he should be fired," as they were optimistic that any backlash would be minimal.[67] Richardson passionately argued for Cox's idea of a panel, but failed to persuade anyone in the room. Sensing that the negotiations were falling apart, Richardson encouraged Wright to talk directly to Cox about the special prosecutor's concerns with the proposal. Wright agreed and Richardson left the White House that evening, frustrated that his efforts to find a compromise had clearly failed. When he returned home, he began to work on the letter with a heading that read, "Why I must resign."[68]

Wright called Cox that evening while the special prosecutor was hosting his brother and his children for dinner. Sitting on the floor, with young children running around him, Cox listened to Wright lay out the proposal, which sounded much like an ultimatum. Under the new plan, only Stennis would listen to the tapes, none of the tapes would be given to the courts, and Cox would have to agree to end his pursuit of any other White House materials. Wright added, "You won't agree to these, and there is no sense in continuing conversations if you don't." After Cox took in the new stipulations, he asked to see the proposal in writing so that he could review it in a better setting. "You catch me in a difficult position, Charlie. I'm sitting on the floor at my brother's house and we're in the middle of dinner. There are children running about. I don't think I ought to be put in a position of responding under these conditions, do you?"[69] Wright agreed and sent in the new proposal the next morning to a perplexed Cox. He had already made concessions in agreeing to work with Richardson on the Stennis proposal, and now Wright had inserted even tougher conditions that would prevent him from seeking access to tapes in the future. It was the first time that the White House had mentioned the stipulation to Cox, who now had every reason to believe that the negotiations were over. By Friday morning, the White House received Cox's letter, which stated that he could not accept the current outline of the Stennis compromise. He reminded Wright that he had promised the Senate to resist the exact offer the White House was now supporting, and stated that he could not break that promise. The White House immediately considered the letter the last straw in their talks with Cox; Wright wrote to Cox, "It is my conclusion from that letter that further discussion between us seeking to resolve this matter by compromise would be futile, and that we will be forced to take the actions that the President deems appropriate in these circumstances."[70]

The previous night, Richardson reflected on the last several months while sitting in his family room that overlooked the Potomac River. Frustrated over the White House's refusal to budge on their proposal, he wrote down his thoughts about his potential resignation. Richardson argued that because he was "by temperament a team player," a special prosecutor was always necessary for the investigation. Anticipating that he would be asked to fire Cox, he wrote that he would only follow the White House's orders "in the case of some egregiously unreasonable action" taken by the special prosecutor. Later on in the note, he sympathized with Cox's position in his negotiations with the White House. "He is, after all, being asked to accept a proposition that would give him significantly less than he has won in 2 court decisions." He concluded that the White House was to blame for the breakdown in communication: "many problems and headaches could have been avoided by cooperating with him [Cox] more and fighting him less."[71]

The next morning, Richardson gave the letter he had toiled over the previous night to his secretary so that she could type it up and hand out copies to Darman, Moore, and Smith. The mood of the meeting was somber as the attorney general recounted the previous day's events to his aides. The pessimism had even reached Ruckelshaus, who upon returning from a short trip to Michigan did not know whether he was now the new attorney general. Amidst the increasing anxiety within the Justice Department, Richardson called Haig and asked for a meeting with the president if negotiations had in fact stalled between Cox and Wright. Within the hour, Haig called Richardson back, told him that the negotiations were "fruitless," and asked him to meet at the White House. Before departing his office, Richardson told his aides, "Until this moment, I haven't been nervous. Now I am."[72]

Arriving at the White House shortly after 10:00 a.m., with his resignation letter in his pocket, Richardson sat down with Nixon's legal team to discuss Cox's letter. When Richardson was given a copy of the letter, the attorney general assumed there had been "a misunderstanding on Cox's part," and pointed out to everyone in the room that he had never told Cox that the agreement would prevent him from seeking other presidential records. Initially naïve to what the White House had done behind his back, he even suggested writing a follow-up letter to Cox to clarify the president's position. Wright then spoke up and informed the stunned Richardson that he had already proposed the stipulation to Cox on Thursday night, and that the president would not participate in any additional negotiations. With the White House united behind their last and most recent offer to Cox, the conversation then moved on to whether Cox would accept the proposal. Richardson told the four men that he believed Cox would resign rather than accept the offer. When asked if he would follow through on the president's order to tell Cox to no longer seek access to any other materials, Richardson remembered that he left "without having given any clear indication of his own views" and "returned to the DOJ to discuss it with his closest advisors."[73]

Others within the room claimed that Richardson committed to carrying out the order. Haig later argued that Richardson "left those present with the impression that he supported the Stennis compromise." He also claimed that the attorney general "suggested that Cox be given a cease and desist order with regard to the tapes."[74] In the weeks after the Saturday Night Massacre, Haig, Garment, and other White House officials repeated their version in an apparent attempt to discredit Richardson. More than thirty years after the meeting, Garment offered up a somewhat different take from the claims that he and others at the White House had propagated in the wake of the Saturday Night Massacre. Instead of calling Richardson a liar, Garment later remembered that the meeting "was one of many occasions where people, including myself, heard what we wanted to hear rather than what was actually said." Garment added, "Richardson was very key. There was a knowledge that if he went, everything was likely to go. And therefore, the recollection of what took place [was] governed by wishful thinking."[75]

Whatever may have transpired during that crucial meeting, it was clear that Richardson did not forcefully support or oppose the White House's plan. After the meeting, he went back to his office and met with Darman, Moore, and Smith, who were surprised that their boss had not already resigned. Sitting in a small dining room just to the side of the attorney general's office, the three assistants carefully went over the details of the meeting, while Richardson doodled on his notepad in the corner of the room. When Nixon's order came up, Moore, who was becoming frustrated with his boss's vague descriptions of the discussion, angrily asked, "You didn't tell them that you were against that. Did you?" Richardson conceded that he did not, but defended himself, arguing that he only told the White House that he would think about it. Moore warned him that his nonanswer would be used against him. "Let me tell you, Al Haig is making the calls right now saying that you agreed to this. I'm convinced of this," Moore remembered saying to Richardson. Looking back on the events of that week, Moore concluded that Richardson "was not inclined to distrust the people he was dealing with. Elliot needed a little more distrust that week."[76] Throughout the rest of the meeting Moore, along with Darman and Smith, helped instill a little more distrust in the attorney general. The three collectively argued that Nixon had been manipulating him the entire week, reinforcing the attorney general's suspicions. They pushed him to follow his instincts and say no to the president if asked to fire Cox. Richardson came out of the meeting convinced that he would not carry out the president's order.

RICHARDSON REFUSES TO FIRE COX

Richardson spent much of the rest of the afternoon on the phone with Haig and Buzhardt. After Haig informed him that the proposal had gained the support of Senators Howard Baker and Sam Ervin, Richardson stated his objections to the "linked proposal." He told Haig and Buzhardt that the plan was "clearly ill-advised," and that the president should know about his stance. Haig attempted to sway Richardson into supporting the proposal by arguing that it would help him with his "constituency." When Richardson asked what constituency he was referring to, Haig replied, "Republicans." Later that day, the attorney general once again argued against the proposal and hoped that he could still have a constructive conversation with Nixon. When Haig called at 7:00 p.m., it was not to negotiate or to set up a meeting with Nixon, but to read a letter from the president. "As a part of these actions, I am instructing you to direct Special Prosecutor Archibald Cox of the Watergate Special Prosecution Force that he is to make no further attempts by judicial process to obtain tapes, notes, or memoranda of Presidential conversations."[77]

Richardson was devastated and said, "Al, given the history of our relationship on this, I would have thought that you had consulted me prior to sending any letter."[78] It had become clear to Richardson that he had been roped in by the White House to build credibility for a proposal that was designed all along to force Cox out. Richardson then called Cox to let him know about the president's order, while also making it clear that he was not "transmitting the instruction to Cox." Cox understood and worked with his staff to plot out their next step. That same night, media outlets began to pick up the White House's press release which announced that the president was ordering Cox "to make no further attempts by judicial process to obtain tapes, note, or memoranda of Presidential conversations." Cox and his staff rapidly worked on a counterstatement that asserted their opposition to the Stennis proposal. Working with his press secretary, Cox was able to send out the press release late Friday night and set up a press conference for the next day.

Richardson returned home after 10:00 p.m., and recapped the day's events to his wife, Anne. When he told her about his refusal to carry out the president's order, she compared her husband's impending exit from the administration to being "buried in a mahogany coffin." Richardson then moved to the family room to write down his thoughts, labeling his note "The Mahogany Coffin."[79] With his yellow legal pad in his lap, Richardson had a drink to calm his nerves, which had left him uncharacteristically rattled for most of the day. Building off of his letter from the previous night, he carefully went over the reasons for why he would resign. The decision was not an easy one for Richardson, as his nagging sense of loyalty to the president filled him with trepidation. Unlike previous times when Richardson chose to remain silent in his opposition, the president's attempt to infringe on Cox's independence meant that Richardson could no longer be a team player. In the note he wrote, "If you fire Cox and then resign you will do two things you had no reason to do," adding, "If you refuse to fire Cox and then resign you will do two things you had reason to do."[80]

As Richardson worked on the note, Haig called to discuss the president's instructions. He asked Richardson about a previous phone call to Nixon's legislative adviser Bryce Harlow, where he said that he had felt shabbily treated by the White House. Richardson attempted to diffuse the situation and said, "Well I'm home now. I've had a drink. Things look a little better and we'll see where we go from here."[81] Haig noticed that the attorney general's speech was "slurred and disjointed," an observation he would later use to spread rumors about Richardson's drinking habits.[82] After the conversation, Richardson returned to his yellow legal pad, and spent the rest of the night working on his letter. When he woke up the next morning, Richardson sat down with his thirteen-year-old son, Michael, and fifteen-year-old daughter, Nancy, to explain that he might have to resign. The children understood, but also sensed that their father was asking for their advice. He was determined to use every resource at his disposal before he officially resigned.

Arriving at his office at 10:00 a.m. the next morning, Richardson called Haig and told him that he was writing a letter for the president that formally stated his opposition to the Stennis plan. Richardson outlined the contents of the letter to Haig, stating that he did not believe that the "price of access to the tapes in this manner should be the renunciation of any further attempt by him [Cox] to resort to judicial process."[83] Before the conversation concluded, Richardson requested an alternative approach to the tapes where Cox's right to ask for future materials would not be eliminated, but was rebuffed by Haig. With the help of his advisers, he went back to work on his letter to the president. Darman, who was furious with Nixon, wrote a version of the letter that was much more negative than what Richardson had in mind. Most importantly to Richardson, Darman's draft began without thanking the president, something the attorney general could not stand for. Instead of adopting a confrontational tone, he began the letter by thanking the president for the order he refused to carry out. "Thank you for your letter of October 19, 1973, instructing me to direct Mr. Cox that he is to make no further attempts by judicial process to obtain tapes, notes, or memoranda of Presidential conversations."[84]

When Richardson completed the letter, Moore called Cox at the National Press Club, just minutes before the beginning of his press conference. Once he was on the line, Richardson read the letter to Cox, who up until that conversation was uncertain as to how his former student would respond to Nixon's order. Richardson told Cox that he would not follow through on a potential order to fire him as he felt there was not a single reason to do so. Cox then walked out on to the stage where he was about to take his case to the Washington press corps and the millions of television viewers watching across the nation. As he sat down in front of the microphone, Cox appeared before the American public not as a vicious partisan, but as a humble, gray-haired professor who was capable of explaining the events of the past week in clear and precise terms. He explained that Nixon's actions amounted to a refusal to obey the courts and that the Stennis proposal would require him to violate the pledge he took to pursue all forms of evidence. Wearing his signature bowtie, he came across as an Ivy Leaguer, but managed not to appear as an elitist. During the press conference he emphasized his respect for the presidency and strongly conveyed his disappointment that his office was forced to enter a battle with the White House. "I read in one of the newspapers this morning the headline, 'Cox defiant.' I do want to say that I don't feel defiant, in fact, I told my wife this morning I hate a fight." He added, "Some things I feel very deeply about are at stake, and I hope that I can explain and defend them steadfastly."[85]

Richardson and his staff watched the nearly hour-long press conference in the attorney general's office. Once it was over, they awaited the inevitable calls from the White House. The first one came from Garment, who first attempted to persuade Richardson to fire Cox and then resign. Garment then argued that the war in the Middle East made it absolutely necessary to carry out the president's order, as a wave of resignations would weaken the country during a military crisis. Richardson said no. After the phone call, Garment reported back to the president, who remarked, "That's typical of Elliot. He [would] rather cover his ass than protect his country."[86] Less than fifteen minutes after Garment's call, Haig contacted Richardson and ordered him to fire the special prosecutor. Richardson once again said no, and told Haig that he would like to meet with the president.

Before going to the White House, Richardson met with Ruckelshaus and Bork, while a few other staff members began to look into the line of succession within the Justice Department. They knew that the deputy attorney general was next in line, but were surprised to find out that Bork would become the next attorney general if both Richardson and Ruckelshaus resigned. Once the line of succession was established, Richardson asked his deputy what he would do if Nixon asked him to fire Cox. Ruckelshaus told Richardson that he would refuse to carry out the order and would follow his lead in resigning from his post. The choice was a relatively easy one for Ruckelshaus, who felt that the White House has clearly crossed a line. "In fact, it really wasn't a very difficult decision as far as I was concerned," he said in an interview just days after his resignation. "It has to really be a matter of conscience, a fundamental disagreement, and my disagreement was fundamental."[87]

Richardson then turned to Bork and asked him if he would follow through on the order. Although he was more sympathetic to the White House's side, the solicitor general was still overwhelmed by the scenario. He was now hours away from making a decision that would shape the future of the Watergate investigation. The attorney general urged Bork to carry out the order since he had never agreed to a charter with Cox, and had never promised the Senate that he would only fire the special prosecutor due to "extraordinary improprieties." There was also a concern about the future of the Justice Department, as both Richardson and Ruckelshaus believed that if Bork refused to fire the special prosecutor, a White House figure would be appointed attorney general, causing an even larger wave of resignations. "The gun is in your hand—pull the trigger!" said Richardson. Eventually Bork told them that he felt that the president had the right to fire Cox because he personally viewed the special prosecutor's press conference as entirely inappropriate. He agreed that he would carry out the order, but also planned to resign afterwards.

He argued that he did not want to "appear to be an apparatchik," referring to his plan as a murder-suicide.[88] He changed his mind after Richardson pleaded with him to stay, telling him that "the department requires continuity."[89] Bork decided to stay on as acting attorney general, but only with the understanding that he would return to being solicitor general as soon as his successor was found. Bork would later be vilified by many who supported Cox, but his actions were connected to Richardson's own pragmatic approach to the whole affair.

Richardson's pragmatism faced its limits when he was brought to the White House at 3:20 p.m. Before meeting with the president, the attorney general was confronted by Haig and Nixon's legal advisers, who repeated the argument that his resignation would have a devastating effect on the Middle East situation. Haig also argued that if he fired Cox, the administration could do him "a lot of good," and specifically "dangled the prospect of White House support" if he chose to run for president in 1976.[90] Haig's arguments had no effect on Richardson, who was then brought into the Oval Office. Seated across from Nixon, the attorney general told the president that he would not fire Cox and had already decided to resign. Nixon coldly said, "I'm sorry that you insist on putting your personal commitments ahead of the public interest." While controlling his anger, Richardson replied, "My President, I can only say that I believe my resignation is in the public interest."[91] After Richardson left the Oval Office, Nixon did not dwell on the meeting, but as Haig remembered, "was remote and controlled, unsurprised by what had happened" as the resignation "seemed to confirm all his doubts about Richardson."[92] For the president, Richardson's actions amounted to a betrayal, and it was one that he felt he should have predicted months ago. More than forty years later, Pat Buchanan remembered a president who was calm, but somber. The White House speechwriter defended Nixon's actions and concluded that Richardson "had switched sides and gone against the President as he realized that keeping his friends and ensuring his future meant defying Nixon and playing the martyr to those who despised Nixon."[93]

"It was an excruciating moment for Richardson," remembered Smith. "It was the only moment when Elliot said something the President didn't want to hear."[94] When Richardson returned to the Justice Department, he referenced *Macbeth* by telling his staff, "The deed is done."[95] His literary references did not end with Shakespeare; he later cited Homer when he called Cox. Quoting *The Iliad*, he said, "Now, though numberless fates of death beset us which no mortal can escape or avoid, let us go forward together, and either we shall give honor to one another or another to us." Although Richardson and Cox were at times at odds over the trajectory of the Watergate investigation, they consistently trusted one another's instincts. Their shared confidence in one another arguably led to a much more fruitful relationship between the sometimes competing interests of Justice Department and the WSPF. Years later, Cox said that he often wondered what would have happened if he had to work with someone other than Richardson. "I'm not sure things would have worked out the same at all."[96]

THE SATURDAY NIGHT MASSACRE

Sitting with Richardson and several other staff members, Ruckelshaus was soon told that Haig was on the line with the order to fire Cox. Ruckelshaus left the attorney general's office, rode the private elevator down to his office, and took the call. As he did with Richardson, Haig first asked him to fire Cox. When Ruckelshaus said no and that he would resign, he was then asked to carry out the order before resigning. Haig also stressed the order regarding Cox was an order from the commander-in-chief and that refusing to carry it out would have a terrible impact on U.S. foreign policy. Ruckelshaus calmly suggested, "Well, then wait a week before you discharge Cox. Why do you have to do it today?"[97] Nearly forty years after his resignation, Ruckelshaus reflected on his decision, reiterating that it did not cause him as much anxiety as Richardson. "There are people who have said no in the government, nobody even realized they've had, and they've left or resigned. This just happened to be a very visible event."[98]

Before the phone call ended, he made sure to mention to Haig that Bork would fire Cox. Ruckelshaus put Haig on hold and rode the elevator back up to Richardson's office, where Bork was sitting. "Get ready for a phone call, Bob," said Ruckelshaus. Bork then got on the elevator to the fourth floor, talked to Haig, and agreed to fire Cox. He was soon picked up by a car sent by the White House that had Garment in the passenger seat and Buzhardt in the back. Bork nervously joked about being "taken for a ride." After dealing with two resignations in one day, the president and his team carefully dealt with Bork, making sure that he would not back out from firing the special prosecutor. In order to ensure Bork's loyalty, the president even offered a Supreme Court seat. "You're next when a vacancy occurs on the Supreme Court," said Nixon, almost five months after making the same offer to Richardson. Bork did not respond, primarily because he did not take the offer very seriously given the current state of the administration. "I hadn't the courage to tell him that I didn't think he could get anyone confirmed to the Supreme Court, and particularly not the person who fired Cox," wrote Bork.[99]

As Bork sat in the White House, Richardson and Ruckelshaus each worked on their letters of resignation, with the former taking much more time to write than the latter. Ruckelshaus soon grew impatient and decided to go home so that he could explain the day's events to his family. As he walked out of the Justice Department, a group of reporters approached him, asking if the activities within his office had anything to with someone being fired. "It might," he said before driving away.[100] Wire services were soon sending out stories with Ruckelshaus's quote and the resignations became national news. Richardson finished his letter later that evening, and sent the two letters to the White House. In his own letter he wrote to Nixon, "It is with deep regret that I have been obliged to conclude that circumstances leave me no alternative to the submission of my resignation as attorney general of the United States."[101] Once the White House received the letters, Haig decided that instead of accepting Ruckelshaus's resignation, they would fire him, telling the president, "We don't owe him anything but a good kick in the ass . . . I don't want him to go back to Indiana and run for the Senate."[102] Nixon agreed, and the deputy attorney general was officially fired. Bork quickly wrote out his letter to Cox, explaining that he was now the acting attorney general of the United States. He added, "In that capacity I am, as instructed by the President, discharging you, effective at once, from your position as Special Prosecutor, Watergate Special Prosecutor Force."[103]

Richardson left the Justice Department shortly before 9:00 p.m., just as FBI agents were sealing off the WSPF's office under instructions from the White House. The order was eerily similar to the May 1 incident when the president was enraged over the presence of agents inside the White House. This time, it was the president who was using the FBI, and their presence at the WSPF further dramatized the events of that Saturday. When the agents arrived, they were confronted by WSPF staff members, who were appalled that their office building was under siege. Cox's press secretary, James Doyle, symbolically took a framed copy of the Declaration of Independence from his office wall, telling one agent to "Just stamp it void and let me take it home."[104] Less than an hour later, FBI agents sealed off the offices of Richardson and Ruckelshaus at the Justice Department, as several employees rushed to collect their personal files. Smith called Richardson and described the scene that surrounded him. "About all I can tell you is they don't have high topped boots on," he said. As the two offices were being closed off, Cox issued one last statement to the press. "Whether ours shall continue to be a government of laws and not of men is now for Congress and ultimately the American people."[105]

The events of that Saturday were soon dubbed the "Saturday Night Massacre," as the media quickly reported on Nixon's attempt to interfere with the Watergate investigation. That Saturday night, each of the three networks interrupted their regular programming to cover the firing of Cox. The American public swiftly condemned the decision to fire Cox. In a poll taken by NBC, 75 percent of those who were surveyed opposed Cox's dismissal. In a separate poll taken by Gallup, the president's approval rating fell from 38 percent in August to a new low of 27 percent.[106] More than 300,000 telegrams, ten times the normal rate, were sent to Congress and the White House, with the overwhelming majority of them calling for Nixon's impeachment.[107]

In the days after the Saturday Night Massacre, the White House realized that they had vastly underestimated the public's reaction to the firing of Cox. Years later, Nixon wrote that he was "taken by surprise by the ferocious intensity of the reaction that actually occurred." He added: "For the first time I recognized the depth of the impact Watergate had been having on America; I suddenly realized how deeply its acid had eaten into the nation's grain."[108]

Besieged by angry letters, George H. W. Bush, the then chairman of the Republican National Committee, urged the White House to rehire Richardson as ambassador to the Soviet Union for damage control.[109] Instead, the White House chose to attack Richardson, spreading stories that were designed to put a dent in his shining armor. Haig, in particular, often claimed that Richardson's actions were purely political, a part of a plan to win either the governorship in Massachusetts or the presidency. Based on Richardson's records, there is little evidence to suggest that Richardson's decision was motivated by his political aspirations, as staff members only began to seriously plan for his future after his resignation. "I don't remember there ever being a discussion about long-term prospects. Not a single word," said Smith.[110] Haig also told several senators that Richardson had been drinking heavily throughout the week, citing his conversation with the attorney general from the night before his resignation. Soon stories began appearing that speculated as to whether or not Richardson had a drinking problem, bringing up his car accidents from his college years as proof that he was an alcoholic. According to his friends and colleagues, the reports about Richardson's drinking habits were greatly exaggerated, and were mostly dismissed as

FIGURE 8. Following the Saturday Night Massacre, the White House received more than 300,000 telegrams, ten times the normal rate. The overwhelming majority of them called for Nixon's impeachment. That fall, bumper stickers like the one above became increasingly popular. (Nixon Impeachment Bumper Sticker [1973]—The Tamiment Library Vertical Files: Subjects; Tamiment #469, Box 6; Folder—Impeachment: Nixon; New York University; New York University Libraries)

a petty attempt by the White House to sully the attorney general's image. Still, the rumors received enough attention that Richardson felt the need to acknowledge them during a post-resignation speaking engagement. "That's water, by the way," Richardson quipped after taking a sip from his glass in the middle of his speech.[111]

In the middle of the White House's PR battle, Nixon invited Richardson to the White House for a final conversation. The president and Richardson talked about foreign affairs, but never addressed any of the events from the previous weekend. Even after resigning, Richardson politely thanked the president for his opportunity to serve the administration and left without ever coming close to raising his voice. Nixon, who felt betrayed by the former attorney general, also remained civil as the two said their final goodbyes to one another. It was an odd but rather fitting end to their working relationship.

The very next morning, Richardson appeared before the national media at the Great Hall of the Justice Department. Leading up to the press conference, many wondered if Richardson would attack Nixon or stick to his usual gentlemanly approach to the presidency. Colson, who was still an informal adviser to Nixon, was worried enough to call Moore to pry information from him about the speech. After pressuring his friend to tell him whether or not Richardson would defend the firing, Moore refused, telling Colson, "I can't give him a fucking script." Just before the speech, Moore briefed Richardson that there were reports that former staff members were planning to boo if he chose to adopt a "conciliatory tone when it came to Nixon." Based on his prior conflicts with the president and general penchant for civility, many were worried that their former boss would let Nixon off the hook. Moore was also anxious, specifically about how Richardson would answer if he were asked by a reporter if he would have acted the same as Cox had. The two argued about the question minutes before the press conference, as Richardson told Moore that he would give a nuanced response that would remain supportive of Cox. Moore argued that anything less than a straightforward answer would allow the White House the opportunity to pounce on the speech and use it as evidence against Cox and the WSPF.[112]

As Richardson walked onto the stage, the room erupted into a roaring applause that lasted for two minutes. Standing in front of a room full of reporters who were anxiously waiting to hear Richardson's first public comments on his resignation, Richardson looked up to the balcony section and saw the individuals he worked with at the Justice Department furiously clapping for his decision to stand up to the president. With his wife and William Ruckelshaus seated to his left, Richardson waited for the crowd to quiet and then gave an outline of his version of the events leading up to that historic Saturday. Visibly moved by the reception, Richardson began by thanking Nixon for the opportunity to serve his country. Throughout the rest of the speech, he stated the reasons for his resignation, while also steering away from any real attacks on the president. No one in the audience booed Richardson's diplomatic approach to the White House, but no one cheered. When it came to the Q&A, Richardson defended Cox, stating that he disagreed with the White House's belief that the special prosecutor was "out to get the President," and declared his support for a new special prosecutor. As Moore predicted, a reporter asked if he would have acted the same way as Cox had. Richardson replied, "I would have done what he has done." Later on, when asked if Nixon should be impeached, Richardson refused to answer and stated that it was "a question for the American people."[113]

Although the president's critics did not get the ammunition they were hoping for, it was also a disappointment for the White House because Richardson made no effort to distance himself from Cox. His unwillingness to publicly condemn the president for his actions may have disappointed some, but the performance sent a clear message to the White House that he was not going to make an attempt to publicly reconcile with Nixon. There was no declaration of war, but after years of compromising with Nixon, Richardson stood in opposition to the president.[114]

THE AFTERMATH

The decision to resign caused Richardson much anxiety, but it had also brought him more stature. As the nation was coming to grips with the trauma of Watergate, the former attorney general became a moral counterweight to the corruption that had enveloped the Nixon administration. Richardson's new role as a Watergate hero was ironic considering that he did not consider himself an expert on the scandal. "I was never in a position where I ever needed to know a damn thing about Watergate. Since I appointed a special prosecutor, he was investigating it," he recalled in 1997. "I have never read any book on Watergate. I know less about Watergate, probably, than many people."[115] Whereas many had previously poked fun at Richardson's lack of charisma, his calm demeanor and ironclad integrity were now celebrated in the middle of a constitutional crisis. The *New York Times* even wrote that "aside from everything else, Elliot Richardson looks like Clark Kent. You can expect him to pop into a telephone booth any minute and come out in his Superman suit."[116]

As a result of his increased fame and semi-superhero status, Richardson received an endless number of offers to speak across the country. Just a few weeks into January, his calendar was practically booked with speaking engagements for the rest of the year.[117] Numerous crowds greeted Richardson with great excitement, hoping that he would unload on Nixon, but they were usually left disappointed. The man who had become a celebrated figure for his decision to stand up to Nixon was not willing to attack the president. While many were hoping for dirt on the White House, Richardson was more interested in ruminating on the Constitution, the U.S. system of government, and the public's increasing cynicism regarding the nation's civic institutions. The speeches came from a sincere place and were representative of Richardson's character and upbringing, but they were also often a bore. "He would get a standing ovation in the beginning, but would rarely get a standing ovation at the end of a speech," said Smith.[118]

In addition to his increased bookings, Richardson's post-resignation glow also led to being courted by a dozen different publishers to write a book. Eventually, he decided to work with Holt, Rinehart & Winston, and published *The Creative Balance: Government, Politics, and the Individual in America's Third Century* in early 1976. As with his speeches, he disappointed many who had hoped for an insider's takedown of the Nixon administration. While Richardson did mention his disagreements with Nixon during his time as attorney general, only one section of the book focused on the Saturday Night Massacre. The rest of the book featured philosophical essays on the nation's system of government, and were an extension of the speeches he had delivered on the lecture circuit. Whether it was through his essays or his public appearances, Richardson

FIGURE 9. Richard Nixon boards a helicopter from the South Lawn of the White House following his farewell address to his staff and resignation, August 9, 1974. (From the Richard Nixon Presidential Library and Museum, WHPO-E3386–35)

failed to capitalize on the momentum that he had accumulated after his resignation.

Despite Richardson's inability to connect with most audiences, rumors still persisted about Richardson's political future. Aside from a single memo that was written in September 1972, Richardson and his staff did not discuss running for president or governor until November 1973.[119] He was in fact interested in exploring the possibility of running for president, but was also realistic about his odds. In late 1973, Moore collected reports on his former boss's future, and for the most part they revealed that Richardson's chances were slim. In a memo written by Moore, the attorney general's assistant wrote to his friend, "I think it will be extremely difficult for you to become a viable candidate for 76," but added that he was "a little more hopeful" when it came to the VP slot.[120] After Nixon's resignation, Richardson was briefly considered for vice president, but the former attorney general felt that it would have been improper to accept the position. "I asked to have my name taken off the list, if it were on it, because I had after all had direct responsibility for getting Agnew out," remembered Richardson.[121] Instead, he indirectly asked, through Governor William Scranton, that the president consider him for "a programmatic task and position" within the administration. In a letter to Ford that recounted the conversation, Scranton wrote that Richardson suggested positions such as special assistant to the president for the NSC, lead negotiator in the SALT negotiations, director of the OMB, or heading up the White House's Domestic Council.[122]

When plotting out his future, Richardson and his staff were also well aware of the growing power of the conservative movement, and the impact it would have on his political aspirations. In another memo that covered Barry Goldwater's recent meeting with several White House fellows, the report focused on when one of the young men asked the senator about Richardson capturing the Republican nomination in 1976. "No! No, no way," said Goldwater. Most polls taken in 1974 and 1975 confirmed that Richardson was a longshot to win the Republican nomination. In survey after survey, Richardson was far behind Ford, Reagan, and even Rockefeller. In one poll of Republican county leaders Richardson only received three percent of the vote, a miniscule number when compared to Reagan's 39 percent, Ford's 24 percent, and Rockefeller's 12 percent.[123] During an interview in early 1974 Richardson did not deny his presidential aspirations but also admitted, "If you were to calculate the odds, you'd have to say that the chances of achieving more or better are unlikely." The poll numbers did not shake his self-confidence; when asked by a reporter if he would be a good president, he replied, "Better than anyone I can think of."[124]

As others continued to speculate on his future in politics, Richardson returned to the federal government when President Ford selected him as ambassador to the United Kingdom in December 1974. Living in London, Richardson was removed from the American political scene. A year later, he officially announced that he would not run for president.[125] After a little more than a year as ambassador, Richardson was selected by Ford to be the secretary of commerce in February 1976, making him the first person in U.S. history to serve in four cabinet-level positions. Months later, Richardson and Ruckelshaus were both included on Ford's short list of candidates for the VP slot for the 1976 campaign. Although the two had been effectively isolated from the Republican Party—Ruckelshaus was working as a private attorney—they held much value, especially if Ford chose to further distance himself from Nixon.[126] However, both had clear negatives: Richardson was considered a poor campaigner and Ruckelshaus did not have enough name recognition to make a big impact in the White House's internal polls.[127] Ford eventually decided to steer away from the GOP's liberal and moderate wings, selecting Kansas senator Bob Dole as his running mate. While the moderates still held much influence in the party, Ford did not want to alienate the increasingly powerful conservative movement. Years later, Richardson stated that he thought Ford made a serious mistake in picking Dole. "I'm convinced that had Ruckelshaus or any of several people been the nominee other than Dole, that Ford would have won," said Richardson. "Ruckelshaus would have been terrific."[128]

Ford's loss to Jimmy Carter meant that Richardson was forced to yet again prematurely leave a cabinet-level position. It would be his last stint in the cabinet, but his stature would earn him a position within the next administration as President Carter's special negotiator at the Law of Sea Conference. After three years on the job, he helped shape a workable agreement among the major nations of the world that would continue to be worked on in later conferences.

Richardson's post–Saturday Night Massacre accomplishments were impressive, but they did not override the fact that his later career was marked by an overriding sense of disappointment. As the conservative movement gained more power within the GOP, an increasing number of Republicans had little use for moderates like Richardson. Although he was still heralded for his past achievements, Richardson was now out of tune with the base of his own party. A few years after Richardson completed his work at the Law of Sea Conference, the Reagan administration chose to leave the conference negotiations due to concerns over the agreement's restrictions on deep sea-bed mining.

Richardson's disconnect with the New Right became even more clear during his failed campaign for the U.S. Senate in 1984. When it came to Massachusetts politics, he had previously seen encouraging signs—one poll showed him leading then governor Michael Dukakis by ten points a year before the 1978 gubernatorial election.[129] Richardson declined to run in 1978, but chose to campaign six years later for a Senate seat that had been vacated by Democrat Paul Tsongas. Early on, Richardson was the overwhelming favorite to win the Republican nomination and was viewed by most party officials as having the best chance to win in November in a Democratic state. His main challenger in the primaries was Ray Shamie, an eccentric conservative businessman who had previously lost to Ted Kennedy during the 1982 senatorial election. Shamie was initially the underdog, with Richardson building up a twenty-point lead in the polls in July, just two months before the primary. The lead soon vanished after Richardson lambasted the party's platform at the RNC as being too far to the right, called Shamie irresponsible for opposing any tax increase, and even came out for stronger efforts to control nuclear arms. Shamie aligned himself closely with President Reagan's conservative philosophy, and ended up winning the primary in a landslide, 62–38 percent, before losing to Massachusetts lieutenant governor and future Democratic presidential nominee John Kerry in the general election.[130]

Throughout the campaign, Shamie echoed Nixon's private views of Richardson. "Elliot represents the establishment," said Shamie. "We have enough professional politicians . . . He's a liberal Rockefeller-type Republican who would be very comfortable in the Democratic Party."[131] Unfortunately, that characterization of Richardson had become all too true within the Republican Party, as Nixon's suspicions about moderate establishment figures had now become a prominent part of the GOP of the 1980s. Richardson's defeat marked the end of his career in politics and signaled the end of his days as a major player within the party. Years after his defeat, during a dinner with Smith, Richardson was asked by his former assistant why he was still a Republican. "He didn't have a good answer," Smith remembered.[132]

. . .

In the final years of his life, Richardson felt even more isolated from his own party. Richardson came of age in the 1950s and 1960, when moderates largely controlled the Republican Party. They still had significant power during Watergate, but the Saturday Night Massacre was arguably one of the last stands for moderates. Richardson may have won the public relations battle against Nixon, but the conservative movement (using some of Nixon's playbook) won the war for the GOP. In his second book, *Reflections of a Radical Moderate,* Richardson took aim at the GOP's Contract with America and the party's approach to poverty. "Since when has it been conservative for Americans to turn their backs on the poor?" asked Richardson. "They are not an alien 'lower class.' They are our neighbors."[133] When Richardson was given the Presidential Medal of Freedom for his public service, it was a Democrat, Bill Clinton, who had decided to bestow him with the award. The ceremony, which was held just nine months before the twenty-fifth anniversary of the Saturday Night Massacre, featured a speech from Clinton that celebrated Richardson's career. "No public servant has shown greater respect for the constitution he has served," said Clinton, who also emphasized Richardson's heroism during the Saturday Night Massacre. "He saved the nation from a constitutional crisis with his courage and moral clarity."[134]

Months after losing his wife, Anne, due to complications related to Alzheimer's, Richardson died of a cerebral hemorrhage on December 31, 1999 in Boston. Much of the media emphasized Richardson's martyr-like status and focused on his refusal to fire Cox. The posthumous tributes may have reminded the public of the crucial role that Richardson played in Nixon's downfall, but his funeral service at the National Cathedral in Washington, DC, truly demonstrated the impact of his life's work. Whether it was a Democrat or a Republican, a former employee from HEW or the Defense Department, the overwhelming majority of the crowd was made up of civil servants who had each been deeply affected by Richardson's career in government. "I watched it in four different departments. He mobilized civil servants," remembered Moore. "I saw swarms of bureaucracies come alive under him. If there was anyone in Washington who fought off cynicism, it was Richardson."[135]

It was Richardson's idealism and integrity that defined his legacy. Richardson's decision to resign from office helped magnify the president's abuses of power to a point where Watergate was no longer just about partisan politics. Whereas others had said no to the president with very little publicity, the attorney general's actions were exceptional in that they were closely followed by a captivated public. The heightened level of fanfare and its direct effect on the Watergate investigation made Richardson's case exceptional, but it was also an extension of the resistance to illegal or unethical orders of other idealistic Republicans in the Nixon administration. Richardson once wrote: "Watergate was a tragedy not so much of immoral men as of amoral men, not so much of ruthless men as of rootless men," warning that there "are thousands more back home where they came from—ready to root their identity in an organization, ready to serve."[136] The legacy of the Saturday Night Massacre should not only be a celebration of its immediate actors, but of all the Republicans who refused to play a part in Nixon's abuses of power.

Conclusion

Nixon's Culture of Loyalty in the Age of Trump

Twenty-six years after the Saturday Night Massacre, the media's coverage of Richardson's death showed that his life was still largely defined by his decision to say no to Nixon. Soon after hearing about his death, President Clinton paid tribute to the former attorney general, stating that he put the "nation's interests first even when the personal cost was very high." The heading of his obituary in the *New York Times* read, "Elliot Richardson Dies at 79; Stood Up to Nixon and Resigned in 'Saturday Night Massacre'." In the obituary, his decision to resign in protest was described as "widely lauded as a special moment of integrity and rectitude."[1] After years of being excluded by a conservative GOP, Richardson's death allowed many to fully appreciate the crucial role he played in Watergate. It is fitting that Richardson is still remembered as one of the Republican heroes of the Watergate era. In many ways he was the embodiment of the liberal and moderate wings of the GOP, the technocratic culture that had defined much of the nation's federal bureaucracy and everything else that Nixon and his allies viewed with great suspicion. He was not the only one.

Richardson's refusal to fire Cox was a monumental decision, but it must be linked to other acts of resistance by Republicans within the Nixon administration. The lesser-known stories of Republicans who refused to carry out Nixon's orders add a different level of understanding to the thirty-seventh president's downfall. Through analyzing their experiences in the Nixon administration, one can truly understand the scope of the president's abuses of power and situate them within a longer history of American politics. It was because of the Republicans who said no to Nixon that the federal government did not participate in full-scale politically based audits or cut federal funds to universities with antiwar protests. It was also because of these Republicans that a credible independent investigation into Watergate was saved from the White House's attacks. They did not block every single one of Nixon's abuses of power, but their collective efforts prevented the president from further damaging key institutions within the federal government.

The battles between Nixon and the moderates were representative of two different cultures: the president's culture of loyalty and a culture of nonpartisan civil service that was embedded within segments of his administration. While Nixon was all too willing to divide his own administration into friends and enemies, the moderates who opposed him were comfortable working with both Democrats and Republicans. They did not use the cultural and political instability of the era to demonize dissenters or adopt extralegal tactics within their offices. They refused to adopt Nixon's ever-present bunker mentality that made enemies out of political opponents. They saw no justifiable rationale in participating in the president's schemes to punish his enemies. Whereas Nixon was on the lookout for any potential signs of disloyalty, the moderates were much more cerebral in their duties. They were an important counterpoint to Nixon's visceral approach to politics. They encouraged an open work environment with a wide range of views. Although some of them gave in to White House pressure on certain orders in an attempt to maintain a positive relationship with the president, they eventually stood their ground when it came to Nixon's more sinister plans. The president may have questioned their toughness and masculinity, but they provided strong and courageous resistance to Nixon's worst instincts, protecting their offices from abandoning a solution-oriented approach to their work.

That adherence to defending a technocratic culture within the federal bureaucracy was at odds with Nixon's plan to expand the powers of the presidency in his second term. Parts of those plans were sometimes carried out by certain loyal figures within the administration, but Nixon ultimately failed to gain full control over the federal bureaucracy. The White House tapes, along with countless memos and other archival records, show that Nixon was the architect of the White House's plan to revamp several government agencies. If one groups all of the president's controversial orders as a whole, and places them alongside some very explicit conversations regarding a second term, it is irrefutable that

Nixon was planning to institutionalize his abuses of power. The Republicans who stood up to Nixon were not just blocking individual abuses of power, but were also countering Nixon's perilous vision of a second term. The American public is still discovering the details of that vision, but several administration officials recognized the danger of Nixon's plans before Watergate became a national story. At a time when very few people were aware of the scope of Nixon's intentions and illegalities, several key Republicans risked their careers to stop his power grab.

Months before his landslide reelection victory over George McGovern, Nixon met with John Connally, the then outgoing treasury secretary. The former Democratic governor from Texas had become one of Nixon's closest allies during his first term, the two bonding over their shared foreign policy views and their mutual disgust toward the liberal establishment. During their meeting, they discussed their shared frustrations with the Democratic Party, and even brought up their fears about the threat of a dictator taking over the country (implying that McGovern fit the bill). Nixon once again repeated that that there were too many Ivy Leaguers within the administration, and Connally agreed that the administration should try to recruit individuals from outside of the nation's traditional elite universities. "Frankly you don't find a lot of radicals in Texas or Ohio . . . The environment is better," argued Nixon. In order to diminish the establishment's influence on his administration, Nixon was considering a wide range of options to build up his "new establishment." At one point, Nixon brought up his plan to ask for the resignation of every presidential appointee after winning reelection. Nixon did decide to carry out the mostly symbolic plan, believing it would send a strong message to various administration officials that things would be different during his second term. Upon facing major resistance to some of his more controversial orders, the president maintained his desire to drastically alter the culture of his administration. "I don't believe that civil service is a good thing for the country," said Nixon. He repeated, "I don't think it's a good thing for the country."[2]

Nixon's remarks about the value of civil service were born out of his frustrations from the previous four years, but more importantly they were also a product of his authoritarian views on governance. By the end of his first term, he was adamant that the White House should seek to weaken the nation's academic and political establishments, especially across the federal bureaucracy. His cynicism regarding public service is a recurring theme throughout the White House tapes, as he rarely could see beyond partisan politics. The unwillingness of Republicans inside his administration to take on the White House's foes meant that they had been corrupted by the poisonous influence of the postwar establishment. The president viewed their acts of independence as blatant signs of weakness and felt that their actions proved they were not tough enough to engage in his war on the culture of the establishment. Since they were unwilling to attack that culture, the moderates were seen as complicit in the White House's problems and were excluded from Nixon's vision of a new, more conservative establishment.

In order to diminish the influence of the liberals and moderates within his administration, the president often relied on the more conservative members of his team, such as Roger Barth, Chuck Colson, and Caspar Weinberger, to carry out the White House special projects that took explicit aim at his enemies. For Nixon, their loyalty trumped their politics, but it was not a complete coincidence that the two often overlapped. Through trying to expand the secret punitive powers of the state, the president aligned himself with the conservatives who wanted to find ways to weaken both the American Left and the liberal establishment by any means necessary. Nixon was not an ideological conservative in the Buckley mold, and his relationship with the conservative movement was often contentious, but his obsession with building an establishment that would counter important elements of postwar liberalism situated him within the culture of the right wing. Notable conservatives such as Barry Goldwater may have eventually opposed the excesses of Watergate in 1974, but the culture that created Watergate was kept alive by much of the later conservative movement. In reality, Nixon may not have been a steady ally of the conservative movement, but because of his enemies, the memory of his presidency became inextricably linked to its cultural conservatism.

Numerous historical documents clearly show that Nixon was all too willing to use the power of the state to fight the cultural and ideological wars of the era. The battles between Nixon and the moderates in his administration reveal just how determined Nixon and the conservatives on his staff were to expand the punitive powers of the government to weaken the moderates and the Left. The stories of the Republicans who blocked Nixon's plan help to explain Nixon's place in the recent history of the GOP and its broader relationship to the state. It is still hard to attach any traditional ideological labels to the thirty-seventh president, but his approach to dealing with his opponents made him an important cultural ally for the modern conservative movement and its use of the federal government. "That's because the Watergate affair turned conservative skeptics of Richard Nixon into hardcore supporters, drawing out the immediate crisis and deepening divisions in the long term," wrote Nicole Hemmer in 2017. She warned readers that the legacy of Watergate among conservatives suggests that Republicans may do the same when confronted with a potentially earth-shattering scandal in the Trump administration. "Conservatives at the time refashioned the scandal into a tale of Democratic hypocrisy and media hostility—a narrative that many Republicans have adopted once again to explain away the emerging Trump scandals."[3] In the wake of the 2016 election, it has become even more clear that cultural conservatism has often outweighed a more well-defined ideological conservatism in the recent history of the GOP.

Conventional wisdom tells us that Nixon has been and will continue to be a complete pariah. More than thirty years after *Time* magazine declared "He's Back" in a profile of Nixon and his rehabilitation campaign, the public still largely holds a negative assessment of his presidency. In 2013, Nixon's approval rating stood at 31 percent, the lowest of all the postwar presidents. In a 2014 Quinnipiac Poll, Barack Obama and George W. Bush were ranked the worst two presidents, but Nixon came in third with 20 percent of the vote.[4] While both Obama and Bush's standings in this particular poll were shaped by present-day politics, the overwhelming majority of Americans still view Nixon in a negative light forty years after his resignation. As important as these polls are in explaining Nixon's overall legacy in the public's imagination, the thirty-seventh president continues to loom large in American culture and politics. Aside from the aforementioned revisionist scholars, Nixon is frequently held up as an exceptional president and something approaching a political martyr by different wings of the conservative movement. While there is no shortage of Republicans who have employed the term "Nixonian" to attack high-profile Democrats, he is still often depicted by conservatives as a skilled manager who did the best he could to combat a tumultuous era. Since the meaning of the 1960s and 1970s remains highly contested, the debate over Nixon's legacy is far from settled. In a 2008 review of Rick Perlstein's *Nixonland* for the *Atlantic*, conservative columnist Ross Douthat critiqued the author's conclusions regarding Nixon and concluded that Nixon was "too small a man to threaten the republic." He added, "His corruptions were too petty; his schemes too penny-ante; and his spirit too cowardly, too self-interested, too venal to make him truly dangerous." Contrasting Nixon's presidency to the political instability of the period, Douthat concluded that Nixon "was a bridge, thank God, to better times."[5]

Given Donald Trump's victory in the 2016 presidential election, Nixon's legacy has become significantly easier to connect to today's politics. Whether it is Trump's supporters in the GOP or anti-Trump conservatives, Nixon's campaigns and his presidency have repeatedly been brought up in an effort to better understand the present. In the buildup to the 2016 GOP primaries, Douthat surveyed the field and argued in the *New York Times* that "there are times, and this might be one of them, when the country needs a little Nixon." As an anti-Trump conservative, Douthat argued that Nixon "knew how to channel an angry, 'who's looking out for me?' populism without letting himself be imprisoned by its excesses." There are meaningful differences between Nixon and Trump—the former was much more refined in his rhetoric, relying on dog whistles instead of blatant racism—but Douthat underestimated the cultural connections between the two divisive figures. He rightly pointed out that Nixon did not rely on explicit "slurs and empty bluster" when campaigning, but that does not mean that Nixon's repeated calls for law and order are completely disconnected from Trump.[6]

Trump and his campaign drew a link between his campaign and Nixon, often emphasizing the connections between 1968 and 2016. From adopting the term "Silent Majority" to the inclusion of advisers such as former Nixon aide Roger Ailes and 1972 campaign staffer Roger Stone, Trump's campaign has acted as a spiritual cousin of sorts to Nixon's campaigns. "I think what Nixon understood is that when the world is falling apart, people want a strong leader whose highest priority is protecting America first," said Trump. He added, "The '60s were bad, really bad. And it's really bad now. Americans feel like it's chaos again." Just days before Trump's convention speech, his then campaign manager Paul J. Manafort specifically cited Nixon's 1968 RNC speech as a source of inspiration. "If you go back and read, that speech is pretty much on line with a lot of the issues that are going on today."[7] Trump's own speech unsurprisingly lacked the sophistication of Nixon's, who was able to balance doom and gloom politics with a healthy amount of optimism, but the campaign's willingness to make the comparison spoke volumes about the cultural connections between the two GOP icons.

While the more pragmatic wing of the GOP and certain liberal scholars have attempted to claim Nixon as their own, more polemical conservative figures such as Ann Coulter, a Trump supporter, have also recently publicly defended Nixon. Rather than distancing herself from Nixon's tarnished legacy, Coulter and others have depicted Nixon as the victim of a liberal conspiracy. At an event that was hosted by the Nixon Foundation in 2013 in the Nixon Library's replica of the White House's East Room, Coulter defended the president from his critics. Instead of lauding the president's positive accomplishments, Coulter distorted the record surrounding Nixon's relationship with the IRS. "For Nixon obsessives, liberals seem to know very little about his presidency. Nixon never had any of his enemies audited," argued Coulter, just yards away from the president's birthplace. Instead of focusing on the actions of George Shultz and Johnnie Walters, Coulter downplayed the president's orders and emphasized the actions of the Democratic Party.

> He went around the Oval Office fuming and saying you know they audited me when I was running for president. They, Democrats audited their enemies all the time. Oh, a tradition that has continued with both Clinton and now Obama. He, so OK, maybe he asked for his enemies to be audited, but you know he surrounded himself with good people and decent people and honest people who said I'm not auditing people for political reasons. No one was ever audited. Nixon himself was audited as president.[8]

Coulter's explanation of Nixon's enemies list project cynically manipulated the facts of the entire affair to portray the president as the victim. While she briefly mentioned the "decent people and honest people" who said no to Nixon during her speech, Coulter quickly gave the president credit for their actions, and misled attendees to believe that the White House did not engage in a prolonged effort to control the IRS. Nixon's repeated attempts to control the IRS were reduced to outbursts that went nowhere. At a higher level, Coulter, like other Nixon supporters, also bent over backward to situate Nixon's abuses of power alongside alleged wrongdoings of other modern presidents. If one is cynical enough about all presidents, even in a vague sense, then Nixon's crimes do not seem exceptional.

Coulter's explanation of the enemies list is even more astonishing in that it took place within close proximity of the Nixon Library's new Watergate exhibit, where visitors can learn about Nixon's attempts to audit his political opponents. The library may now include a nonpartisan take on Watergate, but Nixon's allies are still aggressively fighting the president's last campaign—the rehabilitation of his legacy. Rebranding the president as "RN", Nixon loyalists are repeating the themes of the 1968 campaign within the library's newly renovated museum galleries. With the approval and support of the National Archives, the exhibits depict the president as the man who saved the nation from the civil unrest of the 1960s. "It really sets the stage for what the president walked into," said the Nixon Foundation's current president William H. Baribault.[9] In 2016, at the opening ceremony of the renovated Nixon Library, the politics of the new galleries became a bit clearer. Referring to the library as "the President's Library," Nixon Foundation chairman Ronald H. Walker declared that the new exhibits "brought history alive" in a way that would "help shape the future." The event's final speaker was former governor of California Pete Wilson, a one-time advance man who worked for Nixon's failed gubernatorial campaign in 1962. Calling Nixon "a conservative reformer," Wilson argued that his former boss deserved a museum that defended his legacy, and not one that relied on critical historians. "God knows, the people who presume to tell us what it was all about had better study it carefully and be as dispassionate and fair and honest in their judgment as Bill Clinton was at his funeral."[10] It remains to be seen what happens to the Nixon Library, a facility that like all other presidential libraries is partially funded by taxpayer dollars. Based on recent events, it unfortunately appears likely that it will primarily remain as the geographical center of the rehabilitation of the nation's only president to resign from office.

Nixon supporters can be found across the cultural and political spectrum, but at the heart of the rehabilitation project are Nixon alums, men who are also fighting for their own legacies. Among these figures are individuals whose careers were ruined by Watergate, some by prison sentences they received for their roles in the cover-up. Depicting the president as a pragmatic, sometimes nonpartisan moderate who shielded the nation from civil unrest not only promotes Nixon's legacy, it validates their own time spent in the White House. During a reception to mark the hundredth birthday of Richard Nixon hosted by the Nixon Foundation, high-profile figures such as Pat Buchanan and Henry Kissinger joined other Nixon alums to collectively argue for a broader reevaluation of their former boss. The event was meant to act as the official beginning of the foundation's fundraising effort for the Nixon Library's renovation. It was also an emotional reunion for the administration officials who are still publicly defending Nixon. Former ideological adversaries within the White House, such as Buchanan and Kissinger, had settled their differences from the White House years to act as a united front against the president's critics. Improving their former boss's legacy, as well as their own, overrode any prior policy disputes. Buchanan, who was the only person to briefly mention Watergate during the reception, made sure to attack the press, whom he felt unfairly brought down "the old man." After calling present-day reporters who have asked him to talk about the Watergate scandal "the offspring of the old jackal pack," he quoted Nick Carraway from *The Great Gatsby*. "They were a rotten crowd, sir. You're worth the whole damn bunch put together." The room stood and applauded Nixon's former speechwriter, who ended the speech by proudly arguing, "Nixon, now more than ever!"[11]

In the short term, Nixon's culture of loyalty ultimately lost to a stronger culture of civil service that had shaped parts of the federal bureaucracy. While Nixon's culture was based on anger and cynicism, the moderates who opposed him inspired optimism among their staffs. They were not only well-respected civil servants, but also leaders who motivated others to take civil service seriously and see it as invaluable component of the nation's system of government. The stories of the Republicans who said no to Nixon further suggests that in the end, everything that encompassed what we know as Watergate led to a truly healthy, albeit fragile, response from our democratic institutions. The public's overwhelming opposition to Nixon that eventually forced his resignation was not based solely on partisan politics, but connected to a broader resistance to the president's unethical and illegal orders. This resistance to Nixon was present both inside and outside of the federal government. It was a rejection of Nixon's visions of a second term and it was partially built on the risks that administration officials took to prevent the president's abuses of power.

In light of recent events, it has also become apparent that the resistance to Nixon was deeply connected to the postwar liberal establishment that shaped much of the federal bureaucracy following the New Deal era. The nation's bureaucratic state has been significantly altered in recent decades, and its surviving strands have come under attack by the conservative movement. At a high-profile speech during the 2017 Conservative Political Action Conference (CPAC), then White House chief strategist Steve Bannon declared that the Trump administration would engage in a daily battle for the "deconstruction of the administrative state." The *Washington Post* reported that Bannon argued the postwar "political and economic consensus" was failing the American people and that it should be replaced with a new "system that empowers ordinary people over coastal elites and international institutions."[12] Bannon's nationalistic outlook bears little resemble to Nixon's internationalist foreign policy, but the two men are linked by their shared antipathy toward the liberal establishment and its influence on the federal government. It remains to be seen if today's GOP is at all connected to the ethical civil servants of a previous generation.

Since Trump's inauguration there has been steady stream of comparisons in the media between the current president and Nixon. The similarities between the two seemed especially prescient after Trump fired FBI director James Comey, the top official in charge of the criminal investigation into the president's ties with the Russian government during the 2016 election. Scores of reporters and columnists compared the controversial firing to the Saturday Night Massacre, another moment where a president was interested in blocking an independent investigation.[13] "Richard Nixon Also Fired the Person Investigating His Presidential Campaign" read one headline on Vox shortly after Comey's firing. However justifiable it may be to look back at Watergate to make sense of the present, it is absolutely essential to acknowledge the key differences between the two eras. The Republican Party of the Nixon era was much more ideologically diverse, and maintained a cultural space for those who did not share a Nixonian approach to politics. Trump's GOP may have its highly publicized internal battles, but it is mostly united behind a largely culturally based conservatism whose roots are in the Nixon era. Much like Nixon, Trump's brand of conservatism is primarily defined not by a coherent set of ideological principles, but by what he and his allies oppose. While Nixon felt compelled by the political climate of his era to include figures like Richardson in his administration, the Trump administration recently decided to remove Richardson's portrait from the Justice Department.[14] With the exception of a few outgoing senators, resistance to Trump within the GOP has been severely limited during the first year of his presidency. Without a strong nonpartisan culture, there is little support within the party for those who may be opposed to the current president.

It is worth noting that very few in 1972 would have expected resistance from Republicans in the Nixon administration. With the help of new archival records, we now know the full scope of their actions. George Shultz, Johnnie Walters, Kenneth Dam, William Morrill, Paul O'Neill, William Ruckelshaus, and Elliot Richardson all said no to the president because they were all fiercely dedicated to preserving a strong culture of nonpartisan civil service within the federal government. It was a culture that shaped their careers, and it is one that they felt was necessary to protect. While Nixon did not see any strength in the men who resisted his orders, their collective stand was powerful enough to block the president's attempts to institutionalize abuses of power. They chose integrity over loyalty, and as a result, Nixon was prevented from dramatically expanding his presidential powers. Nixon often complained that there were too many principled men in his administration, but there were also just enough "nice guys" to stop him from dramatically undermining constitutional democracy.

Notes

INTRODUCTION

1. Oval Office, 760–9, August 3, 1972, Richard Nixon Presidential Library and Museum, Yorba Linda, California (hereafter Nixon Library).

2. Evan Thomas, *Being Nixon: A Man Divided* (New York: Random House, 2015), 251.

3. There are multiple accounts of Senator Goldwater and Senator Scott's final meeting with President Nixon. For more information, see *New York Times,* "Nixon Slide from Power: Backers Gave Final Push," August 12, 1974, and Andrew Glass, "When the GOP Torpedoed Nixon," *Politico,* February 7, 2007.

4. July 3, 1971 meeting with George Shultz, James Hodgson, Julius Shiskin, and Charles Colson, Folder Bureau of Labor Statistics II 3 of 3, White House Special Files Charles Colson Box 40, Nixon Library; Oval Office, 801–4, October 17, 1972; Oval Office, 808–5, October 27, 1972, Nixon Library.

5. K. A. Cuordileone, *Manhood and American Political Culture in the Cold War* (New York: Routledge, 2004), 45, 183–86.

6. Rick Perlstein, "The Long Con: Mail Order Conservatism," *The Baffler,* no. 21 (2012).

7. Heather Hendershot, *Open to Debate: How William F. Buckley Put Liberal America on the Firing Line* (New York: Broadside Books, 2016), 219–29.

8. Oval Office, 836–9, January 9, 1973, Nixon Library.

9. Oval Office, 801–24/802–1, October 17, 1972, Nixon Library.

10. Timothy Weiner, *Enemies: A History of the FBI* (New York: Random House, 2012).

11. Beverly Gage, "Deep Throat, Watergate, and the Bureaucratic Politics of the FBI," *Journal of Policy History* 24, no. 2 (2012): 157–78.

12. Oval Office, 801–24/802–1, October 17, 1972, Nixon Library.

13. Justus D. Doenecke, "FDR's Sorry Domestic Spying Record," *Daily Beast,* May 10, 2015.

14. Tim Weiner, "JFK Turns to the C.I.A. to Plug a Leak," *New York Times,* July 1, 2017. Weiner's *Enemies* (cited above) and *Legacy of Ashes: The History of the* CIA (New York: Random House, 2007) offer up detailed accounts of the relationships between different presidents and the CIA/FBI.

15. There are numerous books on the conservative movement, too many to include in a single endnote, but these two represent different ways of studying the rise of the Right: Kim Phillips-Fein, *Invisible Hands: The Making of the Conservative Movement from the New Deal to Reagan* (New York: W.W. Norton, 2009); Lisa McGirr, *Suburban Warriors: The Origins of the New American Right* (Princeton, NJ: Princeton University Press, 2001).

16. Nicole Hemmer, *Messengers of the Right: Conservative Media and the Transformation of American Politics* (Philadelphia: University of Pennsylvania Press, 2016); Kevin Kruse, *One Nation under God: How Corporate America Invented Christian America* (New York: Basic Books, 2015); Jason Stahl: *Right Moves: The Conservative Think Tanks in American Political Culture since 1945* (Chapel Hill: University of North Carolina Press, 2016).

17. Cited in Stahl, *Right Moves,* 67.

18. Hemmer, *Messengers of the Right,* 227.

19. Geoffrey Kabaservice, *Rule and Ruin: The Downfall of Moderation and the Destruction of the Republican Party, From Eisenhower to the Tea Party* (Oxford: Oxford University Press, 2011), provides a comprehensive history of moderate Republicans during the 1960s and 1970s. Leah Wright Rigueur, *The Loneliness of the Black Republican: Pragmatic Politics and the Pursuit of Power* (Princeton, NJ: Princeton University Press, 2014), does not focus solely on liberal/moderate Republicans, but they do make up a large part of her history of the exchange between black leaders and the GOP.

20. Rick Perlstein, *Before the Storm: Barry Goldwater and the Unmaking of the American Consensus* (New York: Nation Books, 2001); Perlstein, *Nixonland: The Rise of a President and the Fracturing of America* (New York: Scribner, 2008); Perlstein, *The Invisible Bridge: The Fall of Nixon and the Rise of Reagan,* New York: Simon & Schuster, 2014).

21. All of the memoirs that were consulted for this project are included in the list of sources. However, it is worth mentioning that the literature surrounding Watergate—from Woodward and Bernstein's still valuable books on Watergate to the wide variety of books from former White House staffers to Nixon's own memoir—was and still is heavily shaped by first-person accounts of the scandal.

22. Stephen E. Ambrose, *Nixon* (New York: Simon & Schuster, 1990–91); Tom Wicker, *One of Us: Richard Nixon and the American Dream* (New York: Random House, 1991).

23. David Greenberg, *Nixon's Shadow: The History of an Image* (New York: W.W. Norton, 2003), 332.

24. Joan Hoff, *Nixon Reconsidered* (New York: Basic Books, 1994), 346.

25. Dean J. Kotlowski, *Nixon's Civil Rights: Politics, Principle, and Policy* (Cambridge, MA: Harvard University Press, 2002); Melvin Small, *The Presidency of Richard Nixon* (Lawrence: University Press of Kansas, 1999).

26. "The American Public's Attitudes about Richard Nixon Post-Watergate," Roper Center for Public Opinion Research, https://ropercenter.cornell.edu/the-american-publics-attitudes-about-nixon-post-watergate/.

27. This argument was made by many in the wake of the Iraq War, but it was explicitly laid out by John Dean in *Worse than Watergate: The Secret Presidency of George W. Bush* (New York: Little, Brown, 2004).

28. Federalist Papers Project, http://thefederalistpapers.org/us/meme-illustrates-difference-between-hillary-and-nixon.

29. Colbert once devoted an entire show to mark the fortieth anniversary of Nixon's resignation (August 4, 1974), which included interviews with Pat Buchanan and John Dean. Colbert explicitly defended Richard Nixon in an interview with Adam Sternberg, "Stephen Colbert Has America by the Ballots," *New York Magazine*, October 16, 2006. During the interview, he argued: "He was so liberal! Look at what he was running on. He started the EPA. He opened China. He gave 18-year-olds the vote. His issues were education, drugs, women, minorities, youth involvement, ending the draft, and improving the environment. John Kerry couldn't have run on this! What would I give for a Nixon?"

30. Thomas, *Being Nixon*, xiv.

31. Thomas, *Being Nixon*, 528–30.

32. Cited in Greenberg, *Nixon's Shadow*, 327.

33. Remarks were delivered during the "Watergate Reexamined" panel discussion at the Richard Nixon Symposium, Hofstra University, November 20, 1987. Video footage can be found on C-SPAN's website.

34. There are several books that deal with Watergate conspiracy theories, but the most popular one is Len Colodny and Robert Gettlin, *Silent Coup: The Removal of a President* (London: St. Martin's Press, 1991).

35. Richard Nixon Foundation, "The Vietnam War—Errors and Omissions," September 25, 2017.

36. Cited in John A. Farrell, *Richard Nixon: The Life* (New York: Doubleday, 2017), 358. The quote is from John Ehrlichman, Richard Nixon Library, Oral History, August 11, 1987.

37. Charles Colson, interview by Timothy Naftali, Naples, FL, August 17, 2007, Richard Nixon Oral History, Nixon Library.

38. Douglas Brinkley and Luke Nichter's two volumes of transcripts of taped conversations—*The Nixon Tapes: 1971–1972* (New York: Houghton & Mifflin, 2014) and *The Nixon Tapes: 1973* (New York: Houghton & Mifflin, 2015)—are both extremely useful, but there is a heavy emphasis on tapes that deal with foreign affairs, especially China and the Soviet Union, and covering the trajectory of the Watergate cover-up.

39. Ken Hughes, *Chasing Shadows: The Nixon Tapes, the Chennault Affair, and the Origins of Watergate* (Charlottesville: University of Virginia Press, 2014); Hughes, *Fatal Politics: The Nixon Tapes, the Vietnam War, and the Casualties of Reelection* (Charlottesville: University of Virginia Press, 2015); Timothy Weiner, *One Man against the World: The Tragedy of Richard Nixon* (New York: Henry Holt, 2015).

40. Farrell, *Richard Nixon*.

41. Peter Baker, "Nixon Tried to Spoil Johnson's Peace Talks in 68, Notes Show," *New York Times*, January 2, 1968.

42. Ken Hughes's two books on Nixon—*Chasing Shadows* and *Fatal Politics*—dive even deeper into the Chennault Affair.

43. See John Andrew, *Power to Destroy: The Political Uses of the IRS from Kennedy to Nixon* (Chicago: Ivan R. Dee, 2002); David Burnham, *A Law unto Itself: Power, Politics, and the IRS* (New York: Random House, 1989).

44. Margaret Pugh O'Mara, *Cities of Knowledge: Cold War Science and the Search for a New Silicon Valley* (Princeton, NJ: Princeton University Press, 2015).

45. Ken Gormley, *Archibald Cox: Conscience of a Nation* (Boston: Addison-Wesley, 1997).

46. During my time at the Nixon Library, Nixon Foundation employees/interns would often monitor the Nixon Library's school tours to pick up on any signs of anti-Nixon bias.

47. For more information about the Nixon Library and the Watergate Gallery, see Andrew Gumbel, "Nixon's Presidential Library: The Last Battle of Watergate," *Pacific Standard*, December 8, 2011.

48. For details regarding Mark Lawrence's candidacy, see Jeffrey Frank, "Who Owns Richard Nixon?" *New Yorker* May 20, 2014; Daniel Langhorne, "Nixon Library Left Leaderless as Foundation, Federal Officials Seek Common Ground," *Orange County Register*, May 11, 2014.

49. Martin Wisckol, "Nixon Library Chief Greeted with Relief, Dismay," *Orange County Register*, January 5, 2015.

50. More information on the Bureau of Labor Statistics order can be found in Timothy Noah, "Nixon's Jew Count: The Whole Story," *Slate*, September 26, 2007, and Noah, "Malek Talks," *Slate*, April 1, 2011. The latter cites Fred Malek, Nixon Library Oral History, Washington, DC, September 17, 2017.

51. Remarks were delivered at the Nixon Library on October 16, 2016. Footage can be found on C-SPAN.

52. The two are listed on the Nixon Foundation's 2016 Tax Statements (Form 990), which can be found on their website.

53. Remarks were delivered during Pat Buchanan's lecture at the Nixon Library on May 22, 2017. Footage can be found on C-SPAN.

54. Chris Woodyard, "Nixon Library Reboots for a New Generation," *USA Today*, November 11, 2016.

55. Chris Haire, "Nixon Library Opening Ceremony for Re-Imagined Galleries Draws Dignitaries, Crowds," *Orange County Register*, October 17, 2016.

56. David Whiting, "Remodeled Nixon Library Makes Peace with Its Past as It Becomes More Modern," *Orange County Register*, July 7, 2016.

1. "AN INDEPENDENT SON OF A BITCH"

1. This recording was released by the Nixon Library in 2011. White House Dictabelt Machine, #DB-480, August 29, 1972, Nixon Library.

2. Johnnie M. Walters, *Our Journey* (Macon, GA: Stroud & Hall, 2011), 79.

3. Oval Office, 498–15, May 13, 1971, Nixon Library.

4. Oval Office, 836–9, January 9, 1973, Nixon Library.

5. July 21, 1969 entry in H. R. Haldeman, *The Haldeman Diaries: Inside the Nixon White House* (New York: G. P. Putnam's Sons, 1994), 73.

6. Interview of Randolph Thrower, September 19, 1973, Folder Witness Statements: Randolph Thrower, Investigation of IRS Witness Statements, Plumbers Task Force Investigation of the Misuse of the Internal Revenue Service Box 1, Records of the Watergate Special Prosecution Force (WSPF), National Archives, College Park, MD.

7. David Burnham, *A Law unto Itself: The IRS and the Abuse of Power* (New York: Random House, 1989), 278.

8. Memorandum to President Nixon, written by Tom Charles Huston, "IRS to Take a Close Look at Activities of Left-wing Organizations Which Are Operating with Tax-exempt Fund," June 18, 1969, Folder FG 12–8 Internal Revenue Service [1969–1970], White House Special Files Confidential Files Box 18, Nixon Library.

9. Jerry Berman, Robert Borosage, and Christine Marwick, *The Lawless State: The Crimes of the U. S. Intelligence Agencies* (New York: Penguin Books, 1976), 198–201.

10. Memorandum to H. R. Haldeman, written by Tom Charles Huston, "IRS & Ideological Organizations Report on Activities of SSS Group," September 21, 1970, Folder Dean Exhibits 2nd, Plumbers Task Force Investigation of the Misuse of the Internal Revenue Service Box 19, Records of the WSPF.

11. Interview of Randolph Thrower, Records of the WSPF.

12. Interview of Randolph Thrower, Records of the WSPF.

13. Henry Hecht, "Procedural Arrangement for Disclosure from IRS," December 7, 1973, Folder Plumbers Task Force Investigation of IRS Planning and Coordination, Plumbers Task Force Investigation of the Misuse of the Internal Revenue Service Box 1, Records of the WSPF.

14. Mollenhoff defended his actions in John Andrew, *Power to Destroy: The Political Uses of the IRS from Kennedy to Nixon* (Chicago: Ivan R. Dee, 2002), 182.

15. Interview of Vernon Acree, July 20, 1973, Folder Acree, Vernon D. Plumbers Task Force Investigation of the Misuse of the Internal Revenue Service Box 2, Records of the WSPF.

16. Oval Office, 504–15, May 27, 1971, Nixon Library.

17. Letter to Jack Caulfield, written by John D. Ehrlichman, May 11, 1972, Folder Jack Caulfield, White House Special Files: White House Central Files—Alphabetical Name Files Box 1, Nixon Library.

18. Interview of Jack Caulfield, September 20, 1973, Folder Caulfield: Interviews and Testimony, Plumbers Task Force Investigation of the Misuse of the Internal Revenue Service Box 14, Records of the WSPF.

19. Letter to John D. Ehrlichman, written by Roger V. Barth, February 8, 1971, Folder IRS, White House Special Files John D. Ehrlichman Box 20, Nixon Library.

20. Andrew, *Power to Destroy*, 187.

21. Memorandum to H. R. Haldeman, written by John W. Dean III, "IRS," December 9, 1970, Folder Internal Revenue Service [Folder 2 of 2], White House Special Files John W. Dean Box 40, Nixon Library.

22. Memorandum to H. R. Haldeman, written by Fred Malek, "Proposed Actions Steps for Resolution of IRS Problem," Folder Internal Revenue Service [Folder 2 of 2], White House Special Files John W. Dean Box 40, Nixon Library.

23. Memorandum to John D. Ehrlichman, written by Jack Caulfield, "Myles Ambrose—IRS White House Office of Drug Abuse Law Enforcement," March 4, 1971, Folder IRS, White House Special Files John D. Ehrlichman Box 20, Nixon Library.

24. Memorandum to John D. Ehrlichman and John Mitchell, written by Fred Malek, "IRS Commissioner," March 8, 1971, Folder IRS, White House Special Files John D. Ehrlichman Box 20, Nixon Library.

25. Oval Office, 464–25, March 9, 1971, Nixon Library.

26. Johnnie M. Walters, interviewed by Timothy Naftali, Greeneville, South Carolina, October 18, 2008, Richard Nixon Oral History, Nixon Library; "8/6/71 Bio Sketch," Folder IRS Commissioner—General, Box 2, Johnnie M. Walters Papers, South Carolina Political Collections, University of South Carolina, Columbia, South Carolina.

27. John W. Dean III, phone interview with author, March 8, 2013.

28. Memorandum to John W. Dean III, written by Johnnie Walters, August 19, 1970; memorandum to Walters, written by Richard Stakem, August 21, 1970; memorandum to Walters, written by Dean, August 28, 1970; memorandum to Dean, written by Walters, September 9, 1970: Folder Correspondence File, General Correspondence, September 1–30, 1970, White House Special Files John W. Dean III Box 9, Nixon Library.

29. Nixon Library Oral History, 2008.

30. Executive Office Building, 247–4, April 13, 1971, Nixon Library.

31. Oval Office, 498–15, May 13, 1971, Nixon Library.

32. Oval Office, 504–15, May 27, 1971, Nixon Library.

33. Interview of Randolph Thrower, Records of the WSPF.

34. Interview of Fred Malek, Records of the WSPF.

35. Walters, *Our Journey*, 75.

36. Nixon Library Oral History, 2008. Johnnie M. Walters, "Note—Walters Recollection of Conversation with John D. Ehrlichman," June 4, 1971, Plumbers Task Force Investigation of the Misuse of the Internal Revenue Service Box 27, Records of the WSPF.

37. Johnnie M. Walters, "Note of Conversation with Malek and Connally," June 11, 1971, Plumbers Task Force Investigation of the Misuse of the Internal Revenue Service Box 27, Records of the WSPF.

38. Memorandum to John D. Ehrlichman, written by Tod Hullin, "Roger Barth and Johnnie Walters," June 16, 1971, Folder 12 May 1971 – 17 June 1971 [3 of 3], White House Special Files John D. Ehrlichman Box 57, Nixon Library.

39. Walters, *Our Journey*, 76.

40. Memorandum to White House, written by Roger Barth, August 26, 1971, Folder 8/26/71—Barth–Walters App. of Wm. Loeb as Dep Comm of IRS, Concerns Dem Control of IRS, Plumbers Task Force Investigation of the Misuse of the Internal Revenue Service Box 3, Records of the WSPF.

41. Memorandum to Bud Krogh, written by G. Gordon Liddy, "Charlie Walker," November 1, 1971, Folder White House Documents, Plumbers Task

Force Investigation of the Misuse of the Internal Revenue Service Box 12, Records of the WSPF.

42. Nixon Library Oral History, 2008.

43. Neil Sheehan, "Vietnam Archive: Pentagon Study Traces 3 Decades of Growing U.S. Involvement," *New York Times*, June 13, 1971.

44. 746–3 Oval Office Nixon, Haldeman, Kissinger, July 1, 1971

45. Meeting Notes, written by H.R. Haldeman, June 23, 1971, Folder H Notes April–June 1971 [May 20, 1971 to June 30, 1971] Part II, White House Special Files H.R. Haldeman Box 43, Nixon Library.

46. White House Telephone, 6–62, June 30, 1971, Nixon Library.

47. Dean, phone interview with author.

48. Memorandum to Bud Krogh, written by John W. Dean III, "Brookings Institution," July 27, 1971, Folder Internal Revenue Service [Folder 1 of 2], White House Special Files John W. Dean III, Nixon Library.

49. Dean's August 16, 1971 memorandum is attached to a memorandum to Haldeman, written by Gordon Strachan. "Dealing with Our Political Enemies," August 17, 1971, Folder Gordon Strachan August 1972, White House Special Files H.R. Haldeman Box 102, Nixon Library.

50. Interview of Larry Higby, August 6, 1973, Folder Witness Statements, Plumbers Task Force Investigation of the Misuse of the Internal Revenue Service Box 5, Records of the WSPF.

51. Executive Office Building, 274–44, September 8, 1971, Nixon Library.

52. Oval Office, 571–10, September 13, 1971, Nixon Library.

53. Oval Office, 572–8, September 14, 1971, Nixon Library.

54. John D. Ehrlichman's Notes of Meetings with the President, September 16, 1971, Folder 08–03–71 to 12–31–71 [2 of 5], White House Special Files John D. Ehrlichman Box 5, Nixon Library.

55. Memorandum to H.R. Haldeman, written by Gordon Strachan, December 1, 1971, Folder Internal Revenue Service [Folder 1 of 2], White House Special Files John W. Dean III Box 40, Nixon Library.

56. Memorandum to John Dean, written by Charles Colson, March 23, 1972, Memorandums to John Dean [1972], White House Special Files Charles Colson Box 7, Nixon Library.

57. Memorandum to H.R. Haldeman, written by William Safire. Included in August 18, 1970 memorandum to H.R. Haldeman, written by John Dean, August 18, 1970, Folder O'Brien, Lawrence: Public Affairs Analyst, Plumbers Task Force Investigation of the Misuse of the Internal Revenue Service Box 8, Records of the WSPF.

58. Memorandum to H.R. Haldeman, written by the President, January 14, 1971, Folder Jan–Feb 71 White House Interest, Plumbers Task Force Investigation of the Misuse of the Internal Revenue Service Box 8, Records of the WSPF

59. Mark Feldstein, *Poisoning the Press: Richard Nixon, Jack Anderson, and the Rise of Washington's Scandal Culture* (New York: Farrar, Strauss and Giroux, 2010), 291–93.

60. Johnnie Walters, June 18, 1974 affidavit about Larry O'Brien, Folder House Judiciary Committee, 1974, Affidavits and Interviews, Walters Papers Box 2, University of South Carolina.

61. Nixon Library Oral History, 2008.

62. Recollections of interview with Gary Sutton of the HJC—Friday May 10, 1974, Folder House Judiciary Committee, 1974, Affidavits and Interviews, Walters Papers Box 2, University of South Carolina.

63. Jay Horowitz, "Summary of O'Brien Case," Folder O'Brien, Lawrence, Plumbers Task Force Investigation of the Misuse of the Internal Revenue Service Box 9, Records of the WSPF.

64. Oval Office, 760–9, August 3, 1972, Nixon Library.

65. George P. Shultz, *Turmoil and Triumph: My Years as Secretary of State* (New York: Scribner, 1993), 23–31.

66. George P. Shultz, interviewed by Timothy Naftali, Stanford, CA, May 10, 2007, Richard Nixon Oral History, Nixon Library.

67. Nixon Library Oral History, 2007.

68. George P. Shultz, interviewed by Henry L. Hecht, April 9, 1974, Folder Witness Files: Shultz, Plumbers Task Force Investigation of the Misuse of the Internal Revenue Service Box 25, Records of the WSPF.

69. Johnnie M. Walters, interviewed by Henry L. Hecht, January 15, 1974, Folder Johnnie M. Walters 1 of 2 Plumbers Task Force Investigation of the Misuse of the Internal Revenue Service Box 26, Records of the WSPF.

70. "Summary of O'Brien Case," Records of the WSPF.

71. Memorandum to Ron Brooks, written by Tod Hullin, "Roger Barth's Interest in Post of Deputy General Counsel," July 20, 1972, Folder 16 June 1972 – 10 August 1972 [2 of 4], White House Special Files John D. Ehrlichman Box 61, Nixon Library.

72. Executive Office Building, 353–18, August 3, 1972, Nixon Library.

73. Oval Office, 763–15, August 7, 1972, Nixon Library.

74. "Summary of O'Brien Case," Records of the WSPF.

75. Oval Office, 767–16, August 11, 1972, Nixon Library.

76. Oval Office, 766–2, August 10, 1972, Nixon Library.

77. Memorandum of interview with O'Brien, August 17, 1972, Folder O'Brien, Lawrence: 8/17/72 O'Brien Interview, Plumbers Task Force Investigation of the Misuse of the Internal Revenue Service Box 8, Records of the WSPF.

78. Camp David Study Desk, 176–10, August 19, 1972, Nixon Library.

79. August 27, 1972 entry in Haldeman, *Haldeman Diaries*, 499.

80. Ehrlichman/Barth telephone conversation, August 28, 1972, Folder O'Brien, Lawrence: Investigation of IRS Witness Statements, Plumbers Task Force Investigation of the Misuse of the Internal Revenue Service Box 8, Records of the WSPF.

81. White House Dictabelt Machine, #DB-480, August 29, 1972, Nixon Library.

82. Oval Office, 772–6, September 7, 1972, Nixon Library.

83. "Summary of O'Brien Case," Records of the WSPF.

84. George P. Shultz, interviewed by Henry L. Hecht, April 9, 1974, Folder Witness Files: Shultz, Plumbers Task Force Investigation of the Misuse of the Internal Revenue Service Box 25, Records of the WSPF.

85. Walters, *Our Journey*, 84.

86. Jay Horowitz, "Legal Research on the Legal Violations Constituted by Politically Motivated Audits by the Internal Revenue Service," November 6, 1973, Folder Enemies List: Legal and Factual Analysis, Plumbers Task Force Investigation of the Misuse of the Internal Revenue Service Box 5, Records of the WSPF.

87. 1973–74—Hearings Investigation into Certain Charges of the Use of the Internal Revenue Service for Political Purposes Prepared by the Joint Com[mittee] on Internal Revenue Taxation by Its Staff, December 20, 1973, Folder IRS (Enemies) Committee Reports, White House Central Files J. Fred Buzhardt Box 22, Nixon Library; Johnnie M. Walters's recollection of April 29, 1974 interview with the House Judiciary Committee, April 30, 1974, Folder House Judiciary Committee, 1974, Affidavits and Interviews, Walters Papers Box 2. University of South Carolina.

88. Johnnie M. Walters, affidavit to House of Representatives of the United States Committee on the Judiciary, May 6, 1974, Folder House Judiciary Committee, 1974, Affidavits and Interviews, Walters Papers, University of South Carolina.

89. Nixon Library Oral History, 2008.

90. Letter to Dr. Laurence N. Woodworth, written by Johnnie M. Walters, July 11, 1973, Folder Watergate Public—Watergate Investigation 1973, Walters Papers Box 2, University of South Carolina; Johnnie M. Walters' Notes of Meeting with John W. Dean III, September 11, 1972, Folder Walters, Johnnie Walters Originals, Plumbers Task Force Investigation of the Misuse of the Internal Revenue Service Box 27, Records of the WSPF.

91. Walters's notes of September 11, 1972 meeting, Records of the WSPF; meeting with Dean and Walters affidavit, May 6, 1974, Folder House Judiciary Committee, 1974, Affidavits and Interviews, Walters Papers Box 2, University of South Carolina.

92. Nixon Library Oral History, 2007.

93. Walters, *Our Journey,* 80–81.

94. Oval Office, 780–7, September 16, 1972, Nixon Library.

95. All references to September 15 conversation are from Oval Office, 779–2, September 15, 1972, Nixon Library.

96. Walters, *Our Journey,* 103.

97. Nixon Library Oral History, 2008.

98. Recollections of interview with House Judiciary Committee, April 29, 1974, Folder House Judiciary Committee, 1974, Affidavits and Interviews, Walters Papers Box 2, University of South Carolina; Johnnie M. Walters' Notes of Meeting with George P. Shultz, September 29, 1972, Folder Walters, Johnnie— Meetings with Treasury Secretary, Plumbers Task Force Investigation of the Misuse of the Internal Revenue Service Box 28, Records of the WSPF.

99. Nixon Library Oral History, 2007.

100. Camp David Hard Wire, 224–1, November 13, 1972, Nixon Library.

101. Executive Office Building, 391–5, November 1, 1972, Nixon Library.

102. Camp David Hard Wire, 225–39, November 16, 1972, Nixon Library.

103. Jack Rosenthal, "Lawyer Slated to Be IRS Chief," *New York Times,* December 24, 1972, 25.

104. Andrew, *Power to Destroy,* 197.

105. Memorandum to H. R. Haldeman, written by Charles Colson, November 13, 1970, Folder Dean Exhibits—Submitted by Colson, Plumbers Task Force Investigation of the Misuse of the Internal Revenue Service Box 19, Records of the WSPF.

106. White House Telephone, 33–108, November 19, 1972, Nixon Library.

107. Camp David Study Table, 155–17, November 20, 1972, Nixon Library.

108. Camp David Hard Wire, 234–10, December 7, 1972, Nixon Library.

109. Executive Office Building, 385–30, December 13, 1972, Nixon Library.

110. White House Telephone, 34–92, December 15, 1972, Nixon Library.

111. Memorandum to the President, written by Fred V. Malek, January 26, 1973, Folder IRS: White House Documents Plumbers Task Force Investigation of the Misuse of the Internal Revenue Service Box 12, Records of the WSPF.

112. Oval Office, 853–12, February 8, 1973, Nixon Library.

113. Oval Office, 854–17, February 13, 1973, Nixon Library.

114. Oval Office, 838–19, January 11, 1973, Nixon Library.

115. Oval Office, 836–9, January 9, 1973, Nixon Library.

116. Memorandum to John D. Ehrlichman, written by Tod R. Hullin, "Commissioner—IRS," January 17, 1973, Folder 2 January 1973 – 31 January 1973 [3 of 5], White House Special Files John D. Ehrlichman, Nixon Library.

117. Oval Office, 854–17, February 13, 1973, Nixon Library.

118. Executive Office Building, 410–14, February 13, 1973, Nixon Library.

119. Oval Office, 871–4, March 7, 1973, Nixon Library.

120. David Cay Johnston, "Donald C. Alexander, 87, Who Resisted Nixon at I. R. S. Is Dead," *New York Times,* February 8, 2009, A21.

121. Memorandum to George. P Shultz, written by Johnnie M. Walters, February 23, 1973, Folder Meetings with Treasury Secretary, Plumbers Task Force Investigation of the Misuse of the Internal Revenue Service Box 28, Records of the WSPF; Executive Office Building, 420–11, March 16, 1973, Nixon Library. The president met with John D. Ehrlichman. During the conversation, Ehrlichman brought up the Hughes investigation. Ehrlichman told the president that they wanted to wait until they have a new commissioner. "We are going to hold off until Alexander is in place."

122. Letter to the President, written by Johnnie M. Walters, March 5, 1973; letter to Johnnie M. Walters, written by George P. Shultz, April 23, 1973, Folder Resignations—1972–73, Walters Papers Box 2, University of South Carolina.

123. Nixon Library Oral History, 2008.

124. Douglas Martin, "Johnnie M. Walters, IRS Chief Who Resisted Nixon's Pressure, Dies at 94," *New York Times,* June 26, 2014.

125. Johnnie M. Walters, affidavit to House of Representatives of the United States Committee on the Judiciary, May 6, 1974, Folder House Judiciary Committee, 1974, Affidavits and Interviews, Walters Papers Box 2, University of South Carolina.

126. Walters, *Our Journey,* 81.

127. Walters, affidavit, May 6, 1974, Folder House Judiciary Committee, 1974, Affidavits and Interviews Walters Papers Box 2, University of South Carolina.

128. NBC Nightly News, "Evidence Shows IRS Resisted Efforts at Misuse," July 16, 1974; CBS Morning News, "Evidence Shows IRS Resisted White House Politicization," July 16, 1974.

129. Bob Kuttner, "White House Pressure on IRS Detailed," *Washington Post,* July 17, 1974, 1.

130. Walters, *Our Journey,* 82.

131. Nixon to Haig, July 7, 1973, Nixon Project WHSF, Pres. Personal File, Box 4, Folder Memos—July 1973, NA.

132. Richard Nixon, interviewed by Frank Gannon, New York, NY, June 10, 1983, Walter J. Brown Archives and Peabody Awards Collection, University of Georgia, Athens, GA.

133. Oval Office, 836–9, January 9, 1973, Nixon Library.

2. "THERE'S NO BASIS IN LAW TO CARRY OUT THIS ORDER . . . AND WE'RE NOT GOING TO DO IT"

1. This recording was released by the Nixon Library in 2011. White House Dictabelt Machine, #DB-075, May 13, 1970, Nixon Library.

2. White House Dictabelt Machine, #DB-076 May 13, 1970, Nixon Library.

3. Oval Office, 822–12, December 13, 1972, Nixon Library.

4. Memorandum to the President, written by Caspar Weinberger, "Federal Aid to Higher Education—Response to Your Questions of February 10, February 13, 1973," Folder February 1–15, 1973, President's Office Files Box 20, Nixon Library.

5. December 1, 1972 entry in H.R. Haldeman, *The Haldeman Diaries: Inside the Nixon White House* (New York: G.P. Putnam's Sons, 1994), 665.

6. Oval Office, 823–1, December 14, 1972, Nixon Library.

7. For more on Nixon's complex relationship with Kissinger, see Robert Dallek, *Nixon and Kissinger: Partners in Power* (New York: HarperCollins, 2007); Richard Reeves, *President Nixon: Alone in the White House* (New York: Simon & Schuster, 2002).

8. Greg Grandin, *Kissinger's Shadow: The Long Reach of America's Most Controversial Statesman* (New York: Metropolitan Books, 2015), 81.

9. Oval Office, 819–2, December 11, 1972, Nixon Library.

10. 821–1, Oval Office, December 12, 1972, Nixon Library.

11. Richard Nixon, *RN: The Memoirs of Richard Nixon* (New York: Simon & Schuster, 1978), 14–15.

12. Oval Office, 819–2, December 11, 1972, Nixon Library.

13. Oval Office, 822–12, December 13, 1972, Nixon Library.

14. Oval Office, 938–3, June 12, 1973, Nixon Library.

15. May 4, 1970, Folder May 1–5, 1970 (1 of 2), Box 5, Kissinger Telephone Conversation Transcripts, Nixon Library.

16. May 5, 1970, Folder May 1–5, 1970 (1 of 2), Box 5, Kissinger Telephone Conversation Transcripts, Nixon Library.

17. May 6, 1970, Folder May 6–9, 1970 (1 of 2), Box 5, Kissinger Telephone Conversation Transcripts, Nixon Library.

18. May 7, 1970, Folder May 6–9, 1970 (1 of 2), Box 5, Kissinger Telephone Conversation Transcripts, Nixon Library.

19. May 5, 1970, Folder May 1–5, 1970 (1 of 2), Box 5, Kissinger Telephone Conversation Transcripts, Nixon Library.

20. May 12, 1970, Folder May 10–20, 1970, Box 5, Kissinger Telephone Conversation Transcripts, Nixon Library.

21. Memorandum to Henry Kissinger, written by Winston Lord, "Reply to Anti-War Harvard Professors," August 21, 1971, Folder Students/Academia (2 of 2), Henry Kissinger Office Files Box 16, Nixon Library.

22. Memorandum to H. R. Haldeman, written by William Safire, "Q and A on Shultz," June 10, 1970, Folder EX FG 6–16 Office of Management and Budget 5/26/70–6/30/70, White House Central Files Subject Files FG–Federal Government–Organization (FG 6–16) OMB, Nixon Library.

23. Oval Office, 481–4, April 17, 1971, Nixon Library.

24. William A. Morrill, *A Journey through Governance: A Public Servant's Experience under Six Presidents* (New York: Cosimo Books, 2013), 4–43.

25. William Morrill, phone interview with author, June 3, 2015.

26. Morrill, phone interview with author.

27. Ron Suskind, *The Price of Loyalty: George W. Bush, the White House, and the Education of Paul O'Neill* (New York: Simon & Schuster, 2004), 10.

28. Elliot Richardson, *Reflections of a Radical Moderate* (New York: Pantheon, 1996), 97.

29. Oval Office, 572–15, September 14, 1971, Nixon Library.

30. Suskind, *Price of Loyalty*, 10.

31. Morrill, phone interview with author.

32. Suskind, *Price of Loyalty*, 167.

33. Memorandum to Caspar Weinberger, written by John Ehrlichman, June 26, 1972, Folder EX FG 6–16 Office of Management and Budget 6/16/72–6/30/72, WHCF Subject Files FG—Federal Government—Organizations (FG 6–16) OMB Box 1, Nixon Library.

34. Oval Office, 836–9, January 9, 1973, Nixon Library.

35. Memorandum to the President, written by Ed Harper, "Federal Funds for MIT and University of California," June 28, 1971, Folder President's Handwriting June 21–30, 1971, White House Special Files President's Office Files Box 12, Nixon Library.

36. Margaret Pugh O'Mara, *Cities of Knowledge: Cold War Science and the Search for the Next Silicon Valley* (Princeton, NJ: Princeton University Press, 2004), 27.

37. "Welcome to the Little Pentagon," Folder Flyers Passed Out 1971–1972, Jerome Wiesner Papers (AC 8) Box 96, Massachusetts Institute of Technology Libraries: Institute Archives and Special Collections, Cambridge, MA.

38. "Pentagonitis at MIT," *Sunday Providence Journal*, January 26, 1969.

39. William F. Buckley Jr., "What's behind March 4-MIT?" *Los Angeles Times*, February 17, 1969.

40. Dorothy Nelkin, "Moral Politics and University Research: MIT and the Instrumentation Library," Folder Draper Laboratory February 1970–July

1972, Jerome Wiesner Papers (AC 8) Box 195, MIT Libraries: Institute Archives and Special Collections.

41. Notes from December 16, 1969 faculty meeting and February 6, 1970 notes for February 11, 1970 faculty meeting, Folder Faculty Meetings (January–March 1970), Jerome Wiesner Papers (AC 8) Box 45, MIT Libraries: Institute Archives and Special Collections.

42. Spring 1970 Faculty Strike Resolution, Folder Spring Student Strike 1970, Jerome Wiesner Papers (AC 8) Box 97, MIT Libraries: Institute Archives and Special Collections.

43. Howard Wesley Johnson and Jerome Wiesner, Note to Faculty, May 4, 1970, Folder Spring Student Strike 1970, Jerome Wiesner Papers (AC 8) Box 97, MIT Libraries: Institute Archives and Special Collections.

44. Nelkin, "Moral Politics and University Research."

45. Michael Albert, "Second Pentagon," Folder Fliers Passed Out 1971–1972, Jerome Wiesner Papers (AC 8) Box 96, MIT Libraries: Institute Archives and Special Collections.

46. Memorandum to John Ehrlichman, written by Jon Huntsman, "University Security Clearances," July 3, 1971, Folder President's Handwriting June 21–30, 1971, White House Special Files President's Office Files Box 12, Nixon Library.

47. Memorandum to John Ehrlichman, written by Pat Buchanan, July 8, 1971, Folder President's Handwriting June 21–30, 1971, White House Special Files President's Office Files Box 12, Nixon Library.

48. John Ehrlichman, July 9, 1971, Folder JDE Notes of Meetings with the President, White House Special Files John D. Ehrlichman Box 11, Nixon Library.

49. MIT News Office, "Assault on the ROTC Building," May 12, 1972, *Tech Talk* vol. 16, no. 45 (special issue), May 15, 1972, Folder Student Unrest 1971–1972 (ROTC Occupation), Jerome Wiesner Papers (AC 8) Box 97; and student flier that describes 1972 graduation ceremony, May 1972, Folder Faculty Meeting–Special (May 12, 1972), Jerome Wiesner Papers (AC 8) Box 46, MIT Libraries: Institute Archives and Special Collections.

50. Thursday MIT's Independent Community Paper, "Schedule of Rallies," April 27, 1972, Folder Faculty Meeting (January–April 1970); Notes of May 12, 1972 Faculty Meeting, Folder Faculty Meeting–Special (May 12, 1972), Jerome Wiesner Papers (AC 8) Box 46, MIT Libraries: Institute Archives and Special Collections.

51. *Tech Talk*, vol. 16, no. 45 (special issue), May 15, 1972, Folder Student Unrest 1971–1972 (ROTC Occupation), Jerome Wiesner Papers (AC 8) Box 97, MIT Libraries: Institute Archives and Special Collections.

52. Oval Office, 720–7, May 5, 1972, Nixon Library.

53. Oval Office, 720–19, May 5, 1972, Nixon Library.

54. May 11, 1972, Folder Telephone Conversations—Chron Files 9–11 May 1972, Box 14, Kissinger Telephone Conversation Transcripts, Nixon Library.

55. Executive Office Building, 339–3, May 15, 1972, Nixon Library.

56. Camp David Hard Wire, 191–18, May 18, 1972, Nixon Library.

57. Caspar Weinberger Appointment Diary Entry, April 20, 1972, Folder—Appointment + Diary Files Diary Notes April–June 1972, Box 220, Caspar Weinberger Papers, Library of Congress (Washington, DC).

58. Caspar Weinberger Appointment Diary Entry, April 24, 1972, Folder—Appointment + Diary Files Diary Notes April–June 1972, Box 220, Caspar Weinberger Papers, Library of Congress (Washington, DC).

59. Caspar Weinberger Appointment Diary Entry, May 1, 1972 Folder—Appointment + Diary Files Diary Notes April–June 1972, Box 220, Caspar Weinberger Papers, Library of Congress (Washington, DC).

60. Caspar Weinberger Appointment Diary Entry, May 5, 1972, Folder—Appointment + Diary Files Diary Notes April–June 1972, Box 220, Caspar Weinberger Papers, Library of Congress (Washington, DC).

61. Caspar Weinberger Appointment Diary Entry, May 8, 1972, Folder—Appointment + Diary Files Diary Notes April–June 1972, Box 220, Caspar Weinberger Papers, Library of Congress (Washington, DC).

62. Memorandum to President Nixon, written by Caspar Weinberger, "Federal Support of MIT," May 5, 1972, Folder—Education, Higher 1972, Box 263, Caspar Weinberger Papers, Library of Congress (Washington, DC).

63. Morrill, phone interview with author.

64. Camp David Study Table, 131–040, Thursday, May 18, 1972, Nixon Library; May 18, 1972 entry in Haldeman, *Haldeman Diaries,* Nixon Library Research Room Copy.

65. Oval Office, May 19, 1972, Nixon Library.

66. Oval Office, 724–5, May 15, 1972, Nixon Library.

67. Oval Office, 746–16, July 1, 1972, Nixon Library.

68. Memorandum to President Nixon, written by Caspar Weinberger, "MIT," August 25, 1972, Folder Pres. Handwriting August 1972, President's Office Files Box 18, Nixon Library.

69. White House Telephone, 33–108, November, 19, 1972, Nixon Library.

70. Oval Office, 819–2, December 11, 1972, Nixon Library.

71. Cabinet Room, 100–1, May 5, 1972, Nixon Library.

72. Oval Office, 798–15, October 14, 1972, Nixon Library.

73. Oval Office, 768–24, August 14, 1972, Nixon Library.

74. Oval Office, 865–28, February 28, 1973, Nixon Library.

75. Memorandum to Charles Colson and Pat Buchanan, written by Larry Higby, December 15, 1972, Folder Lawrence Higby December 1972, White House Special Files H.R. Haldeman Box 106, Nixon Library.

76. Oval Office, 815–19, November 24, 1972, Nixon Library.

77. Executive Office Building, 382–2, December 16, 1972, Nixon Library.

78. "William Bundy Left MIT in 1972 to Teach at Princeton," MIT News Office, October 15, 1972, Folder MIT News Office, Jerome Wiesner Papers Box 96 (AC 8), MIT Libraries: Institute Archives and Special Collections.

79. Memorandum to John D. Ehrlichman and Kenneth Cole, written by President Nixon, December 28, 1972, Folder President's Handwriting December 16–31, 1972, President's Office Files Box 20, Nixon Library.

80. Oval Office, 833–10, January 4, 1973, Nixon Library.

81. Oval Office, 833–10, January 4, 1973, Nixon Library.

82. Oval Office, 833–21(a), January 4, 1973, Nixon Library.

83. Oval Office, 842–13, January 25, 1973, Nixon Library.

84. Caspar Weinberger, Appointment Diary Entry, January 29, Folder—Appointment + Diary Files Diary Notes January–April 1973, Box 315, Caspar Weinberger Papers, Library of Congress (Washington, DC).

85. Note to H.R. Haldeman, written by Caspar Weinberger, February 13, 1973, Folder February 1–15 1973, President's Office Files Box 20, Nixon Library.

86. Memorandum to President Nixon, written by Caspar Weinberger, "Federal Aid to Higher Education—Response to Your Questions of February 10," February 12, 1973, Folder February 1–15 1973, President's Office Files Box 20, Nixon Library.

87. Memorandum to Caspar Weinberger, written by the White House, "Your Memorandum on Federal Aid for Higher Education," Folder February 1–15 1973, President's Office Files Box 20, Nixon Library.

88. *Higher Education and National Affairs*, vol. 22, no. 2, January 12, 1973. Found in Folder Federal Aid to Higher Education, Paul Gray Papers Box 82 (AC 397), MIT Libraries: Institute Archives and Special Collections.

89. Paul H. O'Neill, interviewed by Timothy Naftali, Nixon Library, Pittsburgh, PA, September 21, 2007, Richard Nixon Library Oral History, Nixon Library.

90. Morrill, *Journey through Governance*, 41.

91. Morrill, phone interview with author.

92. O'Neill, Nixon Library Oral History, 2007; Morrill, *Journey through Governance*, 41–42.

93. Nixon Library Oral History, 2007.

94. Oval Office, 884–7, March 20, 1973, Nixon Library.

95. Cabinet Room, 118–1, March 13, 1973, Nixon Library.

96. Oval Office, 941–2, June 14, 1973, Nixon Library.

97. Suskind, *Price of Loyalty*, 169.

98. Memorandum to President Ford, "Spending Actions," February 7, 1975, Folder 1–7 February 1975, Paul H. O'Neill Papers Box 1, Gerald Ford Presidential Library and Museum, Ann Arbor, MI.

99. Nixon Library Oral History, 2007.

100. Morrill, *Journey through Governance*, 41.

101. Morrill, phone interview with author.

102. Morrill, *Journey through Governance*, 154–55.

103. "Caspar W. Weinberger Dies at 88," *New York Times*, March 28, 2006; Neil A. Lewis, "Nixon Tape Shows Vendetta of '72," *New York Times*, May 18, 1993.

3. "GET HIM THE HELL OUT OF HEW"

1. Camp David Hard Wire, 224–15, November 14, 1972, Nixon Library.

2. Oval Office, 791–2, October 3, 1972, Nixon Library.

3. White House Telephone, 45–48, April 30, 1973, Nixon Library.

4. John Thomas Smith II, phone interview with author, July 19, 2013.

5. John Herbers, "Richardson, after Year on Job, Hailed for Ending Chaos at HEW," *New York Times*, June 9, 1971, 22.

6. Richard Nixon, *RN: The Memoirs of Richard Nixon* (New York: Simon & Schuster, 1978), 969.

7. Nixon, *RN*, 1004.

8. Geoffrey Kabaservice, *The Guardians: Kingman Brewster, His Circle, and the Rise of the Liberal Establishment* (New York: Henry Holt, 2004), 33.

9. The District of Columbia Bar, "Legends in the Law: A Conversation with Elliot L. Richardson," *DC Bar Report*, February/March 1995.

10. Neil A. Lewis, "Elliot Richardson Dies at 79; Stood Up to Nixon and Resigned in 'Saturday Night Massacre'," *New York Times*, January 1, 2000, B7.

11. Ken Gormley, *Archibald Cox: Conscience of a Nation* (Boston: Addison-Wesley, 1997), 87.

12. Elliot Richardson, interviewed by Richard L. Holzhausen, Ann Arbor, MI, April 25, 1997, Gerald R. Ford Oral History Project, Gerald R. Ford Presidential Library.

13. Jonathan Aitken, *Nixon: A Life* (Washington, DC: Regnery, 1993), 265.

14. District of Columbia Bar, "Legends in the Law."

15. "Elliot Richardson, "Special to the *New York Times*," *New York Times*, October 12, 1973, 27.

16. Elliot Richardson, *Reflections of a Radical Moderate* (New York: Pantheon, 1996), 141.

17. Jonathan Moore, interview with author, Cambridge, MA, May 22, 2012.

18. Hedrick Smith, "Rogers Picks Bostonian to Be His Chief Deputy: Rogers Picks Top Aid for State Department Team," *New York Times*, January 1, 1969, 1.

19. Moore, interview with author.

20. Jonathan Moore "Miscellaneous Staff Items," March 1, 1969, Folder Personnel General 2, Box I: 100, Elliot L. Richardson Papers, Library of Congress (Washington, DC).

21. January 29, 1970, Nixon, Richard M., Box I: 99, Elliot L. Richardson Papers.

22. Christopher Lydon, "The Choice for H.E.W.: Elliot Lee Richardson," *New York Times*, June 8, 1970, 44.

23. April 29, 1970, Folder April 27–30 1970, Box 5, Kissinger Telephone Conversation Transcripts, Nixon Library.

24. Robert B. Semple Jr., "Nixon Sends Combat Forces to Cambodia," *New York Times*, May 1, 1970, 1.

25. May 2, 1970, Folder Telephone Conversations Chron. File 1–5 May 1970 (1 of 2), Box 5, Kissinger Telephone Conversation Transcripts, Nixon Library.

26. Moore, interview with author.

27. Kabaservice, *Guardians*, 424.

28. Feis—Richardson Papers Box 92 Folder–"F" Misc., May 27, 1970 Letter to Herbert Feis.

29. Interview with Elliot Richardson, May 10, 1970 episode of *Issues and Answers* (ABC Radio, 1960–81).

30. Kathleen Teltsch, "U.S. Official's Plea on Peace Stirs U.N. Interest," *New York Times,* May 3, 1970, 1.

31. May 11, 1970, Folder Nixon, Richard M. Correspondence and Miscellany, Box I: 14, Elliot L. Richardson Papers.

32. Herbers, "Richardson, after Year on Job," 22.

33. Leon Panetta, *Bring Us Together: The Nixon and the Civil Rights Retreat* (Philadelphia: Lippincott, 1971), 368–69.

34. Herbers, "Richardson, after Year on Job," 22.

35. Moore, interview with author; Paul Delaney, "Richardson Firmly in Charge at Health, Education, and Welfare after 6 Months," *New York Times,* November 22, 1970, 77.

36. Jonathan Moore, interviewed by Timothy Naftali, Cambridge, MA, February 11, 2008, Richard Nixon Oral History, Nixon Library.

37. November 1, 1971 entry in H.R. Haldeman, *The Haldeman Diaries: Inside the Nixon White House* (New York: G.P. Putnam's Sons, 1994), 370.

38. Richardson, *Reflections of a Radical Moderate,* 136.

39. Delaney, "Richardson Firmly in Charge," 77.

40. "H.E.W. Chief Vows Integration Push: Richardson Warns Southern Schools of Funds Cut Off," *New York Times,* June 26, 1970, 32.

41. April 20, 1971 entry in Haldeman, *Haldeman Diaries,* 276.

42. James M. Naughton, "Nixon Disavows H.E.W. Proposal on School Busing," *New York Times,* August 4, 1971, 1.

43. Annotated news summary, January 18, 1972, Action Memo-P-1986, Box 50, Staff Secretary Files, Nixon Library.

44. July 13, 1970 entry in Haldeman, *Haldeman Diaries,* 181.

45. Patrick J. Buchanan, *Nixon's White House Wars: The Battles That Made and Broke a President and Divided America Forever* (New York: Crown Forum, 2017), 234.

46. Dean J. Kotlowski, *Nixon's Civil Rights: Politics, Principle, and Policy* (Cambridge, MA: Harvard University Press, 2002), 249.

47. John Ehrlichman, *Witness to Power: The Nixon Years* (New York: Simon & Schuster, 1982), 116.

48. Smith, phone interview with author.

49. Letter from Nixon to Richardson, February 19, 1971, Folder Nixon, Richard M. Correspondence and Miscellany, Box I: 14, Elliot L. Richardson Papers.

50. Nixon Library Oral History, 2008.

51. Richard Lyons, "Richardson Says He'll Fight Cuts," *New York Times,* December 18, 1971, 22.

52. Kotlowski, *Nixon's Civil Rights,* 153.

53. Oval Office, 791–2, October 3, 1972, Nixon Library.

54. Camp David Hard Wire, 225–39, November 16, 1972, Nixon Library.

55. White House Telephone, 33–108, November 19, 1972, Nixon Library.

56. Camp David Hard Wire, 226–24, November 18, 1972, Nixon Library.

57. Oval Office, 819–2, December 11, 1972, Nixon Library.

58. Oval Office, 864–9, February 27, 1973, Nixon Library.

59. Caspar Weinberger, *In the Arena: A Memoir of the 20th Century* (Washington, DC: Regnery, 2001), 217

60. Oval Office, 824–3, December 15, 1972, Nixon Library.

61. White House Telephone, 33–108 November 19, 1972, Nixon Library.

62. Executive Office Building, 384–4, December 10, 1972, Nixon Library.

63. Oval Office, 822–11, December 13, 1972, Nixon Library.

64. Oval Office, 833–10(b), January 4, 1973, Nixon Library.

65. "Memorandum for the President," written by Elliot Richardson, January 8, 1973, Folder Moore, Jonathan, Box I: 143, Elliot L. Richardson Papers.

66. Oval Office, 837–4, January 10, 1973, Nixon Library.

67. Moore, interview with author.

68. Moore, interview with author.

69. Richard Lyons, "Shakeups Are Part of Drive to Streamline H.E.W.," *New York Times*, December 19, 1972, 21.

70. White House Telephone, 45–32, April 26, 1973, Nixon Library.

71. Camp David Study Table, 164–10, April 28, 1973, Nixon Library.

72. Camp David Study Table, 164–48, April 30, 1973, Nixon Library.

73. Camp David Study Table, 164–28, April 29, 1973, Nixon Library.

74. White House Telephone, 45–203, May 10, 1973, Nixon Library.

75. Statement by President, April 30, 1973, Folder Watergate Nomination Hearings and Briefing Book, Box I: 214, Elliot L. Richardson Papers.

76. April 30, 1973, Folder Chron. Files 1973 26–30 April, Box 20, Kissinger Telephone Conversation Transcripts, Nixon Library.

77. Smith, phone interview with author.

78. Elliot L. Richardson, *The Creative Balance: Government, Politics and the Individual in America's Third Century* (Dumfries, NC: Holt, Rinehart & Winston, 1976), 4.

79. Nixon Library Oral History, 2008.

80. April 29, 1973, Folder Watergate SP—Notes of Conversation with Nixon, Box I: 229, Elliot L. Richardson Papers.

81. Richardson, *Creative Balance*, 4.

4. "HE'S GOING TO HAVE TO PROVE HE'S THE WHITE KNIGHT"

1. Memorandum to the President, written by Leonard Garment, May 1, 1973, Folder President's Handwriting May 1973, Box 22, President's Office Files, Nixon Library.

2. Alexander Meigs Haig with Charles McCarry, *Inner Circles: How America Changed the World—A Memoir* (New York: Warner Books, 1992), 335.

3. White House Telephone, 45–93, May 1, 1973, Nixon Library.

4. Oval Office, 911–26, May 3, 1973, Nixon Library.

5. Oval Office, 909–6, May 2, 1973, Nixon Library.

6. Stephen E. Ambrose, *Nixon: Ruin and Recovery* (New York: Simon & Schuster, 1991), 143.

7. Oval Office, 918–15, May 15, 1973, Nixon Library.

8. Elliot L. Richardson's Letter of Resignation to President Nixon, October 20, 1973, Folder Acceptance of Richardson Resignation, 20 October 1973, Box I: 229, Elliot L. Richardson Papers.

9. Elliot L. Richardson, *The Creative Balance: Government, Politics, and the Individual in America's Third Century* (Dumfries, NC: Holt, Rinehart & Winston, 1976), 37.

10. Watergate Special Prosecutor Chronological File of Events, 15–20 October 1973, Box I: 227, Elliot L. Richardson Papers.

11. Statement by Elliot Richardson, May 7, 1973, Folder Watergate Nomination Hearings and Briefing Book, Box I: 214, Elliot L. Richardson Papers.

12. May 11, 1973, Folder WTG SP Special Correspondence Draft Memo to Senate Jud Com., May 11, 1973, Box I: 228, Elliot L. Richardson Papers.

13. May 14, 1973, Folder Watergate SP Draft Release Naming Harold Tyler, 14 May 1973, Box I: 228. Elliot L. Richardson Papers.

14. Ken Gormley, *Archibald Cox: Conscience of a Nation* (Boston: Perseus Books, 1997), 234; James Doyle, *Not above the Law: The Battles of Watergate Prosecutors Cox and Jaworski, A Behind-the-Scenes Account* (New York: William Morrow, 1977), 42.

15. May 7, 1973 List of Candidates, Folder WTG SP Special Correspondence Draft Memo to Senate Jud Com., May 11, 1973, Box I: 228, Elliot L. Richardson Papers.

16. Gormley, *Archibald Cox,* 232.

17. Gormley, *Archibald Cox,* 246.

18. Oval Office, 912–3, May 8, 1973, Nixon Library.

19. Oval Office, 918–15, May 15, 1973, Nixon Library.

20. Oval Office, 923–5, May 19, 1973, Nixon Library.

21. May 25, 1973, Folder Justice Dept. Transition to Atty. General and Congratulations, 23–30 May Replies, Box I: 180, Elliot L. Richardson Papers.

22. White House Telephone, 39–16, May 25, 1973, Nixon Library.

23. Oval Office, 928–12, May 25, 1973, Nixon Library.

24. John Thomas Smith II, phone interview with author, July 19, 2013.

25. Richardson, *Creative Balance,* 36.

26. Doyle, *Not above the Law,* 47.

27. Oval Office, 929–7, May 29, 1973, Nixon Library.

28. Roger Morris, *Haig: The General's Progress* (Chicago: Playboy, 1982), 245.

29. Oval Office, 935–7, June 11, 1973, Nixon Library.

30. Richardson, *Creative Balance,* 38.

31. White House Telephone, 40–86, June 13, 1973, Nixon Library.

32. Spiro Agnew, *Go Quietly . . . Or Else* (New York: William Morrow, 1980), 79.

33. Camp David Study Table, 169–26, June 20, 1973, Nixon Library.

34. Richard M. Cohen and Jules Witcover, *A Heartbeat Away: The Investigation and Resignation of Vice President Spiro T. Agnew* (New York: Viking, 1974), 101.

35. "Nixon Vacation Homes Target of Cox Inquiry" *Toledo Blade,* July 2, 1973, 4.

36. Oval Office, 945–3, June 19, 1973, Nixon Library.

37. Oval Office, 945–5, June 19, 1973, Nixon Library

38. Gormley, *Archibald Cox*, 295–96.

39. Oval Office, 948–14, July 11, 1973, Nixon Library.

40. Oval Office, 948–18, July 11, 1973, Nixon Library.

41. Doyle, *Not above the Law*, 101.

42. Haig, *Inner Circles*, 384.

43. Agnew, *Go Quietly*, 79. The story is also mentioned in a November 20, 1973 memorandum written by Martin Linsky for Richardson, Folder Jonathan Moore, Box I: 253, Elliot L. Richardson Papers.

44. Haig, *Inner Circles*, 357.

45. Richardson's notes of meeting with Cox, September 6, 1973, Folder Cox Notes, Box I: 221. Elliot L. Richardson Papers.

46. Henry Ruth, interviewed by Timothy Naftali, November 12, 2011, Richard Nixon Oral History, Nixon Library.

47. Jonathan Moore, interview with author, Cambridge, MA, May 22, 2012.

48. Richardson's notes of meeting with Cox, October 12, 1973, Folder Memoranda of Conversations General: October 1973, Box I: 205, Elliot L. Richardson Papers.

49. William D. Ruckelshaus, interviewed by Douglas Brinkley, Seattle, WA, August 3, 2011, Ruckelshaus Oral History Project, The William Ruckelshaus Center, Washington State University (Pullman, WA).

50. Aaron Latham, "Seven Days in October," *New York Magazine*, April 29, 1974, 42.

51. Camp David Hard Wire, 225–39, November 16, 1972, Nixon Library.

52. "DOJ Personnel and Your First Meeting with Dean Sneed," written by Jonathan Moore, May 25, 1973, Folder Memoranda of Conversations Special: Haig, Alexander, Box I: 205, Elliot L. Richardson Papers.

53. Oval Office, 819–2, December 11, 1972, Nixon Library.

54. Robert H. Bork, *Saving Justice: Watergate, the Saturday Night Massacre and Other Adventures of a Solicitor General* (New York: Encounter Books, 2013), 13.

55. Bork, *Saving Justice*, 36.

56. Cohen and Witcover, *Heartbeat Away*, 261.

57. Latham, "Seven Days in October," 41.

58. Richardson, *Creative Balance*, 38.

59. Haig, *Inner Circles*, 394–96.

60. Elliot L. Richardson's Timeline of Events Leading up to Saturday Night Massacre, Folder Watergate Special Prosecutor Chronological File of Events, 15–20 October 1973, Box I: 227, Elliot L. Richardson Papers.

61. Latham, "Seven Days in October," 44.

62. Jonathan Moore, interviewed by Timothy Naftali, Cambridge, MA, February 11, 2008, Richard Nixon Oral History, Nixon Library.

63. Latham, "Seven Days in October," 45.

64. Richardson's Timeline of Events.

65. Bork, *Saving Justice*, 78.

66. "The Third Person," letter from Archibald Cox to Elliot Richardson, October 18, 1973, Folder Watergate SP Comments on Stennis Proposal, 18 October 1973, Box I: 228, Elliot L. Richardson Papers.

67. Richardson's Timeline of Events.

68. Richardson's Timeline of Events.

69. Doyle, *Not above the Law,* 158–59.

70. Letter from Charles Alan Wright to Archibald Cox, October 19, 1973, Folder Watergate SP Cox-Wright Correspondence, 18–19 October 1973, Box I: 228, Elliot L. Richardson Papers.

71. "Why I Must Resign," October 18, 1973, Folder Watergate Special Prosecutor chronological file of events, 15–20 October 1973, Box I: 227, Elliot L. Richardson Papers.

72. Latham, "Seven Days in October," 44.

73. Richardson's Timeline of Events.

74. Haig, *Inner Circles,* 400.

75. Leonard Garment, interviewed by Timothy Naftali, New York, NY, April 6, 2007, Richard Nixon Oral History, Nixon Library.

76. Nixon Library Oral History, 2008.

77. Richardson's Timeline of Events.

78. Morris, *Haig,* 250

79. Richardson, *Creative Balance,* 43.

80. James Bennet, "Elliot Richardson, b. 1920: The Longest Day," *New York Times,* January 7, 2001, SM 22.

81. Latham, "Seven Days in October," 54.

82. Haig, *Inner Circles,* 402.

83. Richardson's Timeline of Events.

84. Richardson's Letter of Resignation to President Nixon, October 20, 1973, Folder Resignation Letter, October 20, 1973, Box I: 222, Elliot L. Richardson Papers.

85. 8–16, 10/20/73 Press Conference by Cox re: Refusal to Comply with Compromise, October 20, 1973, VI Massacre—Accordion File, Series I: Watergate Files 1973–1974, James S. Doyle Collection of Watergate Material, Harvard Law School Library (Cambridge, MA).

86. Gormley, *Archibald Cox,* 340.

87. Transcript of William Ruckelshaus's Appearance on the *Today Show,* October 22, 1973, Folder Watergate Special Prosecutor Tapes Compromise, Box 166, Leonard Garment White House Central Files.

88. Bork, *Saving Justice,* 80–82; Moore, interview with author.

89. Robert H. Bork, interviewed by Timothy Naftali, McLean, VA, December 1, 2008, Richard Nixon Oral History, Nixon Library. Other sources, including Moore's 2012 interview with author, match up with Bork's account.

90. Ambrose, *Nixon,* 248.

91. Richardson, *Creative Balance,* 44.

92. Haig, *Inner Circles,* 407.

93. Patrick J. Buchanan, *Nixon's White House Wars: The Battles That Made and Broke a President and Divided America Forever* (New York: Crown Forum, 2017), 358.

94. Smith, phone interview with author.

95. Bennet, "Elliot Richardson, b. 1920," SM22.

96. Gormley, *Archibald Cox,* 377.

97. William D. Ruckelshaus, interviewed by Paul Charles Milazzo and Timothy Naftali, Yorba Linda, CA, April 12, 2007, Richard Nixon Oral History, Nixon Library.

98. Ruckelshaus Oral History Project, 2011.

99. Bork, *Saving Justice*, 84–86.

100. Latham, "Seven Days in October," 57.

101. Richardson's Letter of Resignation to President Nixon, October 20, 1973, Folder Resignation Letter, October 20, 1973, Box I: 222, Elliot L. Richardson Papers.

102. Haig, *Inner Circles*, 419.

103. Letter from Robert H. Bork to Archibald Cox, October 20, 1973, Folder October 20, 1973, Letter to Robert H. Bork, PPF, Box 88, Nixon Library.

104. Morris, *Haig*, 252.

105. Carroll Kilpatrick, "Nixon Forces Firing of Cox; Richardson, Ruckelshaus Quit, President Abolishes Prosecutor's Office; FBI Seals Records," *Washington Post*, October 21, 1973, 1.

106. John Herbers, "Demand Growing for Nixon to Quit; He Drops in Poll," *New York Times*, November 4, 1973, 1.

107. Doyle, *Not above the Law*, 205–6.

108. Nixon, *RN*, 935.

109. Gormley, *Archibald Cox*, 362.

110. Smith, phone interview with author.

111. Christopher Lydon, "Richardson Busy, but Goal Is Unclear on Political: Power Glows in Recognition," *New York Times*, January 13, 1974, 52.

112. Moore, interview with author; Note to Richardson before Press Conference, October 23, 1973, Folder Watergate Final Press Conference, 23 October 1973, Box 214, Elliot L. Richardson Papers.

113. Transcript of Richardson's October 23, 1973 Press Conference, Folder Watergate Final Press Conference, 23 October 1973, Box 214, Elliot L. Richardson Papers.

114. "Excerpts from News Conference by Richardson and Exchange of Letters between Nixon and Richardson," *New York Times*, October 24, 1973, 33.

115. Elliot Richardson, interviewed by Richard L Holzhausen, Ann Arbor, MI, April 25, 1997, Gerald R. Ford Oral History Project, Gerald R. Ford Presidential Library.

116. Clifton Daniels, "The Future of Elliot Richardson: Anthony Eden Recalled Exposure May Help," *New York Times*, October 25, 1973, 43.

117. Lydon, "Richardson Busy," 52.

118. Smith, phone interview with author.

119. In a September 4, 1972 memo entitled "Reflection upon Making of the President," Darman brought up the idea of Richardson possibly being a compromise candidate if there was a brokered convention in 1976. The memo argued that Richardson should depict himself as a centrist, and not as a liberal, in order to appeal to the conservative wing of the party. "The conservatives have a hell of a lot of power in the party. 1976 is fast falling to the Towers, Kemps, Reagans, Agnews of this world," wrote Dick Darman. Dick Darman,

"Reflecting upon Making a President," September 4, 1972, Folder Jonathan Moore, Box I: 253, Elliot L. Richardson Papers.

120. Jonathan Moore, "Random Readings and Thoughts," November 20, 1973, Folder Jonathan Moore, Box I: 253, Elliot L. Richardson Papers.

121. Gerald R. Ford Oral History Project, 1997.

122. Letter from Scranton to Ford, September 16, 1974, White House Central File Name File Elliot Richardson Box 2650, Ford Library.

123. "Reagan Is First in Chairmen Poll," *New York Times*, March 24, 1974, 32. Similar results were found in a July 22, 1974 *New York Times* poll and a March 27, 1975 Gallup poll of potential candidates for the 1976 Republican nomination for president.

124. Lydon, "Richardson Busy," 52.

125. "Richardson Will Not Run," *New York Times*, December 16, 1975, 2.

126. James M. Naughton, "Ford May Consult Foes on Picking Running Mate," *New York Times*, August 11, 1976, 14.

127. Memorandum to the President, written by Robert Teeter, August 16, 1976, and memorandum to the President, written by James Cannon, "Comment from Governor Longley," August 16, 1976, Folder—Political Affairs, Presidential Handwriting Box 37, Ford Library.

128. Ford Oral History Project, 1997.

129. "Richardson Asserts He Won't Run for Governor in Massachusetts," October 6, 1977, *New York Times*, 38.

130. "Elliot Richardson Loses to Shamie in Mass. Primary," *Lewiston Daily Sun*, September 19, 1984, 16.

131. Margot Hornblower, "Election 84," *Washington Post*, June 17, 1984.

132. Smith, phone interview with author.

133. Elliot Richardson, *Reflections of a Radical Moderate* (New York: Pantheon, 1996), 244.

134. William J. Clinton, "Remarks on Presenting the Presidential Medal of Freedom," The American Presidency Project, January 15, 1998.

135. Moore, interview with author.

136. Richardson, *Creative Balance*, 9.

CONCLUSION

1. Neil A. Lewis, "Elliot Richardson Dies at 79; Stood Up to Nixon and Resigned in 'Saturday Night Massacre,'" *New York Times*, January 1, 2000.

2. Oval Office, 722–7, May 9, 1972, Nixon Library.

3. Nicole Hemmer, "A Forgotten Lesson of Watergate: Conservatives May Rally around Trump," *Vox*, May 17, 2017.

4. Roper Center for Public Opinion Research, "The American Public's Attitudes towards Richard Nixon Post-Watergate," August 9, 2014.

5. Ross Douthat, "E Pluribus Nixon," *The Atlantic*, May 2008.

6. Ross Douthat, "Searching for Richard Nixon," *New York Times*, November 21, 2015.

7. Michael Barbaro and Alexander Burns, "It's Trump's Convention, But the Inspiration? Nixon," *New York Times*, July 18, 2016.

8. Ann Coulter, Nixon Foundation Event at the Richard Nixon Presidential Library and Museum, Yorba Linda, CA, November 4, 2013. Video footage of the event can be found on the Nixon Foundation's YouTube page.

9. Details of the Nixon Library's renovation can be found in Christine Mae-Duc, "The 'New' Nixon Library's Challenge: Fairly Depicting a 'Failed Presidency'," *Los Angeles Times*, August 16, 2016; David Whiting, "Remodeled Nixon Library Makes Peace with the Past as It Becomes More Modern," *Orange County Register*, July 7, 2016.

10. Remarks were delivered at the Richard Nixon Presidential Library and Museum in Yorba Linda, CA, on October 16, 2016. Footage can be found on C-SPAN.

11. Molly Ball, "What Would Nixon Say to Today's Republican Party?" *The Atlantic*, January 10, 2013.

12. Phillip Rucker and Robert Costa, "Bannon Vows a Daily Fight for 'Deconstruction of the Administrative State'," *Washington Post*, February 23, 2017.

13. Dylan Matthews, "Richard Nixon Also Fired the Person Investigating His Presidential Campaign," *Vox*, May 10, 2017.

14. Ryan J. Reilly, "Jeff Sessions Started the Week Defining His Agenda; He Ends It Fighting for His Legacy," *Huffington Post*, March 2, 2017.

Sources

ARCHIVES AND COLLECTIONS

Walter J. Brown Archives and Peabody Awards Collection, University of Georgia, Athens, GA.

Gerald R. Ford Presidential Library and Museum, National Archives, Ann Arbor, MI.

Massachusetts Institute of Technology Libraries, Institute Archives and Special Collections, Cambridge, MA.

Richard Nixon Presidential Library and Museum, National Archives, Yorba Linda, CA.

Records of the Watergate Special Prosecution Force, National Archives, College Park, MD.

Elliot Lee Richardson Papers, Library of Congress, Washington, DC.

Tamiment Library and Robert F. Wagner Labor Archives, New York University, New York, NY.

Johnnie M. Walters Papers, South Carolina Political Collections, University of South Carolina, Columbia, SC.

Caspar W. Weinberger Papers, Library of Congress, Washington, DC.

INTERVIEWS

John Dean, phone interview, March 8, 2013.

Jonathan Moore, Cambridge, MA, May 22, 2012.

William Morrill, phone interview, June 3, 2015.

John Thomas Smith II, phone interview, July 19, 2013.

MEMOIRS

Agnew, Spiro. *Go Quietly . . . Or Else.* New York: William Morrow, 1980.

Bork, Robert H. *Saving Justice: Watergate, the Saturday Night Massacre, and Other Adventures of a Solicitor General.* New York: Encounter Books, 2013.

Buchanan, Patrick J. *The Greatest Comeback: How Richard Nixon Rose from Defeat to Create the New Majority.* New York: Crown Forum, 2014.

————. *Nixon's White House Wars: The Battles That Made and Broke a President and Divided America Forever.* New York: Crown Forum, 2017.

Dean, John. *Blind Ambition: The White House Years.* New York: Simon & Schuster, 1976.

————. *Lost Honor.* Los Angeles: Stratford Press, 1982.

Doyle, James. *Not above the Law: The Battles of Watergate Prosecutors Cox and Jaworski, A Behind-the-Scenes Account.* New York: William Morrow, 1977.

Ehrlichman, John. *Witness to Power: The Nixon Years.* New York: Simon & Schuster, 1982

Haig, Alexander Meigs, with Charles McCarry. *Inner Circles: How America Changed the World—A Memoir.* New York: Warner Books, 1992.

Haldeman, H. R. *The Haldeman Diaries: Inside the Nixon White House.* New York: G. P. Putnam's Sons, 1994.

Kissinger, Henry. *The White House Years.* New York: Little Brown, 1979.

Morrill, William A. *A Journey through Governance: A Public Servant's Experience under Six Presidents.* New York: Cosimo Books, 2013.

Nixon, Richard. *RN: The Memoirs of Richard Nixon.* New York: Simon & Schuster, 1978.

Panetta, Leon. *Bring Us Together: The Nixon Team and the Civil Rights Retreat.* Philadelphia: Lippincott, 1971.

Richardson, Elliot. *The Creative Balance: Government, Politics and the Individual in America's Third Century.* Dumfries, NC: Holt, Rinehart & Winston, 1976.

————. *Reflections of a Radical Moderate.* New York: Pantheon, 1996.

Shultz, George P. *Turmoil and Triumph: My Years as Secretary of State.* New York: Scribner, 1993.

Walters, Johnnie M. *Our Journey.* Macon, GA: Stroud & Hall, 2011.

Weinberger, Caspar W., with Gretchen Roberts. *In the Arena: A Memoir of the 20th Century.* Washington, DC: Regnery, 2001.

PERIODICALS

The Atlantic
The Baffler
Daily Beast
DC Bar Report
Huffington Post
Lewiston Daily Sun
Los Angeles Times
New York Magazine
New York Times

Orange County Register
Pacific Standard
Providence Journal
Slate
Toledo Blade
USA Today
Vox
Washington Post

MONOGRAPHS AND OTHER SECONDARY SOURCES

Aitken, Jonathan. *Nixon: A Life*. Washington, DC: Regnery, 1993.

Ambrose, Stephen E. *Nixon: Volumes 1–3*. New York: Touchstone Books, 1988, 1990, 1992.

———. *Nixon: Ruin and Recovery*. New York: Simon & Schuster, 1991.

Andrew III, John A. *Power to Destroy: The Political Uses of the IRS from Kennedy to Nixon*. Chicago: Ivan R. Dee, 2002.

Berman, Jerry, Robert Borosage, and Christine Marwick. *The Lawless State: The Crimes of the U.S. Intelligence Agencies*. New York: Penguin Books, 1976.

Brinkley, Douglas, and Luke Nichter. *The Nixon Tapes: 1971–1972*. New York: Houghton & Mifflin, 2014.

———. *The Nixon Tapes: 1973*. New York: Houghton & Mifflin, 2015.

Brodie, Fawn. *Richard Nixon: The Shaping of His Character*. New York: W. W. Norton, 1981.

Burnham, David. *A Law unto Itself: Power, Politics, and the IRS*. New York: Random House, 1989.

Cohen, Richard M., and Jules Witcover. *A Heartbeat Away: The Investigation and Resignation of Vice President Spiro T. Agnew*. New York: Viking, 1974.

Colodny, Leo, and Robert Gettlin. *Silent Coup: The Removal of a President*. New York: St. Martin's Press, 1991.

Cuordileone, K. A. *Manhood and American Political Culture in the Cold War*. New York: Routledge, 2004.

Dallek, Robert. *Nixon and Kissinger: Partners in Power*. New York: Harper-Collins, 2007.

Davis, Shelley. *Unbridled Power: Inside the Secret Culture of the IRS*. New York: Harper Business, 1997.

Dean, John. *The Nixon Defense: What He Knew and When He Knew It*. New York: Viking, 2014.

Doyle, James. *Not above the Law: The Battles of Watergate Prosecutors Cox and Jaworski, A Behind-the-Scenes Account*. New York: William Morrow, 1977.

Drew, Elizabeth. *Richard M. Nixon: The American Presidents Series: The 37th President, 1969–1974*. New York: Times Books, 2007.

Farrell, Jack A. *Richard Nixon: The Life*. New York: Doubleday, 2017.

Feldstein, Mark. *Poisoning the Press: Richard Nixon, Jack Anderson, and the Rise of Washington's Scandal Culture*. New York: Farrar, Strauss & Giroux, 2010.

Gage, Beverly. "Deep Throat, Watergate, and the Bureaucratic Politics of the FBI." *Journal of Policy History* 24, no. 2 (2012): 157–78.

Gormley, Ken. *Archibald Cox: Conscience of a Nation.* Boston: Addison-Wesley, 1997.

Grandin, Greg. *Kissinger's Shadow: The Long Reach of America's Most Controversial Statesman.* New York: Metropolitan Books, 2015.

Greenberg, David. *Nixon's Shadow: The History of an Image.* New York: W. W. Norton, 2003.

Hemmer, Nicole. *Messengers of the Right: Conservative Media and the Transformation of American Politics.* Philadelphia: University of Pennsylvania Press, 2016.

Hendershot, Heather. *Open to Debate: How William F. Buckley Put Liberal America on the Firing Line.* New York: Broadside Books, 2016.

Hoff, Joan. *Nixon Reconsidered.* New York: Basic Books, 1994.

Hughes, Ken. *Chasing Shadows: The Nixon Tapes, the Chennault Affair, and the Origins of Watergate.* Charlottesville: University of Virginia Press, 2014.

———. *Fatal Politics: The Nixon Tapes, the Vietnam War, and the Casualties of Reelection.* Charlottesville: University of Virginia Press, 2015.

Isaacson, Walter. *Kissinger: A Biography.* New York: Simon & Schuster, 2005.

Kabaservice, Geoffrey M. *The Guardians: Kingman Brewster, His Circle, and the Rise of the Liberal Establishment.* New York: Henry Holt, 2004.

———. *Rule and Ruin: The Downfall of Moderation and the Destruction of the Republican Party, From Eisenhower to the Tea Party.* Oxford: Oxford University Press, 2011.

Kimball, Jeffrey. *Nixon's Vietnam War.* Lawrence: University Press of Kansas, 1998.

Kotlowski, Dean J. *Nixon's Civil Rights: Politics, Principle, and Policy.* Cambridge, MA: Harvard University Press, 2002.

Kruse, Kevin. *One Nation under God: How Corporate America Invented Christian America.* New York: Basic Books, 2015.

Kutler, Stanley. *The Wars of Watergate: The Last Crisis of Richard Nixon.* New York: Alfred A. Knopf, 1990.

———. *Abuse of Power: The New Nixon Tapes.* New York: Free Press, 1997.

McGirr, Lisa. *Suburban Warriors: The Origins of the New American Right.* Princeton, NJ: Princeton University Press, 2001.

Milazzo, Paul Charles. *Unlikely Environmentalists: Congress and Clean Water.* 1945–1972. Lawrence: University Press of Kansas, 2006.

Morris, Roger. *Haig: The General's Progress.* Chicago: Playboy, 1982.

O'Mara, Margaret Pugh. *Cities of Knowledge: Cold War Science and the Search for the Next Silicon Valley.* Princeton, NJ: Princeton University Press, 2004.

Parmet, Herbert. *Richard Nixon and His America.* New York: Little, Brown, 1989.

Perlstein, Rick. *Before the Storm: Barry Goldwater and the Unmaking of the American Consensus.* New York: Nation Books, 2001.

———. *Nixonland: The Rise of a President and the Fracturing of America.* New York: Scribner, 2008.

————. *The Invisible Bridge: The Fall of Nixon and the Rise of Reagan*. New York: Simon & Schuster, 2014.

Phillips-Fein, Kim. *Invisible Hands: The Making of the Conservative from the New Deal to Reagan*. New York: W. W. Norton, 2009.

Reeves, Richard. *President Nixon: Alone in the White House*. New York: Simon & Schuster, 2002.

Rigeuer, Leah Wright. *The Loneliness of the Black Republican: Pragmatic Politics and the Pursuit of Power*. Princeton, NJ: Princeton University Press, 2014.

Small, Melvin. *The Presidency of Richard Nixon*. Lawrence: University Press of Kansas, 1999.

————, ed. *A Companion to Richard Nixon* (Wiley Blackwell Companions to American History). Hoboken, NJ: Wiley Blackwell, 2013.

Stahl, Jason. *Right Moves: The Conservative Political Think Tank in American Political Culture since 1945*. Chapel Hill: University of North Carolina Press, 2016.

Stanley, Timothy. *The Crusader: The Life and Tumultuous Times of Pat Buchanan*. New York: Thomas Dunne Books, 2012.

Suskind, Ron. *The Price of Loyalty: George W. Bush, the White House, and the Education of Paul O'Neill*. New York: Simon & Schuster, 2004.

Thomas, Evan. *Being Nixon: A Man Divided*. New York: Random House, 2015.

Vance, Tom. *Elliot Richardson: The Virtue of Politics*. CreateSpace Independent Publishing Platform, 2014.

Weiner, Timothy. *Legacy of Ashes: The History of the CIA*. New York: Random House, 2007.

————. *Enemies: A History of the FBI*. New York: Random House, 2012.

————. *One Man against the World: The Tragedy of Richard Nixon*. New York: Henry Holt, 2015.

Wicker, Tom. *One of Us: Richard Nixon and the American Dream*. New York: Random House, 1991.

Wills, Gary. *Nixon Agonistes: The Crisis of the Self-Made Man*. Boston: Houghton-Mifflin, 1970.

Witcover, Jules. *The Resurrection of Richard Nixon*. New York: G. P. Putnam's Sons, 1970.

Woodward, Bob. *The Last of the President's Men*. New York: Simon & Schuster, 2015.

———— and Carl Bernstein. *All the President's Men*, New York: Simon & Schuster, 1974.

————. *Final Days*. New York: Simon & Schuster, 1976.

Index